Take Back Your Time

Take Back Your Time

FIGHTING OVERWORK AND TIME POVERTY IN AMERICA

JOHN DE GRAAF, EDITOR

Posters designed by graphic design students
at the University of Minnesota, Duluth

BK Berrett-Koehler Publishers, Inc.
San Francisco

Berrett-Koehler Publishers, Inc.
235 Montgomery Street, Suite 650
San Francisco, CA 94104-2916
Tel: (415) 288-0260 Fax: (415) 362-2512 www.bkconnection.com

Ordering Information
Quantity sales. Special discounts are available on quantity purchases by corporations, associations, and others. For details, contact the "Special Sales Department" at the Berrett-Koehler address above.
Individual sales. Berrett-Koehler publications are available through most bookstores. They can also be ordered direct from Berrett-Koehler: Tel: (800) 929-2929; Fax: (802) 864-7626; www.bkconnection.com
Orders for college textbook/course adoption use. Please contact Berrett-Koehler: Tel: (800) 929-2929; Fax: (802) 864-7626.
Orders by U.S. trade bookstores and wholesalers. Please contact Publishers Group West, 1700 Fourth Street, Berkeley, CA 94710. Tel: (510) 528-1444; Fax (510) 528-3444.

Berrett-Koehler and the BK logo are registered trademarks of Berrett-Koehler Publishers, Inc.

Printed in the United States of America

Berrett-Koehler books are printed on long-lasting acid-free paper. When it is available, we choose paper that has been manufactured by environmentally responsible processes. These may include using trees grown in sustainable forests, incorporating recycled paper, minimizing chlorine in bleaching, or recycling the energy produced at the paper mill.

Library of Congress Cataloging-in-Publication Data
De Graaf, John.
Take back your time : fighting overwork and time poverty in America / edited by John De Graaf.
p. cm.
Includes bibliographical references and index.
ISBN 1-57675-245-3
1. Hours of labor--United States. 2. Quality of life--United States. 3. Work and family--United States. I. De Graaf, John.

HD5124.T35 2003
646.7--dc21

2003045237

First Edition
08 07 06 05 04 03   10 9 8 7 6 5 4 3 2 1

Design and composition: Seventeenth Street Studios
Copyeditor: Bonnie Duncan
Indexer: Jeanne C. Moody

CONTENTS

Take Back Your Time Day

JOHN DE GRAAF

Welcome to the official handbook for Take Back Your Time Day, a new national consciousness-raising event that will be held for the first time on October 24, 2003. The date falls nine weeks before the end of the year and symbolizes the fact that we Americans now work an average of nine full weeks more each year than do our peers in Western Europe. It wasn't supposed to be this way.

Back in the late 1960s, I studied sociology. I remember distinctly some of the class discussions we had then. We were told that American society would be facing a serious social problem by the end of the twentieth century. That problem was *leisure time!* With all our advances in labor saving technology, with automation and "cybernation," we'd be working less than 20 hours a week by the year 2000. Just what would we do with all that leisure time?

It would be a Big problem, one that we sociologists would have to help solve. As you are no doubt aware, it didn't happen. We got the technology but we didn't get the time. In fact, most Americans say their lives feel like a rat race. Millions of us are overworked, overscheduled, overwhelmed. We're just plain stressed out.

It starts at work. Despite those promises of leisure, we're working harder and longer today than we were back in my college days, as several chapters in this book make clear. Americans work more than do the citizens of any other industrial country. Our work days are longer, our work weeks are longer, and our vacations are disappearing. In fact, one quarter of American workers got no vacation at all last year. Even medieval peasants worked less than we do!

My personal interest in this issue was re-kindled in 1993 when I coproduced a PBS documentary called *Running Out of Time* that explored the epidemic of overwork that seemed to be sweeping America. Then followed another documentary called *Affluenza,* which looked at our obsession with achieving ever-higher material standards of living at the expense of other values we once held dear. Working on those programs allowed me to meet many people who were trying to find more balanced lives amid the pressure to work and spend, amid the constant barrage of messages urging all of us to work and buy more and more and more and . . .

These were people who were beginning to ask big questions, and the biggest of them was: *what is an economy for?* Why for the sake of "the economy" were we caught up in patterns of life that force us to pay an enormous price in terms of our health, our families and communities, and the earth itself, and that, in fact, leave us less happy than we were decades ago when we had half as much stuff or less?

About two years ago, I was invited by Vicki Robin, one of the authors of this book, to join an organization called the Simplicity Forum, made up of recognized "leaders" of the voluntary simplicity movement. I ended up as the co-chairperson of the Forum's Public Policy Committee. The Committee was formed because all of us had become aware that simplifying our lives wasn't a purely personal choice.

We knew that for millions of Americans simplicity was anything but voluntary. We knew that the rising cost of key necessities (such as housing and health care) in America kept many people struggling to make ends meet. We knew that sprawl, well-meaning but misguided zoning laws, and poor public transportation made it difficult for us to reduce the amount of driving we did, despite our concerns about energy use, the Arctic National Wildlife Refuge, or global warming.

As we talked about what we might do to help create a more simplicity-friendly society with more balanced, healthy and sustainable lifestyles, it became clear that we couldn't just stand *against* overconsuming. We needed to be *for* something, something that was clearly missing in our society despite all its material wealth. Most of our committee felt that something was *time.*

Many of us were overworked ourselves and constantly rushed. Others saw the phenomenon among our friends; every time we wanted to get together with them they'd have to take out their calendars and look weeks ahead for a little white space amid work and scheduled appointments.

We also talked about our lives outside of work, about how time-pressured and overscheduled even our children's lives had become, despite warnings from prominent child psychologists that kids need time just to be kids. We were shocked to learn that many school districts had even eliminated recess in a misguided effort to make their students "more productive."

As we shared experiences and further researched the issue, we came to understand that overwork, overscheduling, and time poverty threaten our health, our marriages, families and friendships, our community and civic life, our environment, and even our security. I promise that you'll see what we mean as you read through this book.

At a meeting in Kalamazoo, Michigan, in March of 2002, we came up with an idea. Why not try to create a national dialogue about our national time problem and how we, as Americans, might begin to solve it? We talked about the first Earth Day in 1970, when, in communities throughout America, people came together to discuss the harm we were doing to the earth and how we might improve our environment.

We knew that within two years of that outpouring of public concern, Congress passed, and a conservative Republican president signed, the most significant environmental legislation in American history—the Clean Air and Water Acts, the National Environmental Policy Act, the Endangered Species Act, and other similar laws.

If Earth Day could do that, we thought, what about a Time Day? Anders Hayden, a member of our group and author of one of the chapters in this book, suggested we hold the event nine weeks before the end of the year—symbolizing the fact that we Americans now work nine weeks more each year than do our trans-Atlantic neighbors.

Thus was launched the first official national initiative of the Simplicity Forum—Take Back Your Time Day.

Since we came up with the idea, thousands of Americans from all corners of our country have joined the Take Back Your Time Day campaign. They will hold teach-ins at colleges all across the country and speak-outs at labor halls and churches. The outpouring of interest has indeed confirmed our feeling that this is an issue people feel deeply even if they are often shy about expressing their frustrations.

A manager at an aircraft company called to say he'd just suffered a third heart attack and that his physicians blamed his increasingly long work hours and stress on the job. A veterinarian wrote us about seeing animals who had literally chewed off their fur out of boredom, after being left alone for long periods by their "too-busy" owners.

We began hearing from people from all walks of life, from accountants to schoolteachers. Career counselors, therapists, personal coaches, and corporate human resources managers wrote or called to say they were witnessing a major increase of clients or employees who were working beyond what their bodies and minds could endure.

Volunteers joined the campaign, allowing us to build a major event with almost no money. Art students at the University of Minnesota, Duluth have designed our logo and produced the posters and other visual materials for the campaign. You'll see their work throughout this book. Environmental journalism students at Western Washington University devoted an issue of their award-winning quarterly magazine to the Take Back Your Time effort. Representatives of unions, family organizations, churches and environmental groups readily joined our steering committee.

Take Back Your Time Day is a *strictly* nonpartisan event. All differences in viewpoints will be welcome—the important thing is to start the dialogue. We will help people to come together and talk about their overworked, overscheduled lives and how personally, or through collective bargaining or legislation, they might find more time for things that really matter. Already, some creative legislation is being developed in Congress—believe it or not!—and at the state level.

The movement for a more balanced American life will begin on Take Back Your Time Day, but it won't end there. In every community, Take Back Your Time organizations will develop local campaigns to win back time. They'll help people act at personal, cultural, workplace and legislative levels. By Take Back Your Time Day, 2004, we intend to ask every candidate for office, and especially the Presidential nominees, what they intend to do to help bring work/life balance to America, providing us with what Europeans already take for granted.

Take Back Your Time Day will produce a broad coalition for change. This issue can unite groups who seldom talk to each other—family values conservatives and the women's movement, labor unions and environmentalists, clergy and doctors, advocates for social justice, enlightened business leaders, and the "slow food" and "simple living" movements. It is an issue that crosses ideological lines. Nobody has any time out there!

As this book makes clear, countries like Norway, the Netherlands, France, and Germany have shown that shorter work time and a balanced life is possible and that it can even be good for business. In fact, most of them are more productive per worker hour than we are!

Shortly after the first mention of Take Back Your Time Day in the press, I received an email of "solidarity" from an organization in Norway called 07-06-05, one that clearly illustrates the gulf that exists between Americans and Europeans where the issues of work time and consumption are concerned. Norwegians may not be the best in the world at coming up with titles for organizations, but they do have the world's shortest working hours—already. And they aren't resting on their laurels.

07-06-05, it turns out, stands for June 7, 2005, the one hundredth anniversary of Norway's independence from Sweden. By that time, 07-06-05 leaders hope Norway will be well on its way to environmental sustainability. They hold up two pillars as the key to achieving their goal—reducing working hours and reducing consumption, so that more of the world's resources will be available for the world's poorest countries.

As I read the 07-06-05 call to action, I thought it must have come from some radical green group, some Norwegian Ralph Nader, maybe. But it turns out that

07-06-05, a campaign complete with TV, radio, and print advertising campaigns throughout Norway, is fully funded by the Norwegian Environment Ministry and endorsed by the prime minister!

Can you imagine an American president of any party actually suggesting we might be better off as a nation if we worked and consumed *less*? But in fact, as this book suggests, such a proposal by an American leader would be music to millions of ears all over the world.

We talk so little publicly about this issue that people often feel they are alone in their concerns about time. But time, or rather, or lack of it, is the big skeleton hidden in our national closet. Let it out! Talk about this issue around the dinner table and the water cooler, at PTA meetings, union meetings, and book clubs. Use this book, and others recommended in it as resources to help others understand that they are not alone in the time crunch they face, and that they can do something about it.

Join the Take Back Your Time Day campaign, and don't wait, because there's no present like the time!

Visit our Web site: www.timeday.org

One-half of all author royalties from this book will be contributed to Take Back Your Time Day.

Take Back Your Time Day is an initiative of the Simplicity Forum, and a project of The Center for Religion, Ethics and Social Policy at Cornell University.

Acknowledgments

Few books get written without the help of a lot of people, and this one is no exception. I want to thank as many of you who helped as I can remember and beg the forgiveness of those who, in my many senior moments, I forgot.

First of all, of course, a humongous thanks to the nearly forty separate authors of this book for cheerfully volunteering to do your chapters, getting them in to me promptly, and doing an excellent job in a short period of time. You rock!

Many of this book's authors are on the steering committee for Take Back Your Time Day, but I'd like to thank the other members of the steering committee as well, for their efforts to make Take Back Your Time Day a reality and a success. You'll find their names on our Web site (www.timeday.org).

Special thanks are due steering committee members Dave Wampler, whose tireless work got our Web site up, running, looking good and functioning marvelously; Joellyn Rock, our national art coordinator; Gretchen Burger, our underpaid national staff person; Bill Doherty; Cecile Andrews; and Tom Turnipseed.

Vicki Robin and Carol Holst deserve special thanks too, for establishing and leading the Simplicity Forum, of which Take Back Your Time Day is a national initiative. So does my Simplicity Forum Public Policy Committee co-chair, Jerome Segal.

Thanks also go to Take Back Your Time Day's intrepid student interns from The Evergreen State College—Mark and Tressie Schindele and Nicole Bade—and their faculty sponsor Nancy Parkes.

Additional thanks to the non-profit sponsor of Take Back Your Time Day—the Center for Religion, Ethics and Social Policy (CRESP) at Cornell University, and to CRESP staff members Anke Wessels and Beatrice Boes.

Thanks also to the staff of the Center for a New American Dream, and especially Sean Sheehan, Eric Brown, Betsy Taylor, Monique and Dave Tilford and Megan Waters.

My heartfelt appreciation to Joellyn Rock's University of Minnesota—Duluth art students who contributed all of the remarkable visual images you'll see in this volume. You rock too!

Thanks to copy editor Bonnie Duncan for her careful and cheerful efforts, to wunder-designer Lorrie Fink and her associates at Seventeenth Street Studios—Bob Giles, Kevin Stoffel, and Valerie Winemiller, and to everybody at Berrett-Koehler Publishers—especially, but not only, Steven Piersanti, Jeevan Sivasubramaniam, Ken Lupoff, Kristen Frantz, Robin Donovan, Richard Wilson, María Jesús Aguiló, Pat Anderson, Jenny Hermann, and Brenda Frink. Thanks also to the editorial readers whose suggestions were most useful: Jennifer Liss; Paul Wright; Sandy Chase; Joe Webb and Perviz Randeria.

And finally, apologies to my colleague, Hana Jindrova, for my preoccupation with Take Back Your Time Day, and a special thank you to my family, Paula and David, for their patience while I've been over-working to end overwork.

My heartfelt appreciation to all of you, and my apologies to anyone I've forgotten and for any mistakes in this book, for which the responsibility is mine.

John de Graaf
May, 2003

Introduction

JOHN DE GRAAF

In this book, you'll find a wide range of perspectives regarding time poverty and begin to see the connections between all of them. Frances Moore Lappé pointed out to me the critically important observation by farmer and environmental writer, Wendell Berry, that in the United States, we too often solve problems issue by issue when it would be more effective to solve them by "pattern." What is it about the *pattern* of our lives that exacerbates so many of our social and environmental problems?

This book suggests that a key aspect of our pattern problem comes from an unconscious choice we've made as a nation since World War II. Without thinking about it, Americans have taken all their productivity gains in the form of more money—more stuff, if you will—and none of them in the form of more time. Simply put, we as a society have chosen money over time, and this unconscious value pattern has had a powerful and less than beneficial impact on the quality of our collective lives.

True, we didn't all get the money; in fact, the poorest among us actually earn fewer real dollars than they did a generation ago. Our most significant financial gains went to the richest 20 percent of Americans. Nevertheless, as a whole society we now have much more stuff and considerably less time than we used to.

That's the pattern, and this book shows that the consequences have been and continue to be troubling. The argument here is that if we begin to change the *pattern* in favor of more time rather than more stuff, a host of other beneficial changes in the quality of our lives will follow.

A Collection of Essays

This book is a collection of essays written by academics, religious and labor leaders, activists, work/life and family counselors and personal coaches, physicians, and journalists. Most have devoted years of their lives to thinking deeply about the issue of time and Americans' lack of it. The views of all writers, including myself, are theirs alone, not official positions of Take Back Your Time Day, and not necessarily shared by other writers in this book, although I suspect you'll see considerable agreement as you read along.

You will see, too, that styles differ; some chapters focus on factual data, others on anecdotes and personal stories. Some are conversational, others more academic in approach. Each can be read alone and fully understood, but the whole here is greater than the sum of its parts. As you read along, you'll clearly see how connected these issues are. You'll find some repetition because these glimpses into various aspects of time famine do overlap, but, I trust, not too much.

A word about statistics: you may discover in reading this book some differences in the working hour statistics presented by different authors. As Juliet Schor explains in Chapter one, measuring work time is an inexact science. For example, measuring working hours per job will result in statistics showing shorter hours of work than will measuring hours per worker, since nearly ten percent of Americans hold more than one job. Estimates using the Current Population Survey of the United States show longer working hours than do Time Diary studies. International Labor Organization (ILO) reports on annual working hours show longer hours than do those of the Organization for Economic Cooperation and Development (OECD). Nonetheless, the central point the book makes—that American working hours are getting longer—is backed up by all measurements, although only recently in the case of Time Diary studies. Moreover, the ILO and OECD both show the same *gap* between American and western European working hours, approximately 350 per year. About the fact that Americans work considerably longer hours than the citizens of any other modern industrial nation, there is no longer any debate.

Structure of the Book

The book starts with work-time issues, demonstrating clearly how American working hours have risen since the 1960s. You'll see how American vacations have become an endangered species—the Spotted Owl of our social lives—and how millions of workers face steadily increasing "mandatory" overtime demands that leave them exhausted and leave you less safe and secure.

The next series of chapters examines the impact of overwork *and over-scheduling* on our families, children, communities, citizen participation, and even our treatment of animals.

Health and security concerns follow. A criminologist suggests that long working hours make us less safe, while two doctors examine the impact of our rush, rush, work, work, hurry-up existence on our health as individuals *and* as a nation.

We explore the environmental impact of overwork, and the time cost of our sprawling land use patterns and automobile dependence. We reveal a new study showing that people who work fewer hours are not only happier than are the overworked, but also more benign in their environmental impact.

Two chapters explore history and tradition. For more than half a century, the United States was the *leader* in the worldwide movement for shorter work time. Moreover, our great religious and spiritual teachings all emphasize the need for rest from work, for time to *be* instead of to *have*.

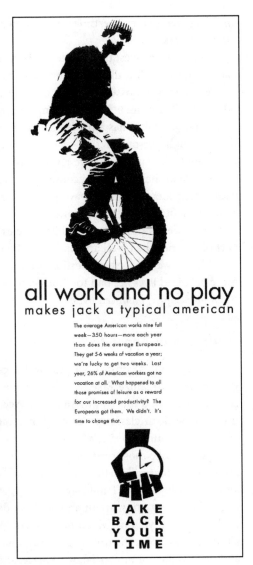

all work and no play
makes jack a typical american

The average American works nine full week—350 hours—more each year than does the average European. They get 5-6 weeks of vacation a year; we're lucky to get two weeks. Last year, 26% of American workers got no vacation at all. What happened to all those promises of leisure as a reward for our increased productivity? The Europeans got them. We didn't. It's time to change that.

**TAKE
BACK
YOUR
TIME**

But this is also a book about solutions, and they start with personal choices and responsibility. We see how our spending patterns and unconscious acceptance of the plethora of consumer messages we get each day actually *cost* us time. Thousands of Americans are finding out how to simplify their lives and sharing their ideas with others.

Others are finding ways to share jobs and win more flexible work schedules through negotiation with their employers.

We present the case for phased retirement options and for sabbaticals—for ordinary workers, not just academics. We find out what labor unions are doing to challenge mandatory overtime and win more family time for their members and other workers.

Some critics suggest that shorter working hours would be bad for the economy, bad for business. But this book counters that assumption.

We also look at possibilities for cultural change, seeing how the "slow food" and "slow cities" movements are changing everyday life in ways that give us time.

But Public Policy has a place here as well; many Americans will not win more time through personal action or even workplace bargaining alone. We examine the enlightened laws that have given Europeans the choice of far more balanced lifestyles than their American counterparts enjoy—shorter working hours, longer vacations, generous family leave policies, and other innovative approaches that assure benefits for part-time workers.

Can we develop American public policies that put work in its rightful place, as part of life, not the be-all and end-all of life? We offer some bold ideas to do just that. Finally, we ask the big question: some economists say shorter work hours and more balanced lives are bad for "the economy," *but what's an economy for anyway if not for happier, balanced lives?*

A Practical Appendix

The appendices comprise a practical organizer's toolkit, giving you the ideas you'll need to organize Take Back Your Time Day activities in your community or college (you'll find more of them at our Web site: www.timeday.org.) You can use this handbook in classes or discussion groups. You'll find suggested discussion questions on our Web site, as well.

If you are like most readers, you will find many things to agree with here, and other points that call forth exclamations of "no way!" But the point of this book, and of Take Back Your Time Day, is not to get us all to agree on everything, but to begin the conversation about an issue that deeply affects the great majority of us in this country, yet one which our leaders seem not to think and speak about at all. We cannot solve the time crunch until we talk seriously about it as Americans and make it part of our social, workplace, and political agenda. Let the discussion start with this book.

PART ONE

Overwork in America

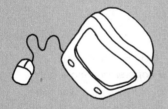

CHAPTER 1

The (Even More) Overworked American

JULIET SCHOR

I consider Juliet Schor to be one of America's intellectual treasures—a scholar whose profound gifts have been devoted to making ours a happier and more balanced society. I first met her in 1991. Then an economist at Harvard, she was just finishing her powerful book, The Overworked American, the first to document and challenge the steady rise in hours worked by Americans since the late 1960s. Her book impressively examined the high price Americans are paying for their new epidemic of overwork, and it suggested a strong connection between long working hours and consumerism—what Schor called "the work-and-spend cycle." Schor's work has been a wake-up call for many Americans, including myself, but sadly, the problems she analyzed have only grown worse, and are in even greater need of attention today. —JdG

One of the most striking features of American society is how much we work. Now the world's standout workaholic nation, America leads other industrial countries in terms of the proportion of the population holding jobs, the number of days spent on those jobs per year, and the hours worked per day. Taken together, these three variables yield a strikingly high measure of work hours per person and per labor force participant.

In 1996, average U.S. work hours surpassed those in Japan. And they haven't stopped climbing. Through booms and busts, both work hours and employment have continued to rise for more than three decades.

The Rise of Annual Work Hours

Just over ten years ago, I published a book entitled *The Overworked American*, in which I argued that contrary to the conventional belief that leisure time was increasing, U.S. working hours had begun an upward climb following the 1960s. My estimates caused a firestorm of controversy, but subsequent years confirmed the trend I identified. Work hours are indeed rising, and significantly so. And the trend has continued. Americans are now working even more than they did when *The Overworked American* was published.

The data I relied on were from the Current Population Survey (CPS) of the United States, a household survey. The Economic Policy Institute in Washington, which originally published my estimates, has continued to update them (see Table 1 for their latest calculations). What the data show is that from 1973 to 2000, the average American worker added an additional 199 hours to his or her annual schedule—or nearly five additional weeks of work per year (assuming a 40 hour workweek).

Since the 1980s, work hours have risen steadily by about half a percent per year, a reality attributed both to the fact that weekly hours have gone up (about a tenth

TABLE 1 / Annual Hours in the United States, 1967–2000

YEAR	ANNUAL HOURS
1967	1716
1973	1679
1979	1703
1989	1783
1995	1827
2000	1878

Source: Mishel et al 2002, Table 2.1, p. 115

Note: The International Labor Organization (ILO) estimates current U.S. annual work hours as even higher (at 1979), but shows the same upward trend since the 1960s

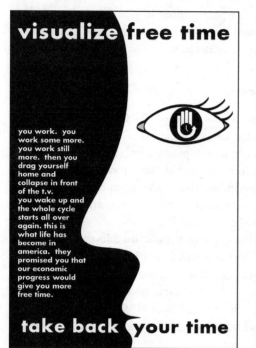

of a percentage point a year), and that people are working more days and weeks each year.

Viewed from the perspective of the household, which incorporates the rise in the participation of mothers in the labor force, the added burden of work has been even greater. Among all married-couple households, with heads of households in the 25–54 age range, total annual hours of paid work by both husbands and wives rose by a whopping 388 between 1979 and 2000, a gain of nearly 12 percent.

The increase has been even larger for some subgroups. Among those in the mid-point of the income distribution (the famously "squeezed middle class") the average increase in hours worked annually was 660 per year, a rise of just over 20 percent.

The Controversy about Time-use Trends

As mentioned earlier, some researchers challenged my findings, most notably Thomas Juster, Frank Stafford, Geoffrey Godbey, and John Robinson. They all believed that Americans were actually gaining leisure time at a rapid clip. They based their conclusions on a different type of data—daily time diaries in which survey participants recorded their activities in fifteen minute time blocks.

My source of data, the Current Population Survey (CPS), was a large, representative sample of households. Respondents gave retrospective estimates of how many hours they had worked in the previous week. The time-diary researchers believed that people were over-estimating their work time in the CPS data.[1]

Some of the claims of the time diary researchers were easy to refute. Juster and Stafford, for example, argued against my conclusions on the basis of data which were already a decade out of date (ending in 1981), and which missed the large work-time increases of the 1980s. Similarly, time diaries do not measure annual hours, but only weekly ones. Given that the larger part of the increase in

---

1. *Growth in Annual Hours and Productivity in the United States, 1967–2000.* For a comprehensive discussion of this debate, see the work of J.B. Schor.

annual hours occurred because people were working more days per year, their emphasis on weekly estimates was misleading.

Another limitation of the time diary research was that it has never taken into account the substantial influence on hours of work that comes from variations in the rate of unemployment or the stage of the business cycle. Time-diary researchers compared hours at the peak of business expansions (longer) with hours in the midst of recessions (shorter). My methods corrected for all these macroeconomic influences.

Finally, the time-diary samples have been much smaller and unrepresentative of the whole country in ways which bias the results. One important virtue of the CPS is that it is a very large, representative survey.

On the other hand, time-diary researchers did have an important point. Diary data is superior to recall data, and their claims that people overestimate their working hours may be true. However, the issue under debate was less the *actual amount* of work-time than *trends*. As long as the tendency to overestimate is stable, the upward trend of the CPS data is still a valid indicator.

Furthermore, some researchers have argued that the general claim of an "overworked American" obscures important differences in experience by education and income level. Yet my original research found that virtually all subgroups in the labor force experienced an increase in hours, with the exception of the partially-unemployed.

Eventually, the controversy died down. The ongoing estimates of the Economic Policy Institute, as well as estimates provided by other economists, supported the finding that work hours were increasing. And by the mid-1990s, the change was recognized even in the time diaries. In the second edition of their book, *Time for Life*, Robinson and Godbey reported that their additional data collection efforts during the '90s were yielding a new trend: the number of hours that women worked each week had begun to rise dramatically.

The Ironic Effects of Laborsaving Technologies

Of course, there is a certain irony in all the work that Americans are doing. The U.S. led the world in the technological revolution of the 1990s, as the Internet, computers, wireless, bio-informatics, and science were supposed to yield stupendous productivity gains that delivered us from excessive labor. This was both a promise and a prediction. Consider Jeremy Rifkin's book, *The End of Work*, which predicted that widespread technological change would increasingly make human labor superfluous.

As it turns out, however, the labor requirements of technology have very little to do with how many jobs an economy generates or how long people work at those jobs. Indeed, the first Industrial Revolution of the nineteenth century and the

Technological Revolution of the late twentieth century teach us an important lesson: the introduction of labor-saving technologies are frequently the impetus for massive increases in work.

What accounts for this paradox? On the one hand, the new technologies of the late twentieth and early twenty-first century provided new opportunities for making money. As firms seized those opportunities, they required long work hours from their employees, especially in the high-tech sectors, and in better paid manufacturing industries, such as auto or steel, where heavy overtime became a permanent feature of life.

Employers were able to elicit those extra hours because structural changes in the labor market made it hard for people to resist. There were far fewer unions, while part-time, contingent, and temporary work had become more prevalent. Even at the end of the 1990s boom, Americans felt more insecurity about their job status than in previous decades. Finding a full-time job with good security, benefits, and promotional possibilities had gotten harder and harder over time. Landing one of those plums meant that long hours came with it.

At the same time, the booming economy reinforced a powerful cycle of "work-and-spend," in which consumer norms accelerated dramatically. People needed to work more to purchase all the new products being churned out by a globalizing consumer economy. And they responded to their stressful working lives by participating in an orgy of consumer upscaling. There was an upsurge in luxury goods consumption, but now the aspiration to own these status items had become widely shared. Over the last thirty years, real consumption expenditures per person have doubled, from $11,171 to $22,152.

Conclusion

Recent trends in working hours are almost astonishing. Unlike the century between 1850 and 1950, when productivity improvements translated into considerable reductions in hours of work, the last three decades have witnessed steady increases in work time.

Between 1969 and 2000, the overall index of labor productivity per hour increased about 80 percent, from 65.5 to 116.6 (1992 = 100). That index represents economic progress, indicating that the average worker in 2000 could produce nearly twice as much as in 1969. Had we used that productivity dividend to reduce hours of work, the average American could be working only a little more than twenty hours a week. That's the most extreme assumption—all productivity increases channeled into shorter hours.

And what if that had happened? Our material standard of living would have stabilized. Americans would be eating out less, house size wouldn't have grown by 50 percent, and kitchen cabinets might still be made of formica. We also wouldn't be heating up the climate as rapidly, because expensive gas-guzzling SUVs wouldn't have become so popular. We wouldn't need to replace our computers every two to three years either, which might not be such a bad thing, at least from an environmental point of view. (A recent report suggests that the average computer uses a total quantity of material resources equivalent to the average car, or more.)

It's worth noting that stable incomes do not mean static consumer choice. Certainly, Americans would be consuming a different mix of goods and services than in 1960. But in the aggregate, taking all productivity growth as leisure time would have led to a stable real level of income.

But rather than focus on the stability of income, why not consider the temporal gains? The normal workweek could go as low as 20 hours, plus seven weeks of vacation. Two-income households with children could easily do without paid child care, because their work-time commitments would be low. People would have plenty of time for community and volunteer work, perhaps meaning less need for government social spending. It would be easy to pursue a passion, like playing music or woodworking, or quilting, or fishing.

We could become lifelong learners, or make up for our chronic national sleep deficit. All that free time could also go into pleasurable activities that provide additional income or consumption—like gardening, or making crafts for sale, or building furniture, or sewing—but that increasingly few people have time for now. There would also be fewer work-related expenses which would make stable salaries more bearable.

Americans could actually get back to eating dinner together, talking, and visiting friends—all activities that have been pushed out by excessive work time. From today's vantage point, a time-surplus society may seem utopian, almost unnatural. But that's only because we've been going at 24/7 for too many years and have lost sight of other possibilities.

It's not too late to stop and smell the roses. The time has come to take back our time.

TABLE 2 / Growth in Annual Hours and Productivity in the United States, 1967–2000 (average annual change)

PERIOD (1)	CHANGE IN HOURS (2)	CHANGE IN PRODUCTIVITY (2)	PRODUCTIVITY MINUS HOURS -(1)
1967–1973	-0.04	2.5	2.46
1973–1979	0.2	1.2	1.4
1979–1989	0.5	1.4	1.9
1989–1995	0.4	1.5	1.9
1995–2000	0.6	2.5	3.1

An Issue for Everybody

BARBARA BRANDT

One sometimes hears that the issue of time pressure in America is primarily an upper middle-class concern, without meaning for the rest of society. But as Barbara Brandt points out, overwork and time pressure may have even greater impact on poor Americans, many of whom need to work at least two jobs to rise above the poverty level. For me, the most wrenching story in Michael Moore's recent film, Bowling for Columbine, *addressed just this issue. Moore showcased a recent tragedy in his hometown of Flint, Michigan, where a six-year-old girl was shot to death by a classmate. While call-in show listeners demanded that the boy who killed her be tried as an adult, both the prosecutor and the sheriff in the case spoke to the underlying cause of the incident.*

The boy's mother, a single parent, had been moved from "welfare to work" in response to recent welfare reform. The only job available was a 90-minute bus commute from her home so she was away for at least eleven hours a day, could not afford Childcare, and had to leave her son unsupervised for long periods. In fact, her full-time job paid so little she fell behind on her rent payments and had to move in with her brother who kept a gun collection. The boy found one of the guns and took it to school. The rest was tragedy.

Although work is preferable to charity, circumstances such as these raise the question, Should mothers of young children be required to spend so much time in the workplace regardless of the impact on their children?

For more than 12 years, Barbara Brandt, the National staff person for the Shorter Work-Time Group, has tirelessly investigated the issue of shorter work time from the perspective of overworked Americans at all income levels and in all walks of life. As she points out, people in different situations are affected differently; solutions that can help poor Americans escape the overwork treadmill will not necessarily be the same as those that help the more affluent. Instead, any broad discussion of this issue must include consideration of "living wages," assuming that no American needs to work more than full time to escape the burdens of poverty. —JdG

In the early 1990s, US Airways was near bankruptcy. To keep the company afloat, employees made numerous concessions. Their holidays and vacations were cancelled, and their wages slashed. One employee movingly described how, after the wage cuts, he had to work enormous amounts of overtime in order to meet his expenses. This was taking a terrible emotional toll on his family life. He and his wife were drifting apart, and he rarely saw his two teenage daughters. With tears in his eyes, this man told company executives, "I want to be able to fall in love with my wife again. I want to be home with my daughters." His desire for more time is anything but unique.

Overworked, stressed-out, rushed, harried Americans today include millions of men and women of all ages, races, and classes, at all income levels and in all occupations, married and single, with and without children. They range from Fortune 500 CEOs and high-powered, high-tech professionals to garment workers in grimy sweatshops; from truck drivers and autoworkers to medical professionals, both doctors and nurses, forced to keep working even though bleary-eyed and exhausted; from well-to-do lawyers, middle managers in retail and other service industries to office workers on our new "electronic assembly lines," and low-paid men and women who must combine multiple poorly paid jobs to get by.

They include the millions of Americans who want more time with their families, whose children reside dawn to dusk in day-care centers or hang out unsupervised after school; the millions of people who are emotionally exhausted and stressed out because they can't meet all their responsibilities at work and at home; those who develop Repetitive strain injuries from long hours of performing the same work movements with their hands and arms; and the numerous Americans who don't have enough time to visit with friends, participate in their communities, or even to vote.

But the problem of overwork affects not only those who have to work long hours. Overwork also affects the unemployed and the underemployed: the millions of Americans in the contingent workforce who are struggling to subsist on insecure, low-paid temporary or part-time work, and the millions of people who are seeking work, but remain jobless.

Families

Families are especially hard hit by our rising work hours. The typical family of the 1950s and 1960s—at least in the popular mythology—consisted of a bread-winner who supported his family with one full-time job, while his wife worked "mothers' hours" or was a full-time homemaker so she could raise the kids. By the 1990s, the typical family had become the dual-earner family, with both adults working, often full time, or longer. Thus, families as a unit are now putting in more paid work time than ever before in recent history.

This is a particular burden for working women who in general still take primary responsibility for housework and childcare after all their paid work. But as it becomes more acceptable for men to share housework and childcare, both men and women are expressing the desire to work less.

The *1997 National Study of the Changing Workforce* reports that today's working American man puts in an average of 49.4 hours on the job per week while today's working woman puts in an average of 42.4 hours per week on the job. Both men and women would like to work about *eleven hours less* per week. Long work hours are especially hard on single parents who now head about 27 percent of our families—22 percent headed by mothers alone, and five percent headed by fathers alone.

Wageworkers and Professionals

The Fair Labor Standards Act (FLSA), passed by Congress in 1938, established the 40-hour "full-time" workweek, and mandated time-and-a-half pay for "over-time"—any work over 40 hours per week. While this "overtime penalty" was supposed to discourage employers from overworking existing employees, and instead hiring more workers when needed, it has become increasingly irrelevant. With the high cost of job-related benefits (health insurance, paid vacations, etc.), it is now more cost-effective for employers to overwork their current employees and pay them overtime, rather than hiring additional full-time employees with all the benefits that would include.

When workers are unionized, they can attempt to bargain for reasonable limits to their work hours. But in recent years, employers have often been able to insert mandatory overtime into their contracts, far beyond the amounts that workers want to put in. Furthermore, the Fair Labor Standards Act only applies to employees who are paid by the hour. It does not cover the salaried professionals, administrators, executives, and managers who make up one-third of our workforce. Since these millions of "FLSA-exempt" employees have no legal protections, they can be forced to work as many hours as their employers want—and they do not even have to be paid for their overtime work.

Public Health and Safety

Forcing people to work excessively long hours causes fatigue, impairs judgment, and leads to accidents and injuries. Not only workers, themselves, but the people they work with, and even the general public, can suffer due to overwork-related errors and accidents.

A few years ago, a member of a Hollywood film crew fell asleep in his car and died in a crash while driving home from a 19-hour work day on a movie set—one of a string of extremely long work days demanded by the producers in order to meet their deadlines. His colleagues began circulating a petition to limit their work hours to a maximum of 14 hours a day. Over 20,000 members of the International Alliance of Theatrical Stage Employees in Hollywood, along with members of the Screen Actors Guild and the Directors Guild have since signed this petition. Movie crew members on the set are now wearing buttons that say, "We came to work, not to die."

On May 11, 2000, after a grueling seven weeks on the picket line, 600 Registered Nurses at St. Vincent's Hospital in Worcester, Massachusetts won a bitter strike against their for-profit management's demand that they work eight hours of

mandatory overtime on top of their regular eight-hour shifts. These nurses—and others in Washington, D.C., Flint, Michigan, and elsewhere in the U.S.—were striking because management's proposal would use mandatory overtime not to deal with occasional emergencies, but as a regular staffing strategy.

Even more importantly, the nurses emphasized that they were striking for patient safety, because exhausted nurses cannot stay alert or make good decisions. Overtime is rising in every industry, commented Carolyn McVay, President of the California Nurses Association. "But in this one, if you're tired and you make a mistake, it can mean a life." Because of the issues involved, nurses' strikes against mandatory overtime around the U.S. have received widespread community support.

Part-time and Temporary Workers—The Underemployed

While hours for full-time workers have been rising since the 1970s, we've seen a simultaneous increase in part-time and temporary work, often referred to as "contingent employment." Some estimates claim that the contingent workforce now includes approximately 30 percent of all U.S. workers, primarily women and people of color.

But even contingent workers are affected by overwork. Not only has it become more profitable for employers to require their regular full-time workers to work excessive hours, it is also profitable to supplement the regular staff with part time or temporary workers who, according to current law, do not have to receive benefits, and who are often paid lower hourly rates than their full-time colleagues for doing the same job.

The Underemployed

Overwork and joblessness are often two sides of the same coin, as employers increasingly choose to limit the number of employees hired while requiring those already on the job to work extended hours. Although unemployment affects Americans of all ages and skill levels, people of lower-income and communities of color are the hardest hit. Black men, especially younger ones, suffer from our nation's highest unemployment rates.

Furthermore, over the last 20 years, unemployment has also impacted hundreds of thousands of formerly secure, well-paid workers due to corporate mergers, takeovers, or "restructuring." In order to maximize profits, companies are "downsizing"—laying off as many employees as possible and *overworking* those who remain. As many "survivors" say, "One person is now doing the work of two." The events of September 11, 2001, and the accompanying economic slowdown have led to additional widespread layoffs.

Might it be possible for well-paid but overworked employees to "just say no" to their long hours, give up their extra pay, and demand instead that their work be shared with those who don't have jobs? Not only is this possible, it has actually happened.

In 1986, autoworkers from UAW Local 95 at the General Motors plant in Janesville, Wisconsin were jubilant when they signed an agreement with GM for a four-day workweek: four 10-hour days and three days off per week. The contract also provided for a fifth 10-hour day if GM felt it was needed. At first, workers were able to enjoy their great schedules, but after a few years, GM began pushing them to work five, six, even seven days a week, sometimes up to 80 hours a week.

Even though these workers made $27.75 an hour in overtime pay for Saturday and weekday overtime, and $37 an hour for working Sundays and holidays, many preferred to give up the extra hours and income so they could have more time with their families. In November 1994, Local 95 voted to go on strike to reduce excessive overtime hours and to get GM to hire additional workers.

Local 95 was inspired by another dramatic strike one month earlier. At GM's enormous "Buick City" plant in Flint, Michigan, workers were forced to put in 11-hour days, six days a week or more, and their fatigue, repetitive strain injuries, and stress-related illnesses were rising. Buick City had not hired any new workers since 1986, instead taking on occasional temporary workers for limited periods of peak demand.

On September 29, 1994, the 11,500 members of Local 599 struck Buick City. After five days, during which production in GM plants across the U.S. was shut down, the strike ended when GM agreed to help those already injured, prevent such overload in the future, and hire back 779 full-time workers who had long been unemployed.

Low-income Workers

The Economic Policy Institute reports that approximately 24 percent (almost one-fourth) of all American workers today earn below-poverty incomes ($8.71 an hour or less). Low-income workers tend to be women and people of color, and their low incomes often result from low hourly wages at contingent, short hours or temporary jobs (usually without benefits). For low-paid workers, long work hours—if they can get them—are often essential.

On Chicago's South Side, a mother (we'll call her Jane) and her two children—an eight-year-old boy and a six-year-old girl—live in a very dangerous neighborhood. Due to commonplace drugs and shootings, Jane has to be around to watch them when they get home from school at 3 P.M. Since she can't find a regular job while they're in school, she leaves them home alone at night while she works the night shift at a retail drugstore. Her work number is posted between the kids' beds on a nightstand by the phone. But her $200-a-week night job isn't enough to pay her bills, so she also finds part-time work cleaning apartments during the day. She sleeps when she can.

Low-income workers like Jane sometimes juggle two, or even three, part-time jobs in order to support themselves and their families. When they do so, the government officially counts them as "part-time workers," even though they may actually be working more than 40 hours a week (more than "full-time"), while still receiving low pay and no benefits from any of their jobs.

While people at all occupational and income levels suffer from the problems of overwork, lack of time, and related physical and emotional stress, low-income workers and their families bear a special burden. If you are overworked but well paid, you can use your income to purchase conveniences and amenities that help you cope with your lack of time, and you can hire others to provide essential household services, such as cooking, cleaning, and childcare that you do not have time to perform. Lower-income workers, however, may not only lack time, but also the ability to pay for the services and conveniences higher-income workers take for granted.

There is nothing wrong with part-time work that pays well and provides benefits. For many overworked individuals, being able to do their jobs less than full-time, while still receiving benefits and promotions, is an ideal solution for better work-life balance. But for lower-income workers, shorter hours alone are no solution unless accompanied by higher wages. Understanding this, many American communities have passed "living wage" laws, requiring minimum rates of pay that lift full-time workers in their communities above poverty levels.

The Good News

Some big corporations are finding that allowing high-powered employees to work less actually improves their performance. And these employees report that their scaled-back workweeks do not inhibit their career advancement. Such findings come from a recent study of 87 corporate professionals whose employers developed "customized work arrangements" that allow them to work less than full time, at proportionally reduced wages. These "downshifting" professionals include women who are starting families, and men seeking more time with their kids or greater community involvement.

In an industry notorious for its long work hours, SAS, a privately held computer software company in Cary, North Carolina, decided to improve employees' well-being by limiting their weekly work hours, starting with its CEO. Hours were reduced first to 40, then 35 per week. The company switchboard got turned off at

5 P.M., and the gate was locked at 6 P.M. The result has been programmers who are more alert, fewer programming errors, and millions of dollars saved due to extremely low employee turnover. Originally viewed as crazy by its competitors, SAS has since been profiled by "60 Minutes," and studied by many other firms interested in duplicating its unique approach to productivity.

But bigger struggles still lie ahead, as Americans of all backgrounds bring the problems related to overwork and lack of time into widespread public discussion, question the workaholic values and assumptions of our culture and economy, and begin to propose a range of shorter work-time solutions for a public policy agenda that can benefit all workers. Take Back Your Time Day presents an exciting opportunity to move this process forward.

CHAPTER 3

The Incredible Shrinking Vacation

JOE ROBINSON

Back in 1992, a San Francisco lawyer named Richard Such had a great idea. A trip to Germany had made him aware of how much more vacation time Europeans get compared to Americans. So, Such tried to get an initiative on the California ballot that would have required a six-week vacation for all workers in the state. I met Such while he was seeking signatures for the initiative at a transit stop in downtown San Francisco. Though many people were adding their names, business opposition and a lack of money prevented Such from getting enough signatures to bring the issue to a vote.

More than 10 years later, the situation has not improved. Instead, the average American vacation is even shorter. But another Californian, Joe Robinson, an energetic writer and adventurer from Santa Monica, is trying to change that. He is the leader of a national campaign advocating minimum paid vacation legislation. The campaign has attracted 50,000 petition signers and considerable media attention. In this chapter, Robinson points out how far behind the rest of the world we Americans are when it comes to time for life, and what we can do about it. —JdG urtis Krizer is an aerospace engineer, a parent, a Republican—and livid. The volatile economy and, in particular, the gyrations of defense contracts, have made it practically impossible for him to be at a company for the five years needed to get more than two weeks off. This is a fact of life for most of us now in a world where the average worker will go through seven *careers*, and many more jobs, in a lifespan. With each new employer, his accrued vacation time shrinks to zero, and he's back to grubbing for a week or two of vacation.

Sometimes pulling 80- and 90-hour workweeks, Krizer is furious that he never has any extended time to recover from the pounding or to spend with his wife and family as real quality time. His company's policy of two weeks, he tells me, is "hilarious, because that only applies to the U.S. Our company has a division in Germany where they get four- to six-week holidays."

American Exceptionalism

As the world shrinks in the global marketplace and many of us work for multinational companies, more and more American workers across party lines are discovering just how out of whack paid-leave policies are in the U.S. compared to the rest of the world, and often to what European and Australian fellow workers in their very own companies receive.

While colleagues in Paris or Melbourne get four to five weeks of paid leave by law each year—six and more by collective agreement—Americans are stuck with 8.1 days after the first year on the job, and 10.2 days after three years, according to the Bureau of Labor Statistics, by far the shortest vacations in the industrialized world. It's becoming clear that this miserly state of affairs doesn't jibe with our professed belief in equal treatment, family values, justice, or engaged citizenship.

As one worker wrote to Work to Live, the campaign I started to address our vacation deficit disorder with a minimum paid-leave law, "It makes my blood boil to know that European workers for my company receive three times the vacation time I do, and it makes me feel like a big, fat sucker."

Workers like these know the lie behind the stinginess of American paid-leave— that we could never have long vacations like the Europeans because it would kill profitability and reduce us to living on Spam for the rest of our lives. In fact, hundreds of American companies operate successfully in Europe while providing employees with four to six-week vacations as required by local law.

It's been going on for decades, and the European divisions of Ford, Xerox, Microsoft, Coke, and Pepsi have all managed to avoid apocalypse, as have thousands of corporations in the U.S. who offer their top executives four weeks vacation or more—a routine part of incentive compensation for the brass. It's proof positive that four-week vacations are not only doable, but are in fact being done on a regular basis.

No Legal Protections

So it's not that U.S. companies *can't* implement real vacations. They just don't want to. And if they don't want to, they don't have to, because we are the only country in the industrialized world without a minimum paid-leave law. Even the Chinese get a mandated three weeks off. With vacation time left solely to the whim of employers, we are forever left in the position of begging for it, and now as never before. In the 24/7 workplace, where, according to *U.S. News & World Report* and the *National Sleep Foundation*, almost 40 percent of us put in more than 50 hours a week, it's becoming harder and harder to get the leave coming to us. Vacations are increasingly on paper only.

"They tell you, 'we can't really let you take that time off now, because we're short'," fumes Troy Overfield, a managed care administrator. "It's life that's too short. I worked for 10 years with no vacation. I'm not accepting that anymore."

The manic lust to reach the next quarter's earnings estimates so the brass can cash in astronomical bonuses and stock options, combined with the false urgency of ubiquitous instant communications, has chilled our already paltry vacations further. Managers stall, sow doubt, and cancel paid leave, making it seem like you're a company saboteur simply for taking the time the company originally offered you.

"They make you feel like the whole place is going to fall apart if you leave," notes Matt Fahrner, a systems technician for a national leather retailer. "You'd be causing a hardship for other employees. There's always a big project that needs to be done. The way that business is structured today there's always something more to do. You're never finished. Therefore, when you take a vacation, it's a bad time, no matter what. So there's this guilt associated with it."

Downsizing-fueled job insecurity has led some Americans to work through their vacations in a practice known as "defensive overworking," a futile attempt to insulate themselves from future layoffs. On average, according to a study commissioned by Expedia.com, Americans *gave back* 175 million days of paid vacation to employers last year—time they already had coming. It was a $20 billion gift to business.

It's no surprise in this climate of fear and paranoia that some 26 percent of American workers don't take any vacation at all. And for the rest, well, it's not much better, as this mind-boggling stat reveals: Half of all travel by Americans is now in two or three-day microscopic bits, reports the Travel Industry Association of America. The average vacation span now is a long weekend. This helps to explain another staggering statistic: Only eight percent of Americans have passports. In Australia, more than 40 percent of the population has passports. It's tricky to see the world in a weekend.

Europeans joke that Americans come in only two ages: college student or senior citizen. As if out of some lost *Twilight Zone* episode, every Yank without a student ID or jug of Metamucil has gone missing. Unfortunately, we know all too well where they are, sucked up by the career black hole that passes for life for Americans between the ages of 25 and 65.

Out of Balance

The only thing valued in the mindset that fuels our overworked land is productivity. Unless we're hyperventilating away on productive activity, we are worthless. This has led us to the truly psychotic state whereby enjoyment—intrinsic satisfaction without objective end—is a cause for guilt, twitchiness, and unhappiness, because it's seen as a violation of productive purpose.

When the point of all our work, enjoyment of the fruits of our labor, has become something to fear, we have succeeded in sentencing ourselves to a "life" of hard labor. Even if we manage to take a vacation, we're too guilty to really relax and allow ourselves the release from the endless cycle of fear and anxiety our bodies need to recover from a year of stress.

We are definitely a piece of work.

The Engine of Creativity

As with any behavior as psychologically twisted as this, there's a lot going into the pot: the fact that we have so much of our esteem and self-worth wrapped up in what we do, instead of who we are. There's the superstition about free time—that it's evil because it's non-productive. But it's really the opposite. It's the engine of creativity, energy, and innovation. And there's the illusion that more material stuff, prestige, and money will make us happy when, as all the science shows, they won't.

We could begin to stick our toe in the water of real vacations and enjoyment, and not feel guilty about it, if we could simply legalize them. Because we have no paid-leave law, the message is very clear: Vacations are not officially sanctioned. Instead, they are left with the distinct odor of illegitimacy, particularly as we have to go through such a stink to get them from people who don't want us to take them.

When you have to twist arms, run a gauntlet of slacker cracks, and then—the final insult—feel unproductive and paranoid when you're on your vacation, it feels about as legitimate as a bank heist. But it's you who has been robbed of the peace of mind to enjoy the time of your life.

How Europe Does It

It's all so pointless when you realize how easy it could be for us to take real holidays. The difference between being a zombie with a week or two of guilt-wracked vacation and having four to six legal weeks to savor and indulge as the Europeans do comes down to two amazingly simple workplace practices: *planning* and *cross-training*.

Unlike in the U.S., where companies don't want you to be gone, and so don't plan for it, turning even a few days off into utter chaos, real vacations work in Europe because companies actually plan for it. Employees put in their holiday requests at the beginning of the year and figure out among themselves and management who goes when.

"We would sit down and say, 'well, there's a conflict here; we can't have as many people gone in that time frame'," recalls Elliot Robertson, an American technology buyer who worked in Germany for eight years. "So then we'd ask who's willing to give and take. If people had kids, you made sure that those guys got first dibs on the times when their children were out of school. It worked very well." Robertson and his family were able to enjoy six weeks off every year.

Holiday scheduling is built into the workflow for the year. "It's an integral part of the work planning," explains Danish labor expert Kim Benzon Knudsen. "Five to six weeks holiday here is 10 percent of the year, and management must provide that the workforce of the company has the ability to cover people while they're gone to that extent."

Vacations are factored into budgeting, production, and all phases of the operation. The absence of any thought or planning in American companies for the vacation benefits they supposedly offer illustrates not only how poorly managed things are here, but also why there's that panic and pile-up when you try to take a holiday. A paid-leave law would legitimize vacations so that they would become a normal part of the work year and planning, not an afterthought that makes your supervisor steam like a jilted lover. Holidays would no longer be thought of as mutinous interruptions, but routine, covered events.

Cross-training

The other part of the solution is cross-training, a concept that makes for better athletes in the sporting world and more well-rounded, and certainly more relaxed, employees at the office. European companies use cross-training to spread the knowledge and skills around, so that when someone is on a holiday other people know enough about their job to pick up the slack while they're gone.

Elliot Robertson raves about the wonders of cross-training, which he first discovered in the U.S. Army (which, by the way, offers four weeks vacation the first year on the job). "Everyone in my department knew pretty much the mechanics of each other's jobs," he says. "So we could cover somebody else while they were on their holiday, and business wouldn't suffer."

Juergen Lattenkamp, a medical assistant who operates MRI equipment at a radiology practice in Mannheim, Germany, spreads his job among three different people to give himself six weeks and more of holiday time each year. "If nobody can do your job, you're stuck," Lattenkamp points out. "It's very important to delegate. If you give up some responsibility, you have more free time."

If it was any more elementary, we'd need coloring books. Ron Keleman, a financial services entrepreneur in Salem, Oregon, knows planning and cross-training can work here, because that's the policy at his company, the H Group. He's gone from being someone who almost never took a day off to somebody who savors a month off each year. He's now working on taking every Friday off, too. His staff gets almost a month of paid leave.

"It's made me more productive," enthuses Keleman. "It's made me happier. I've accomplished more in the last seven years than I did in the previous twenty. It's fun to be here. It's all about quality of life."

For Cincinnati cleaning company, Jancoa, Inc., cross-training combined with three-week vacations for all 468 people at the company has resulted in increased morale, productivity, and profits, which are up 15 percent. It cut turnover at the company from 360 percent to 60 percent in a notoriously revolving-door industry. The company hardly has any overtime or recruiting costs anymore.

It should be clear to anyone that real vacations and the planning to make them work definitely can get done here at almost no cost. Instead of destroying productivity, as the Chicken Littles of the business world claim they will, evidence shows that three- and four-week vacations actually increase production and profits. In fact, when you get into the research, you realize the complete fraud of the bill of goods we're sold on productivity. It's not how long you work, but how well you do the job, which is a function of how rested and energized you are.

Continuous time on a task causes us to get overtasked. CAT scans of fatigued brains look exactly like those that are sound asleep. One Department of Labor study found that the average amount of productive time in a typical working day is 4.8 hours. Another study revealed that someone working seven straight weeks of 50-hour weeks would get no more done after two months than if they had worked 40 hours a week, because the productivity level is so bad in the fried haze of overtime.

Jobs done late at night and over the weekend frequently have to be redone later. Curtis Krizer has seen it many times. "We waste a lot of money on overtime, tons

TIME IS A FAMILY VALUE
TIME IS A FAMILY VALUE
TIME IS A FAMILY VALUE
TIME IS A FAMILY VALUE
TIME IS A FAMILY VALUE
TIME IS A FAMILY VALUE
TIME IS A FAMILY VALUE
TIME IS A FAMILY VALUE
TIME IS A FAMILY VALUE
TIME IS A FAMILY VALUE
TIME IS A FAMILY VALUE
TIME IS A FAMILY VALUE

www.timeday.org

TAKE BACK YOUR TIME
TAKE BACK YOUR TIME
TAKE BACK YOUR TIME

of money," he says. "You make many more mistakes. Work on the weekend has to be redone on Monday. You're spending astronomical amounts if you're paying contractors because of the extra time. It's a waste."

Chronic overtime and skipped vacations don't make us more productive. Our bravado act only produces more medical bills which is one of many reasons why we need real vacations. They keep the health tab down by breaking up stress and healing bodies and minds battered by pointless masochistic behavior. Studies have shown that men who took an annual vacation reduced the risk of heart attack by 30 percent, while frequent vacations cut women's risk of death from heart disease in half.

Half of all U.S. workers are said to be suffering from symptoms of burnout today. Burnout occurs when stress has exhausted all your emotional resources. A study by the University of Tel Aviv's Arie Shirom and S. E. Hobfoll documented that one of the remarkable features of a vacation is that it helps to gather lost emotional resources crashed by burnout, such as social support and a sense of mastery, and that *it takes a minimum of two full weeks for the emotional restoration process to occur.* That's why long weekends are not vacations. You need time to fully unwind and restore your mind and body. Vacations are a simple antidote to the crushing epidemic of burnout.

Vacations are also your best chance in the year to get in some real living, to get out of the job-as-life box, off automatic pilot, and rediscover your passions, enthusiasms, friends, family, and the vitality of partaking in the world outside career brainlock. Social scientists have found that leisure experiences increase positive mood, act as a buffer against life's setbacks, and open the door to the best times of our lives. When we are fully involved in the direct experience of intrinsic pursuits, we come as close as we can to happiness and well-being—to optimum living.

Believe it or not, we almost had paid-leave protection back in the 1930s, when European nations began to enshrine their vacation policies into law. In 1936 the Department of Labor formed the Committee on Vacations with Pay which issued a report blasting our lack of paid-leave legislation pointing out that 30 other countries had laws on the books. It recommended that the Secretary of Labor draft legislation, but the ball was dropped and nothing ever emerged.

It was a huge lost opportunity, the fateful moment that consigned us to micro-vacations ever since. If our lack of paid-leave protection was a scandal seven decades ago, it's little short of barbaric today. We're way overdue to join the ranks of the civilized nations of the world and offer the planet's hardest working people, the folks who create our national wealth, without whom there would be no productivity rates to argue about, a minimum paid-leave law.

That's why tens of thousands of people signed Work to Live's petition for a minimum paid-leave law. I hope you will join with them at www.worktolive.info and help make this initiative a reality.

Work to Live has proposed legislation to amend the Fair Labor Standards Act to mandate three weeks of paid leave for anyone who has worked at a job for a year, increasing to four weeks after three years. It's a modest step in the direction of the rest of the industrialized world. The law would:

Protect you against any retaliation for taking all the vacation coming to you, and end the fear of replacement, demotion, or promotion fallout from taking a vacation.

Protect you against employers stalling or chilling vacations with chronic cancellations.

Prevent your vacation from shrinking when you change jobs. You will always get three weeks after you spend a year at a job.

Provide that after three months with a company and up through the first year you would receive a pro rata share of vacation. For example, at six months you would get 1.5 weeks off.

These provisions aren't pie in the sky. Every other industrialized nation has them. We can have the same protections if we can create a lobbying effort that can form a national consensus around this issue, enough to convince politicians that time for our lives, families, health, and communities is important enough to swing votes.

Congresspersons who talk about family values should be supporting legislation to curb what is by far the biggest cause of home-wrecking today—missing parents caused by overwork, and families who share no more than a long weekend together of quality time the whole year. According to Joan Williams, author of *Unbending Gender,* high-hour parents have more incidence of divorce, with 40 percent of the kids of divorce winding up in poverty with their mothers.

Join together with Work to Live to press the case for minimum paid leave. The majority of working Americans want more time off (75 percent in an Expedia.com survey). We have the votes. Let's use them to take back our time!

CHAPTER 4

Forced Overtime in the Land of the Free

LONNIE GOLDEN

Not long ago, I gave a speech about Take Back Your Time Day *at Southern Utah University. The large student audience was quiet, but very sympathetic, as shown by written comments that were sent to me. However, one professor of economics challenged my support of European laws ensuring vacations and reasonable working hours. It was, he said, a matter of "free choice." American workers, by agreeing to contracts with their employers, freely choose the hours they work. Why did I want to force them to choose fewer hours? The "free choice" mantra is often raised when one talks about working hours, but as Lonnie Golden (who has carefully researched the issue for the Economic Policy Institute) makes clear, for more and more Americans, long overtime hours are hardly freely chosen.—JdG*

On December 12, 1999, grim news came from the state of Maine. Following a winter storm, Brent Churchill, a telephone lineman working almost continuously (with only five hours of sleep in the previous two-and-a-half days), reached for a 7,200 volt cable and was electrocuted. In response, Maine became the first state to limit the number of involuntary *overtime* hours employers could require from an employee, capping them at 80 hours within any two-week period.

Though not exactly a "new deal" for the American worker, the new law drew public attention to the real risks of excessive work hours and helped launch a surge of legislative reform proposals across the U.S. to limit compulsory overtime. Nevertheless, long hours of work are still too often considered just a part of our existence like the weather, the proverbial problem that "everyone talks about but nobody does anything about."

In the U.S., it is entirely legal for an employer to require an employee to work beyond his or her scheduled shift time with no advance notice, *and* to take disciplinary action against a worker who refuses. Reprisals for refusing overtime assignments may range from demotion, assignments to unattractive tasks or shift times and reduced access to promotion, to outright discharge.

Such mandatory overtime may be just the tip of the iceberg. With the increase of dual-working couples in the work force, the dangers of long hours of work and fatigue have become greater. The goal of this chapter is to investigate whether long, involuntary overtime work in the U.S. is indeed prevalent, harmful, and avoidable.

Clarifying the Problem

Many analysts do not regard long hours as a problem at all. Indeed, they argue, such schedules may reflect a healthy work ethic, serve to enrich and enhance the skills of the labor force, and facilitate an economic boom, such as that observed in the 1990s. Thus, we need first to systematically clarify the extent, potential risks, and problems of long hours.

Too often used synonymously, there are three distinct, albeit related, notions of excessive hours of work—*overtime, overwork,* and *overemployment.* Over*time* refers to working hours beyond some standard or norm. For employees on payrolls, this standard is widely considered 40 hours, embodying the spirit of the Fair Labor Standards Act (FLSA) standard workweek.

But for employees "exempt" from the Act's coverage, such as those in managerial, administrative, and professional jobs, the notion of overtime may start at more than 40 hours per week. The list of occupations with the longest hours is headed by clergy, physicians, and firefighters.

The causes behind more overtime are both economic and cultural. For example, escalating costs of health care plans and training for new employees render all but impotent the FLSA's time-and-a-half pay premium as a deterrent to employers' demanding overtime hours. Moreover, as real wage rates for hourly workers have stagnated for almost three decades, working overtime often became the only means by which lower-paid workers could stay ahead of inflation and their increasing, burdensome debts.

Furthermore, the well-documented, rising inequality in wages among workers within a given occupation has increased the rewards of putting in longer hours. Thus, the perpetuation of overtime work is a tango which takes two, if perhaps unenthusiastic, partners.

The connotation of over*work* is somewhat different. Overwork occurs when longer hours per day, week, or year begin to have deleterious effects on the individual, family, community, and economy. The line between work and overwork is crossed when fatigue and stress build up, often cumulatively, leading to a greater risk of mistakes, accidents, injuries, health problems, reduced quality of workmanship, and diminished productivity per hour worked.

Overwork

Overtime, even if voluntary, can inevitably lead to overwork when people work more than is healthy—physiologically or psychologically—for themselves, their families or the public. Indeed, while traveling the towns of Britain as far back as the early 1770s, Adam Smith observed, that with the "encouragement of high wages . . . workmen are very apt to overwork themselves, and to ruin their health and constitution in a few years."

Employees who work overtime on a regular basis reported they are twice as likely (62 percent versus 34 percent) to find their jobs highly stressful, according to a 1991 Northwestern National Life study. Those working more than eight hours per day reported feeling more fatigued and depressed. A critical fatigue point tends to occur after the ninth hour of work in a given day, depending on the working conditions and tasks. This is not surprising given the higher rates of accident and injury and lower productivity per hour during overtime. Overtime has been identified as a factor contributing to safety incidents at nuclear power plants, manufacturing plants, and in hospitals among anesthetists.

The cumulative effects of long hours take their toll via the development of health conditions, such as high blood pressure, heart attacks, and occupational burnout. Moreover, fatigue contributes to road accidents among truck drivers and commuters. Finally, nurses on variable schedules (such as mandated overtime shifts) report being twice as likely to have accidents, errors, and near misses, largely due to "frequent lapses of attention and increased reaction time." Medical residents cite fatigue as a cause for their serious mistakes in four out of ten cases. Lack of control over one's scheduling of work can exacerbate the adverse effects of overwork.

Overemployment

Third and finally, the problem of over*employment* refers to a situation where workers are willing but unable at their current jobs to reduce the amount of time they devote to earning an income. Many people go through a spell at some point when they would prefer shorter work hours. They are prepared to sacrifice income to attain it in order to avoid the more costly step of leaving an occupation or withdrawing from the labor force entirely.

People who remain overemployed tolerate longer hours because they either expect their overemployment to be brief (such as temporary care-giving), or figure that part-time or reduced hours status involves too large a sacrifice in terms of benefit coverage or job status.

Thus, overemployment involves involuntary hours of work, even if no overtime *per se* is involved and even when symptoms of overwork are not yet present. Suffice it to say that the main cause of overemployment is the inherently inflexible nature of most jobs, workplaces, corporate cultures, and work-scheduling structures. But overemployment not only reduces the well-being of workers, but also of others whose employment and income-earning prospects are thereby diminished.

Unfortunately, the establishment of an *eBay*-type mechanism for trading unwanted hours does not appear to be on the horizon. In addition, a large part of overemployment stems from the noncompliance of employers with existing work regulations—violating the FLSA guidelines for providing overtime premiums.

The Extent of Overtime, Overwork and Overemployment

What is the current extent of overtime work, overwork, and overemployment? Regarding overtime, almost one-third of the U.S. workforce regularly works more than the standard 40-hour workweek. In fact, nearly one in five workers now spend more than 50 hours per week at work.

There has been a gradual, yet detectable upward trend in this percentage over the last decade. *Average* overtime hours in manufacturing industries reached a record high of about five hours per week in the late 1990s, with hourly workers putting in 25 percent more overtime than they were a decade previously.

Compared with overtime, the extent of overwork is less easily measured. It can be observed mainly indirectly, through the individual and social costs of long hours, such as risks to worker and public safety and health. A recent study found that 28 percent of American workers reported feeling overworked often or very often in the last three months. This proportion rises to 54 percent who felt overworked sometime during the last three months. Thus, a good deal of the work force feels chronically overworked.

To measure the rate of overemployment among the labor force, we have only periodic snapshots from various one-time surveys, asking people if they are prepared to reduce their work hours and income. Because the question has not been worded uniformly, estimates of the extent of overemployment are all over the map. For example, in one study, as many as 50 percent of wage and salary workers who follow a fixed hour schedule expressed a willingness to work fewer hours for proportionately lower pay. Not surprisingly, this willingness diminishes with the size of the income sacrificed. While 35 percent would give up 10 percent of income for 10 percent more free time, only 17 percent would accept a 20 percent pay cut to get a four-day workweek.

The Extent of Mandatory Overtime

The extent of the most troubling aspect of overemployment, mandatory overtime work, is even less well documented. The last time a thorough attempt was made to directly measure the extent of mandatory overtime work in a nationally representative sample was a 1977 Quality of Employment Survey (QES). At that time, 45 percent of workers said overtime work was "mostly up to their employer" versus 44 percent that said it was "up to them," and 11 percent that said "both." An average of about 24 percent reported that they would suffer a penalty if they refused the overtime work, while 44 percent indicated that they "suffered no penalty." Men and blue-collar workers had a greater likelihood of facing mandatory overtime, as did workers who had medical or pension plans, while unionized workers had a lower likelihood.

The incidence of mandatory overtime has risen more or less commensurately with overtime itself. A recent survey found 45 percent of workers having to work overtime with little or no notice. A particularly informative 1999 Cornell University survey of 4,278 unionized hourly workers, concentrated mainly in the Northeast and in six industries, found that 60 percent worked some overtime in the previous month. About a third of these workers were putting in 11 or more hours of overtime per week.

The survey included specific questions regarding overtime work, attempting to disentangle voluntary from involuntary overtime. About a third of the 60 percent of workers involved in overtime reported being compelled by their employer to work overtime. Workers employed in transportation and emergency health services faced the most pressure from employers.

The damage done by involuntary overtime becomes apparent in the Cornell survey. Workers reporting high pressure to work overtime experienced double the work injuries suffered by those who were not. Similarly, as supervisory pressure to work overtime increased, workers reported higher levels of somatic stress, depression, job-escape drinking, work-family conflict, and absenteeism due to illness.

In the healthcare sector, overtime work is widespread among nurses, medical residents, and doctors. A survey of nurse professionals found that 64 percent have worked mandatory overtime. About one quarter worked mandatory overtime once or twice a month, while another quarter worked it once or twice a week. About 14 percent worked additional mandatory hours every day. Perhaps it is no coincidence that nurse's aides were second only to truck drivers in the total number of cases of disabling injuries and illness.

Solutions: Innovations in Collective Bargaining Agreements

The remedy to excessive hours does not lie in individual responses, such as job switching, downshifting, or negotiating an informal arrangement with one's supervisor. Rather, it involves collective action—using the innovations introduced by recent collective bargaining agreements to adopt legislation and effectively enforce regulations. The goal should be to keep overtime "safe, legal, rare, and a voluntary choice."

Examples of collective bargaining innovation include the following:

Hospitals and Health Services

At Boston University Medical Center, hospital administrators cannot mandate overtime for nurses for more than four hours beyond their normal shift, and at Tenet Healthcare and its affiliate, St. Vincent's Hospital in Worcester, MA, involuntary overtime is permissible no more than twice every three months. The hospital has the right to assign up to two hours of mandatory overtime, but an additional two hours only if the nurse feels capable of doing so safely. In some cases, nurses' contracts may have outright bans on mandatory overtime, with special exceptions for emergencies.

Telecommunications

The Communications Workers of America (CWA) agreement with Verizon in 2000 resulted in reduced mandatory overtime "caps" from 15 to 7.5 hours a week. At Southwestern Bell, mandatory overtime caps at 10 hours per week for seven months a year and 15 hours for the other five months. The company agreed to give at least 2.5 hours advance union notice if overtime is required.

The CWA contract in New Jersey provides the right to refuse overtime one time per month. At Michigan Bell, the contractual limit on mandatory overtime is nine hours per week for eight months a year and 14 hours per week for four months a year. The CWA contract with BellSouth specifies that no mandatory overtime will be assigned to service representatives with less than 24 hours notice, except for emergency conditions.

Airlines

Northwest Airlines permits employees to refuse overtime if they provide reasons that cannot be altered on short notice, such as childcare. In an agreement between United Air Lines and the International Association of Machinists and Aerospace Workers, "employees will not be required to work overtime against their wishes, except in emergencies . . . and until all readily available employees . . . have been offered an opportunity to work the overtime hours . . . "

Postal Services

The American Postal Workers Union (APWU) and National Association of Letter Carriers (NALC) agreed with the United States Postal Service to require overtime only from members who sign up on an "overtime desired" list.

Manufacturing

The United Steelworkers negotiated a cap on mandatory overtime at FMC, a Baltimore pesticide plant. USW agreements at Fording Coal Ltd. and Highland Valley Copper require that overtime shall be on a voluntary basis only. Washington-Baltimore Newspaper Guild Local 320-35 and the publisher Bureau of National Affairs negotiated a voluntary overtime arrangement, where members have a right to be excused from overtime work, unless no other appropriate employee is available.

Food and Retail

The United Food and Commercial Workers won agreements that stipulate "overtime work shall be kept to a minimum . . . and no employee shall be compelled to work overtime or be discriminated against for refusal to work overtime." The Teamsters also won some new restrictions on forced overtime in their recent United Parcel Service (UPS) contract for full-time package-car drivers.

These agreements represent progress, but to keep all of this in perspective, no more than nine percent of first-time negotiated union contracts in the private sector contain any provision limiting mandatory overtime, and only about 20 percent of all U.S. union members have contracts that include restrictions on mandatory overtime.

Solutions: State and Federal Legislative Reforms

California is the only state to limit the workweek by law, and has established a limit of 72 hours. By contrast, the Canadian provinces of Manitoba, Ontario, and Saskatchewan grant workers a right to refuse overtime after working 44 or 48 hours in a week. Similarly, the European Union's Working Time Directives implemented in 1998 set 48 hours as the weekly maximum *and* gave workers the right to a minimum of daily rest periods, at least one day off per week, and four weeks paid vacation per year.

The primary approach to curb mandatory overtime in the U.S. has been to target the healthcare service sector. A few state-level bills have attempted to place caps on the number of overtime hours per week for all hourly health workers. The *Registered Nurses and Patients Protection Act* in the House and the companion, the

Safe Nursing and Patient Care Act of 2001 in the Senate, introduced into the 107th U.S. Congress, would limit the amount of forced overtime that licensed health care providers could work.

Some states have proposed raising the pay premium to double time once work time has crossed a certain threshold, such as 12 hours per day. But the current bills are all quite tame compared to proposals introduced into state Houses in the past, such as a 1983 bill in Pennsylvania that would have banned the institution of mandatory overtime until all employees on layoff are recalled.

Conclusions

The phenomena of overwork and overemployment should be addressed with policies that curb involuntary overtime and increase shorter-hour options. There is broad public support in America already for limiting hours of work by industry and occupation. For example, 68 percent favor capping shifts at eight hours for aviation, 50 percent for health care, truckers, and police officers.

Legislation or collective agreements that make overtime voluntary should start with healthcare then spread to other industries, occupations, or job classifications, not only where public health and safety is at risk, but among workers where overemployment generally is high. At the very least, for safety's sake, workers should be allowed to refuse to work after a certain number of hours. Recent private sector innovations such as work-sharing or individualized reduced hours are useful models.

But the Fair Labor Standards Act itself should be updated to include a protected right of refusal, minimum advance notice, and new pay penalties for systematic overtime work. Unfortunately, the current Congressional leadership is trying to *narrow* the FLSA's overtime provisions, while they should actually be expanded to encompass white-collar jobs, as well.

Long marches all begin with significant first steps. The struggle against forced overtime is no exception.

PART TWO

Time is a Family Value

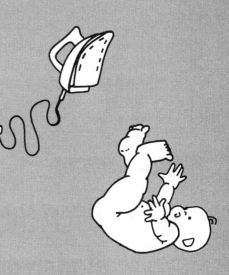

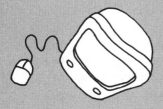

CHAPTER 5

Overscheduled Kids, Underconnected Families

WILLIAM DOHERTY AND BARBARA CARLSON

Americans talk a lot about family values these days, but often leave one out—perhaps the most important one for keeping families together and raising children to be happy and healthy adults. Time is a family value, and family time is perhaps the most obvious victim of overwork in America. Recent studies suggest that dual-income couples find only 12 minutes a day to talk to each other. Advertising, always sensitive to national trends, now frequently focuses on the loss of family time to overwork. Mothers can now leave cards for their children in the morning, apologizing for not tucking them in at night and for leaving for work before they wake up. Many parents, wishing they had more time for their families, give their children material gifts in an attempt to relieve guilt.

Overwork is clearly a culprit in this, but as the next two chapters of this book point out, not the only one. Sadly, we Americans are imposing our hurry-up, overworked lifestyles on our children, with rueful consequences. Taking back our time means changing cultural practices as much as it means reducing overwork. —JdG

A Houston mother recently recounted with pride a scheduling breakthrough with her six- and eight-year-old sons. Their after-school and evening schedules were already crowded with sports and music lessons, but Timmy needed tutoring for reading and Matt had trouble finding time for his homework in the evening.

Her solution was creative; she found a tutor who would meet with Timmy at 6:30 A.M. while Matt did his homework outside in the waiting car. This allowed for an efficient use of early morning hours and no interference with after-school and evening activities. Mom was proud of this scheduling coup.

But Kathy, a California mother, took a different approach. After Little League baseball for 11-year-old son, Josh, reached a fever pitch of scheduling one year, she and her husband said "Enough." Family dinners were vanishing. Evening and weekends were spent on the road and at ball fields. With two working parents, another son's activities to schedule, and a community with overcrowded highways, baseball was pushing everyone to the edge.

Kathy and her husband decided to reclaim family time by not enrolling their son in Little League. But when the new season started, they discovered that they had violated a community standard for good parenting, as evidenced by the shock and dismay of other Little League parents. When Kathy told another mother at the local supermarket about the family's decision, the stunned neighbor replied, "Can you do that?"

We hear these stories all the time, even more so since we helped start the organization, *Putting Family First* (www.puttingfamilyfirst.info), in suburban Minneapolis, and wrote the book, *Putting Family First,* from which this chapter is adapted. Good parents have created schedules for their kids that only CEOs used to keep. When asked by a journalist about a schedule that sometimes combines seven after-school activities for her three children, one mother answered cheerfully, "We like to keep them active and busy." Why so many activities? "We want our kids to be happy," she stated confidently. "We want them to be well-rounded. They seem well-adjusted. And we think we're doing a pretty good job." When questioned again about whether the kids' schedules might be a bit crowded, she responded perhaps a bit defensively, "They like these things. It's not like we're forcing them to go."

The Cart Before the Horse

In today's America, frantic families have become the norm. Well-intentioned parents are acting like recreation directors on a turbo-charged family cruise ship. Family life today revolves around children's activities rather than these activities revolving around the family's schedule. It wasn't always this way. The cart and the

horse have switched positions in the last two decades, with hardly anyone noticing until recently.

Many parents mourn the old family time priorities, but feel helpless to get off
the merry-go-round. We hear parents complain about running all the time, having dinner in the car between practices, and missing out on summer vacations
because of sports tournaments and specialized camps. Although children get used
to whatever family life they receive, we are even beginning to hear them ask to
slow down.

A six-year old gets her first daily planners, and then asks for time just to play.
A nine-year-old boy, in his wish list of birthday presents, places "more time at
home" as number three. A twelve-year old sheepishly asks her parents if it's okay
not to try out for the traveling soccer team. One grandfather shares with sadness
that the only way he gets to see his grandson is from the stands at hockey games.

When so many outside activities compete with one another, things really get
crazy for today's families. Reflecting our competitive culture, many of us want
excellence for our children in every area. And each activity leader feels that his or
her activity requires a good deal of time and commitment.

Kids are torn between hockey practice and Confirmation classes, between
homework and violin practice, between cheerleading and the fall musical. In the
face of these competing demands, time is lost for family activities like dinners,
weekend outings, vacations, and visits to relatives. And there's no time to just hang
out. We end up with overscheduled *and* underconnected families. Though overwhelmed, we still don't think we are doing enough for our children.

Researchers are beginning to catch up with this problem. A national survey
conducted by the University of Michigan's Survey Research Center, finds that
since the late 1970s, there has been a remarkable change in children's schedules
and family activities. Children have lost 12 hours per week in free time, including a 25 percent drop in play and a 50 percent drop in unstructured outdoor
activities.

During the same period, time devoted to structured sports doubled and "pas-
sive, spectator leisure" (watching others play and perform, but not including television) increased from 30 minutes to over three hours per week. In other words,
children make up their own play activities a lot less, engage in supervised sports a
lot more, and spend a whole lot more time watching passively from the sidelines.

It isn't just that children are busier; families spend less time together often
because parents are working more now than ever. According to the Michigan survey, household conversations between parents and children—time for just talking—have dropped nearly off the radar screen, *and there has been a 28 percent
decline in the number of families taking vacations.* Other national surveys have
found a one-third decrease in the number of families who say they eat dinner
together regularly.

What's the Problem?

This change in American family life is deep and broad, cutting a wide swath across income groups and ethnic groups in the population. The very poor do not have the resources to be overscheduled, but they face similar challenges in finding time to connect as a family. The loss of family time has come upon us with amazing speed.

But is this change unwelcome? Is it a problem, or just an inevitable part of modern life? We believe it's a serious problem.

The effects of overbusy family lives on child development are just beginning to be studied by academic researchers, but already the data shows the importance of regular family dinners. The University of Michigan study mentioned earlier found that time eating as a family was a far stronger factor in young children's academic success and psychological well-being than time spent in school, doing homework, and participating in sports, arts, and religious activities.

A large national study of American teenagers found a strong link between regular family meals and a wide range of positive outcomes: academic success, psychological adjustment, and lower rates of alcohol use, drug use, early sexual behavior, and suicidal risk. On the flip side, not having regular family meals was associated with higher risks in all of those areas.

This study defined a family meal as one in which the teenager ate with at least one parent. Given the documented decline in family dinners, it is not surprising that a national poll of teenagers, funded by the White House in Spring, 2000, found that over one-fifth rated "not having enough time with parents" as their top concern, a percentage that tied for first (along with education) on their list of worries.

We also know that children who eat dinner regularly with their families do better nutritionally. One study found that these children have more healthful dietary patterns in a number of areas: more fruits and vegetables, less saturated fat, fewer fried foods and sodas, and more foods rich with vitamins and other micronutrients. Like the other study cited above, these findings held across family income levels.

If you listen to parents, as we do, you know that many feel burdened by crammed schedules and feel a severe loss of family connections. If you listen to teachers, as we do, you know that they see a generation of students weary from schedules that even many adults couldn't handle. A woman from a community near Albany, New York, a teacher of second graders for thirty years, used strong language: "This is an abused generation," she said at a public meeting. She went on to explain that, after thirty years of teaching the same age group, she has never seen children so tired and burdened from being up too early in the morning, going to bed too late at night, while being crunched in between by extremely competitive activities.

The National Association of Elementary School Principals is now weighing in on the problem of overscheduled children. It has issued a recommendation of one activity at a time for young children, with that activity meeting only once or twice a week. If you want your child to experience more than one activity, the Association recommends a different activity each season rather than more than one activity in a single season. These recommendations seem wildly removed from the current schedules of many children and families.

Something is out of whack in American family life, but it's not because parents are enrolling their children in bad activities. We know from common sense and a lot of research that extracurricular involvement is good for kids. Sports, music other fine arts, and religious involvement all contribute to a rich life for a child. The issue is one of balance. And balance requires setting priorities. In our view, there is a serious imbalance and a confused set of priorities in the raising of this generation of children.

What Happened, and When?

How did we get here? It is easier to document the problem of overscheduled kids and underconnected families than it is to explain how it came upon us. There are many explanations, many factors contributing to the problem, and not one decisive cause. We have asked hundreds of parents at community events for their explanations of the social change we have described. Here is what they've said, followed by our own observations:

- More opportunities for children, especially for girls. There are more activities to choose from today than twenty years ago. One mother in North-field, Minnesota, said that she counted fourteen community activities for three-year olds.

- More intense sports activities. Sports used to be seasonal; now many are year round. Traveling teams were unheard of twenty-five years ago, outside of varsity sports. As one veteran coach told us, we have lost the distinction between competitive sports and recreational sports. And this has spilled over to activities such as dance programs and gymnastics which travel to compete. Practices for all kinds of activities now occur three or more times per week, with weekend competitions even for seven-year olds!

- Competition for sports facilities and performance halls means invasion of family time. Take hockey, for example. Limited ice facilities combined with high demand means that some kids practice at 6 A.M. or 10 P.M. And dinner gives way to swimming, music, basketball, and all the rest.

- More working parents. Parents need to fill children's time after school with structured activities. Of course, this does not explain the over-scheduling of

MORE TIME. LESS STUFF.

There's no doubt about it.
When it comes to stuff per capita,
Americans are number one.
But, possessions don't translate into
happiness. What does? A good family
life, meaningful relationships, hobbies,
volunteering for the common good.
It's time we traded some of our
productivity gains for time instead of
money and stuff. We'd all be happier.

10.24.03   TAKE BACK YOUR TIME DAY

evening and weekend hours. Nor does it explain why families with a stay-at-home parent are often as frantic as families with two working parents or single working parents.

- Parental guilt. Parents who feel too busy themselves with work or other activities do not want to deprive their children of any worthwhile opportunity. One mother with a full-time professional job told us that she was determined that her children would not miss out on any opportunities because of her career. She then admitted that the family rarely has dinner together and has a crazed schedule.

- Overreaction to the message that kids do better if they are busy and involved in the community. The word has gotten out to parents that structured outside activities get children involved with other adults and expand their horizons beyond staying home and watching television. What those messages do not emphasize is when to say "enough."

- A sense of danger in the neighborhood. Many parents remember playing freely in their neighborhoods as children, but keep their own children at home or in structured activities to avoid possible danger. These fears are no doubt well-founded in some neighborhoods, but often extend to areas where violent crime is quite rare.

- Fear that one's child will miss out or get left behind. This fuels early, intense involvement in activities, with parents worrying that delaying the start of a sport or musical instrument may doom their child to not being able play competitively at all in the future.

- Increased emphasis on the capabilities of very young children. The preschool years now receive far more emphasis on child development, and parents feel a cultural expectation to get their preschoolers involved in enriching activities. One mother of a four-year old said that she is getting the message from friends and relatives that her daughter (whom the friends and relatives see as athletic) is already behind in gymnastics because she did not start at age three.

- Pressure on contemporary children to "succeed." From having to know the alphabet and colors before going to school, to worrying about a college resume in the sixth grade, to having to compete at high levels in athletics, this is a generation of children and parents who are preoccupied with visible signs of success.

- The expectations of elite colleges for "well-rounded" applicants. During the 1980s and 1990's, these colleges began to emphasize the breadth of students' non-academic records. One sport was not enough. Neither was only one musical instrument or just one leadership position in the school. Community service became a must, with yearbook editorship on the side. Interestingly, in the fall of 2000, Harvard's admissions office published a report saying, in effect, "Enough! We've created a monster." The report described arriving students who are decidedly not well-rounded and who are already burnt out when they enter college.

- Parental peer pressure. All of the forces we've mentioned tend to influence parents most strongly through their peers, that is, from parents of children of similar ages. Parents watch other parents and listen to what other parents say. Look at how holiday letters glowingly describe the plethora of activities in which our children are involved.

All of these factors, and more, contribute to the problem. But what's the big picture? We believe that the adult world of hypercompetition and marketplace values has invaded the family. Of course, parents love their children and try to do what is best for them. But we are raising our children in a culture that defines a good parent as an opportunity provider in a competitive world. Parenting becomes like product development, with insecure parents never knowing when they've done enough and when their children are falling behind.

One parent told us recently that in her upper middle-class community, people no longer brag about the size of their house or the model of their car; they brag about how busy their family is. Parenting has become a competitive sport, with the trophies going to the busiest.

When one parent, in mock complaint says, "We're so busy right now," another parent tops it with a more extreme story. And in a market-oriented, money-driven culture, we can point more readily to things we pay for—equipment, registration fees, traveling expenses, coaches' salaries—than for low-key family activities like hanging out together on a Sunday afternoon or playing a board game on a Friday night.

It's the same with children's play time: we don't easily assign ourselves "parent points" for providing our children with time to daydream and make up games to play with the neighbor's kids. It goes on. A stressed seven-year old whispers to a neighbor parent that she wishes her mother would let her quit scouts. A mother remarks ruefully that her family lives so much in the minivan that she should decorate it! A coach trying to bring balance to his community is dismayed when he comes upon a schedule for 11-year-old boys who practice at 10 P.M. on Thursday nights at a facility 45 minutes from home.

Parents say they hate these schedules but don't know how to change them without depriving their children of opportunities. Everyone is afraid to be the first to cut back. A sane lifestyle looks strange in an insane world.

Enough, we say. Let Take Back Your Time Day be the start of a widespread citizen movement wherein parents reclaim their family time from a world of scheduled hyperactivity and false promises of individual gain.

CHAPTER 6

Recapturing Childhood

BETSY TAYLOR

Until recently, Betsy Taylor was the director of the Center for a New American Dream in Takoma Park, Maryland. The Center (www.newdream.org) is working to redefine core American values—steering them away from a dream centered on money, stuff, and, endless material growth, toward a dream of sufficiency, family, community, and nature. Center organizers, concerned about the harmful impacts of overwork on American life, decided that they would have a four-day workweek (four eight-hour days), with Fridays off. As such, they've been able to attract an immensely able and dedicated workforce, and have created a model for other nonprofits, many of which are as guilty of overworking their employees as any big corporation.

The Center and Betsy Taylor have long been troubled by the corrosive effects of the old, materialistic, American dream on our children. And, as Betsy argues in this chapter (which includes excerpts from her recent book, What Kids Really Want That Money Can't Buy), *they are equally concerned about the new time pressures our children face. —JdG*

Adults aren't the only ones who need to reclaim time. Children are in the same time squeeze. Gone are the days of spacious, unstructured afternoons—time to explore meadows and creeks, or to meander to a museum, or just to hang out at a soda fountain with friends.

There are many reasons for this time scarcity. Overprogramming and the pressure always to advance to higher academic, artistic, and athletic achievement keep kids in a permanent race. Computers, television, and electronic entertainment have replaced unstructured leisure time. On top of this, a growing number of teenagers hold down jobs while attending school. Sadly, many kids are losing touch with life's simple pleasures. They no longer have ample time to explore, play, learn household skills, garden, stay connected with friends and relatives, and keep a slower pace. Kids are being programmed for the rat race, but at what cost?

The Importance of Play

The slogan and bumper sticker adopted by my organization, the Center for a New American Dream, is "More Fun, Less Stuff." Who doesn't want more fun in the midst of our multitasking and rushed daily lives? Adults and kids, alike, need to play; yet kids today are increasingly denied this simple, but essential part of childhood. "Play is the most powerful way a child explores the world and learns about himself," says T. Berry Brazelton, a renowned pediatrician at Harvard Medical School and author of several books on parenting. Unstructured play encourages independent thinking, creativity, positive social relations, and connection to nature, but is becoming a rare phenomenon.

Since the 1980s, hundreds of elementary schools have eliminated recess and parents are enrolling young toddlers in a myriad of "precurricular" activities. There is extraordinary cultural pressure to put kids on the fast track by the age of two. Pediatrician and author Ralph Minear has studied children who exhibit signs of physical and emotional stress, and concluded that much of their problems often stem from being given or asked to do too much.

Sometimes, kids themselves ask for all these activities, yet many sign-up because they feel pressure from parents or from peers to keep up the pace. "Children being pushed too hard may not be able to articulate their feelings, but the signs are there. They become emotionally volatile or complain of aches and pains. They can't sleep. They lose touch with their friends," says Jack Wetter, a clinical psychologist in West Los Angeles. Wetter believes the current flood of children being diagnosed with attention deficit disorder may be misleading. Many of these children, he says, "just don't know how to express their frustration. By the time they are 16, many are burned out, antisocial, and rebellious."

There is pressure on kids to gain a competitive edge in all parts of life. Though benefits may accrue from this push to stay ahead of the curve, the push also typically eliminates free time. What is life for? Kids may be high achievers, but do they know the pleasure of digging in the dirt, building a playhouse from cardboard, playing hide-and-seek in a park, and of all the other crazy, wonderful, creative, nongoal-oriented things kids do when given a chance?

Sleep

Many adults walk around feeling sleep deprived and tired most of the time. Kids feel the same way. How many parents are familiar with the daily struggle of getting everyone out the door and to school on time? It's not surprising that 71 percent of American teenagers polled by the Gallup organization in 2001 said they think it would be a good idea if schools started an hour or two later so that students would be able to get more sleep. According to the National Sleep Foundation, students need nine hours of sleep to be completely energized and ready for school. Yet only 15 percent of adolescents get the sleep they need. Will Wilkoff, a pediatrician and author of *Is My Child Overtired?*, says that about 80 percent of the children in his Maine practice are not getting enough sleep. Statistics such as these lead many to worry about the long-term health effects on children of our frenzied lifestyles.

Homework

Many kids put in the equivalent of an adult workday at school only to come home to hours of homework. There is no question that homework is another major culprit putting the squeeze on kids' time. Homework has intensified for several years, in part because of reports that suggest U.S. schoolchildren don't compare favorably to their international peers. Furthermore, in a dog-eat-dog world, everyone feels compelled to stay ahead of everyone else. Advanced Placement classes, accelerated academic programs, and a nationwide preoccupation with incessant testing leaves kids breathless in the battle to stay on top of homework and ahead of the pack.

The homework battle often pits parents who are fighting for quality time with their kids against educators and others who are trying to ensure that students make the grade. According to a University of Michigan study, students spend eight hours more a week in school than kids did 20 years ago, and homework time has nearly doubled. In 1981, six- to nine-year olds averaged 44 minutes a week of homework; in 1997, more than two hours. Study after study indicates that average daily and weekly homework loads are rising for children of all ages, yet the measurable benefits are questionable at best. John Buell and Etta Kralovec, teachers and authors of *The End of Homework,* argue that "both research and historical experience fail to demonstrate the necessity or efficacy of ever longer hours of homework." They say many students, especially junior high and senior high students, are suffering from the "fatigue factor" of putting in 50 or 60 hours a week of class time and homework time which may burn them out before they go to college.

And too many kids exhaust themselves working late into the night, leaving them stressed out much of the time.

Denise Clark Pope, a lecturer at Stanford University and a high school curriculum expert, studied five motivated and successful students through a year of high school and concluded that kids feel stuck in a "grade trap" that pins future success to high grades, test scores, and Advanced Placement courses. As Pope explains in her book, *Doing School,* "These kids are caught in a system where achievement depends more on doing—going through the correct motions—than on learning and engaging with the curriculum." One student summed it up this way, "People don't go to school to learn. They go to get good grades which bring them to college, which bring them the high-paying job, which bring them to happiness, so they think." The truth is, quantity of work and homework does not equal quality of education. And sometimes, less really is more.

Many parents are asking school systems to review homework policies. The notion that more is always better is under hot debate. In my son's middle school in Takoma Park, Maryland, parents protested heavy homework loads and, in response, the principal asked teachers to cut back on excess assignments. In northern Virginia, the Arlington school district also assessed homework loads and decided to impose some modest restrictions. From Scarsdale, New York to Los Angeles, parents have held protests and meetings to examine how homework is eating up their children's time.

Holding Down Jobs

One 1992 survey found that five million kids between the ages of twelve and seventeen had part time jobs, a third of them for more than 20 hours per week. A more recent study of 14- to 17-year olds found that 34 percent were employed sometime during the year.

Part-time jobs often foster independence, responsibility, and good work habits, but may also eat up too much of our kids' free time. Interestingly, teenagers from both low- and high-income families devote their income to personal items such as clothing, cars, food, entertainment, and in some cases, drugs and alcohol, rather than college savings or family expenses. Parents can help kids assess their desire for spending money versus their need for free time and make adjustments as necessary.

Adult Work Patterns

Parents' work habits are part of the free time problem, too. The majority of school-age children have both parents in the workforce, often by necessity. Typically, children need to be enrolled in after-school programs until the parents can arrive to pick them up sometime after 5 P.M. Many of these programs are terrific, yet the fact remains that they are more structured than the environments of kids with parents who can be home immediately after school.

In response to this situation, some parents have started after school co-ops with participating parents taking turns watching three or four kids at a time. This way, children can be in a home after school with a supervising adult, but not feel required to be part of something more structured. Parents save money by avoiding baby-sitting costs while giving their kids more unstructured time with friends. It does mean that one parent has to negotiate unusual work hours, say from 7 A.M. to 3 P.M. for one day each week. Other parents are simply cutting back to spend more time at home, opting to make less money, but gaining more time for their own and their children's lives. That may not be possible or even desirable for every family, but exploring the possibilities can often lead to new and satisfying arrangements for kids and adults alike.

Electronic Escapes

Television, computers, and electronic entertainment absorb a huge portion of our kids' time. According to one study, 32 percent of 11- to 20-year olds spend 10 to 20 hours a week on-line. A 1998 study by Roper Starch Worldwide provides further insights into the habits of children ages 6 to 17 years: 86 percent have access to a VCR; 70 percent have a video game system at home; 32 percent have a video game system in their own rooms; 50 percent have a TV in their own rooms; 40 percent have their own portable cassettes or CD players; and 35 percent have their own stereo systems. Kids, like adults, are becoming more isolated due to computers, video games, television, and other supposedly "interactive" electronic equipment. Interacting with a machine bears little resemblance to the rewards of interacting with other people, and instant messaging cannot replace one-on-one human contact. Machines are changing the experience of childhood itself, supplanting traditional activities such as reading, playing, and outdoor exploration.

While watching TV or surfing Web sites does constitute free time, it isn't the kind of free time many kids themselves are asking for: the spacious, slow time just to be themselves, and be with friends. Stuart Brown, a retired psychiatrist and founder of the Institute for Play, fears that too little old-fashioned play can lead to depression and the loss of "the things that make us human beings."

Complete withdrawal from our electronic world isn't necessary, but moderation will help free up the time kids say they want. Parents and teachers have a crucial role to play in limiting time with electronic screens of all kinds. By setting limits both on television and computers, parents and teachers can send an important message about life's priorities. In saying no to digital distractions, we can say yes to other things, like playing a game of catch, pulling out the scrabble board, organizing a fishing trip, or encouraging teens to get together after school to make a robotic car, fashion a homemade pizza, or practice dance steps in the living room. Instead of listening to music, make it. Instead of sending instant messages for hours, get together. Instead of playing computer games, get outside and play, or meet at a friend's home for an afternoon of nonelectronic games.

Our children receive nonstop messages and images pouring from the television and computer, but there is another kind of information, what author and social critic Bill McKibben calls "missing information." It can only be discovered when electronic screens are turned off and we have the time to slow our pace and pay attention to the real world, not the artificial one. McKibben says the

noise of the modern world makes it harder to hear, but the natural world's signal is still there, broadcasting around the clock, if we can just help our kids hear it. It's the inspiration that humans have always found, through silence, music, deep sharing with friends, playing with pets, the sound of the wind, and the spaciousness of the sky. We must hold fast to these experiences in the midst of our media-dominated lives. Ultimately, the trick is to help our kids navigate the good parts of this media revolution while creating some shelter against the powerful electronic forces that distract our children from deeper, nonmaterial pleasures.

Kids need time. We all do. It's worth pausing to ask why our kids are being pushed to accelerate ever faster in all fields of endeavor, from algebra to athletics. What's behind the pressure for longer schooldays and years, for more homework, nonstop extracurricular activities, and the incessant chase to do and achieve more? Is it pressure from the federal government and corporate America to ensure our competitive edge at the international level, economic fear brought on by the continual erosion of our societal safety nets, or a quest for a high standard of living for our kids sometime in the distant future? No doubt, many children in overdrive are developing extraordinary skills and talents, but at the cost of healthy daily rhythms? Why is our society apparently willing to jeopardize the emotional and physical well-being of our children by placing the highest value on the pursuit of more, and structuring educational and social expectations accordingly? Are our children losing out in the process?

Parents and teachers who are weary of the race must begin to ask these fundamental questions if we hope to turn things around. President Nixon predicted years ago that we would all have a four-day workweek and that leisure would define life in the twenty-first century. Instead, our furious productivity leaves adults and kids feeling depleted and yearning for balance and free time. We have taken most of our productivity in the form of increased material goods rather than in leisure. This core issue of minimal free time is taking a toll on all of us, and our children are crying out for change.

CHAPTER 7

What about Fluffy and Fido?

CAMILLA H. FOX

I have to admit it. Despite years of interest in the issue of overwork and time pressure, I'd never given a thought to its impact on animals. But when talking to an old friend about Take Back Your Time Day, she told me that "this issue is even important to pets." In her affluent California community, the fastest growing business was professional doggy-walking! "Sometimes you see a person being pulled down the street by five or six dogs," she said. "People are so busy they have no time for their pets." I called Camilla Fox, a friend and professional animal advocate for confirmation of animal neglect due to overwork. She agreed that it was a growing problem and offered to write something about it. —JdG

Often, pets are our best barometers—reflecting our mental and physical state of being. My dog Zaela, for example, is my daily gauge. If you want to know how I'm feeling today, just look at my ever-present four-legged companion. When Zaela is grinning and wagging her tail, you can be pretty sure I'm in a good mood. A forlorn, listless Zaela, however, may indicate it's not the best day to approach me for a raise.

I hate to admit it, but I'm probably a workaholic. Workaholics tend to be oblivious to their surroundings, and Fido and Fluffy are often the first to enter our blind spots. Chronic neglect of our pets' emotional and physical needs can result in their developing behavioral and physical abnormalities, including obesity, diabetes, separation anxiety, and other maladaptive disorders.

I bore witness to this phenomenon in my own home. One morning, while groggily brushing my teeth, I nearly stepped on a large brown "surprise" that had been neatly deposited in the center of the bath mat by my housemate's cat, Echo.

Okay, I thought, no big deal; cats occasionally have accidents in the wrong place. I cleaned it up with little afterthought. But when little brown "surprises" reappeared in the same spot each morning for a week, I knew something was amiss. Echo was trying to say something—and was in fact "echoing" my housemate's stress over her job and relationship. Ann, wrapped up in her own distress, had been oblivious to her cat. When Ann was able to step outside herself and spend more time with Echo, the problem ended.

While Ann's response to her cat's abnormal behavior was to pay it more attention, a growing number of Americans choose quick fixes to deal with stressed-out pets. Dogs suffering from separation anxiety are pumped full of Prozac-like antidepressants or, worse, dumped at the local animal shelter by guardians who believe the behavior irremediable. A reported 20 to 40 percent of pets, primarily dogs, suffer from separation anxiety. Canine separation anxiety, today's number-one doggie behavioral problem, has been linked to absentee caretakers.

Obesity in pets is another reflection of a society deeply out of kilter. Thirty to 40 percent of pets brought to veterinary clinics today are obese. A serious medical problem, obesity has been linked to poor diet, lack of exercise, and anxiety-based overeating. Overweight dogs are more at risk in surgery, more prone to injury, and have more stress on their hearts, lungs, livers, kidneys, and joints. As in people, obesity in dogs and cats can lead to diabetes and heart disease.

Is it fair that our companion animals suffer physically and emotionally because we don't make time for them?

Clearly, many Americans feel that it isn't fair. Some guilt-ridden, overworked, pressed-for-time humans find relief in the burgeoning pet-sitting business. Pet sitting is one of the fastest growing sectors of the pet service industry (and in some upscale communities, the fastest-growing business around).

Two national professional associations, Pet Sitters International and the National Association of Professional Pet Sitters, boast a combined membership of 6,000. Services offered for canines range from dog walking and feeding to full-time doggie daycare, complete with playgroups, snacks, leash walks, and snuggle time.

Mechanized gadgets for pets are also taking the place of time-stressed humans. The billion-dollar pet supply industry has produced an array of toys (costing as much as $500 each) that don't require the presence of humans at all. From mechanized tennis ball throwers to voice-activated "Talk to Me Treatballs" and

mouse-shaped machines that whip pieces of string around for hours, the toy-makers are taking advantage of guilt-ridden dog and cat guardians. Animal care-takers spend over $30 billion each year on their beloved furry companions—more than is spent annually on toys for children.

There's a dark side to this: *The Wall Street Journal,* in a story about mecha-nized pet sitters for overworked owners, showcased some products that will actu-ally *shock* your dog if he or she gets on the couch or enters some other restricted zone in your home. The shocks aren't supposed to hurt Fido, but I admit to being a little bit skeptical.

While it's perhaps refreshing that people care enough for their companion ani-mals to lavish money on them, the increase of services and supplies that attempt to replace the animal-human bond is a disturbing trend, one that may indicate a deeper systemic imbalance within our society. Western civilization's overemphasis on work and productivity has led to a diminution of social interaction, and unfor-tunately humans are not the only species that suffer as a result.

There is, however, reason for hope. While many Americans have left Fluffy and Fido in the lurch, others are discovering the benefits of spending time with non-human animals. "Pet-Assisted Therapy" has gained increasing attention in recent years for a wide variety of human patients, including people with AIDS or cancer, the elderly, and the mentally ill. Stroking a dog, watching a kitten play, or observ-

ing the hypnotic explorations of fish can reduce stress and loneliness, and shift our focus beyond ourselves, helping us to connect to a larger world.

Animals can evoke people's nurturing instinct, making them feel safe and providing unconditional, nonjudgmental love and affection. In nursing homes, animals are known to boost peoples' moods and enhance their social interaction. Research shows that heart attack victims who have companion animals live longer, in part because they may feel needed and responsible, which can stimulate their survival instinct.

Physiological tests have shown that petting animals can improve people's general health, lower their blood pressure, and reduce their anxiety and stress levels.

Companion animals may actually help prevent human illness and disease. A 1990 study of 1,000 Medicare patients revealed that people with dogs visited their doctors 16 percent less often than those who didn't have a dog. A UCLA study found that people with dogs required much less medical care for stress-induced aches and pains than those without a canine companion. A 1991 study in England confirmed these findings, demonstrating that over a 10-month period, dog guardians had fewer small-scale health problems and took more and longer walks than people without dogs.

Dogs and cats aren't the only beneficent animals. Simply watching a tank full of tropical fish may temporarily lower one's blood pressure.

Must it take illness or old age for us to recognize the mental and physical benefits we gain from slowing down and interacting with nonhuman animals? Imagine if the 63 million households that have companion animals were all to stop what they're doing at this very moment—get out of their SUVs, hang up their cell phones, unplug their laptops and TVs—and spend the next hour interacting with their dogs, cats, parrots, or fish.

Imagine how many hearts would relax, how many foul moods would cheer up, how many uptight, pressed-for-time bosses would lighten up, and how many smiles and laughs would erupt. Wouldn't it be a sight to behold?

One hour is not enough, however. Providing a lifetime of adequate care and attention to our furred, feathered, and finned friends may require changing our habits and behavior. A little creativity can go a long way in finding innovative ways to spend more time with our companion animals. Ideas include working at home or arranging a shorter work week with the boss; getting a "pet friendly" policy in place at work; or establishing shared companion animal-care arrangements with friends, family, or neighbors.

In our overworked, rush-rush society, pets are silent losers. As a *PARADE* magazine article recently pointed out, more and more of them are being abandoned at pet shelters by people with no time for them. And though most are victims only of neglect, some suffer actual physical abuse from stressed-out owners who strike out at the nearest possible victims.

It's sad but true: *Even a dog's life isn't what it used to be.*

So the next time Fido sits pleadingly at your feet while your nose is in your laptop, or Fluffy leaves a "surprise" on your bathroom rug, don't dump them at doggie-daycare or the pound. Turn off the computer, put aside your personal and professional problems, and spend some quality time with your pet. You'll be surprised what this interaction can do for your mind, body, and spirit *and* for your furry friend.

Enough already! Now it's time for me to do just that!

PART THREE

The Cost to Civil Society

CHAPTER 8

Wasted Work, Wasted Time

JONATHAN ROWE

Jonathan Rowe is one of the most original thinkers in America today. His insights shine a light on our society that is refreshingly unique and penetrates far more deeply than most of our popular pundits. I first got a glimpse of his thinking when I read "If the Economy is Up, Why is America Down?" an article in the October, 1995 issue of The Atlantic Monthly. In the article, Jon and coauthors, Ted Halstead and Charles Cobb, Jr., dissected that demigod of progress, the Gross Domestic Product or GDP. They showed conclusively that the GDP is anything but a measure of real economic and social health, pointing out that family break-ups increase the GDP, as do environmental disasters. Even cancer is a plus, with the massive medical bills it produces. Certainly, in the eyes of the GDP, leisure time is wasted time. In terms of our real needs, however, it is anything but. And, as Jonathan Rowe points out here, our overwork—often in pursuit of trivial ends or in response to someone else's desire for profit—takes time away from volunteer activities that really could improve our quality of life. —JdG

In the water law of the Western United States, there is a strange concept of waste. The West is the most arid region of the country. Water is precious. Yet in the courts of those states, waste is not water that you use needlessly. Rather it is water that you don't use at all.

If you have rights to water, you keep those rights so long as you use them. It makes little difference what you use the water for. You can pump out groundwater for an Olympic-size swimming pool for your mistress, or for a golf course in the desert. If you have used the water, the law pretty much assumes that you have used it "beneficially," and so extends your rights to it.

But if you don't use the water, the consequences are severe. You are deemed to have wasted the water and can lose your rights as a result. To conserve is to waste, and to waste is to conserve. Rarely have the rules of law been so starkly at odds with the laws of nature and of common sense.

VACATION
An Endangered Species
TAKE BACK YOUR TIME DAY

And rarely has the mentality that underlies this thing we call "the economy" been so starkly on display. That mentality operates entirely on the focal plane of money. It assumes that the only activities that have reality and value are those in which money changes hands. Activities that do not involve money dwell in a kind of netherworld where they await the beckoning of the market to attain actuality and life.

As with water, so too with time. Divert time from its native flow, deploy it in a process in which money changes hands, and then, and only then, does it become useful and productive where the dominant mentality is concerned. It makes little difference where the time goes and what exactly it produces. It could go to thinking up new ways to seduce children into drinking more cola, or plotting ways to subvert the clean air laws.

So long as the time has flowed into the market and increased the churn of money there, it has been used beneficially where the economic mind is concerned. By contrast, time not so engaged is deemed a state of inertia, a kind of temporal primal sludge.

Economists will deny this, and journalists too. But it is the embedded narrative in much of what they say. Just observe the daily media. When a new diversion of temporal resources comes onto the scene—video games for adults, for example, or more choices to make regarding retirement accounts—does anyone stop to ask where this time is coming *from?* Does anyone ask what life function is going to get *less* time so that the market can get more? Much as economists assume that natural resources such as water and air are infinite, they assume that temporal resources are infinite too, so that when the market takes more there is no deficit anyplace else.

But time is not infinite, just as air and water are not. It can be depleted if not husbanded with care. Nor is time wasted just because it does not go to market use, anymore than water is. Water left in a river or aquifer is working all the time. It sustains fish, forests, wildlife, and ultimately humanity. It provides rest to the eyes and activity for the body. Such functions are no less beneficial than are the golf course and swimming pool.

And so with time. Time not diverted to the market is not necessarily lost to lethargy and waste. When we are not working for, or spending money, we often are doing more genuinely useful things. We might be working on a project with our kids or attending a town meeting or fixing a banister for an elderly neighbor. We might just be sitting on a front porch or stoop, providing watchful eyes that help keep the neighborhood safe.

This simple fact is obvious to most of us. But it usually is lost on the policy experts who define the master script for the media, which is to say, who define the way the nation sees its own time. Every new diversion of time gets cheers as a new source of economic "growth" without regard to where the time comes from and the effects of that diversion. It is as though the nation were drawing down a temporal bank account, and no one thought to ask how much was left.

Depletion of the Temporal Commons

No man is an island, the poet John Donne wrote, and neither is the market. It needs a realm outside itself—a *commons*—for sustenance and life. It needs a natural commons, in the form of water, air, space, and the like. It needs a social commons, in the form of language, sidewalks, community, an ambient civility and respect for law, and so on. A market also needs a *temporal* commons, a pool of time available for work that the market neglects. If this work does not get done— if no one cares for the young and old, serves as neighbor and friend, and attends to the work of citizenship in the community—then the market itself will eventually collapse.

There is a symbiosis, in other words, between the market and the temporal commons, and in recent decades that balance has gotten seriously out of whack. The market has been claiming more and more of the nation's time, just as it has been claiming more of nature. Never before in history has a society expended so much time and energy on work of dubious value—pitching junk food to kids, for example—*while neglecting so much work that really needs to get done.*

The data is not easy to assemble, and this, itself, is symptomatic. The U.S. government tracks employment in the market practically down to the last soda filler at McDonalds. But regarding work in the social commons—the vast and crucial realm of family and community—it does very little. Push junk at kids and you count. Give your time to them and you don't.

One recent effort to fill the gap was the book, *Bowling Alone,* by Robert Putnam of Harvard University, which documents a pattern of widespread civic and community decline. Compared to previous decades, Putnam shows, Americans are less involved in community and civic causes, from the NAACP to the PTA. Paid professionals do much of the work of democracy; most of us sit home and watch a scripted version of it on TV, when we pay attention at all.

"For the first two-thirds of the twentieth century," Putnam says in summary, "a powerful tide bore Americans into ever deeper engagement in the life of their communities, but a few decades ago—silently, without warning—that tide reversed and we were overtaken by a treacherous rip current. Without at first noticing, we have been pulled apart from one another and from our communities."

Putnam's thesis provoked controversy when he first published it in the mid-1990s. But for most Americans, I suspect, it confirmed a gnawing sense of social deficit and loss. Putnam cites recent polls showing that some two-thirds of Americans think that civic and community concern has declined. "More than 80 percent said there should be more emphasis on community, even if that put more demands on individuals," he observes. Polls are suspect. But I doubt many Americans think that the nation's social and community needs are adequately met.

The Labor Department released a survey of volunteer work not long ago, for the first time in thirteen years. (By contrast, the Department releases market employment data every three months.) It purported to show that some 59 million Americans—about one in four—did volunteer work "at some point" over the previous year. One out of four is not an inspiring record; and it is even less so when we consider that a much smaller percentage did the heavy lifting. Some 22 percent spent only 1 to 14 hours in volunteer work for the year. The Labor Department data was squishy to begin with. People reported their volunteer hours for the whole year, from memory.

Whether the social commons has declined in absolute terms is not really the question anyway. The question is whether the time we devote to this work has kept pace with the need. By that standard, it would take a true Pollyanna to contend that all is well. A decade ago, the Ford Foundation found that the U.S. had a deficit of some one million volunteers in the area of day care alone, and the situation has worsened since then. When more than two hundred foster children are missing in the State of Florida, it does suggest that America's temporal resources are not deployed to meet its human needs.

The Work Place, The Whole Place

Time is the awareness of space between events. As our lives get more cluttered—more filled with stuff, entertainments, and commercial come-ons—it is not surprising that the sense of time diminishes, even if actual clock hours do not.

Putnam says that time spent at work does not alone explain the depletion of the civic commons, and he probably is right, strictly speaking. But work time isn't what it used to be. For one thing, we spend more time getting to and from work. All told we spend some 72 minutes a day in the car, and Putnam notes a 10 percent drop-off in civic engagement for every additional ten minutes so spent.

For another thing, technology has broken through the guard rails that used to keep work within its temporal bounds. Thanks to e-mail and the cell phone, many Americans functionally are on call 24/7. During the latter part of the 1990s, a scene became familiar in the coffee shops of downtown San Francisco where I lived. A family of tourists would be sitting at a table—the parents and two kids. Mom would be nursing her coffee. The kids would be picking at their muffins, feet dangling in the air. The mood would be desultory, even a bit sullen. Meanwhile Dad would be pushed back from the table, talking business into a cell phone. He was physically present but not really there.

Technology slosh is just one way that the workplace has become the whole place. More broadly, corporations have contrived to claim our time even when we do not officially work for them. They have turned us into an unpaid work force that helps produce the products that we ourselves buy. For example, corporations used to have telephone operators to direct our calls. Now we must navigate labyrinthine answering systems, step by exasperating step, and often several times over.

Then there are the hours and days we spend dealing with problems that corporations should have fixed before they let their products out the door. As I was writing this, I got a pop-up message from the Microsoft Corporation informing me that my system needed an upgrade. Generally I don't let Bill Gates get any closer to my computer than he already is. But I had been reading about security glitches and secret back doors, and thought maybe I'd better download this fix.

Very big mistake. The download froze. When I exited I got the kind of ominous message on my screen that makes me want to dump the whole computer revolution into a Waste Management truck. According to the man on the Dell help line, Microsoft was sending out a defective fix. Maybe. Maybe not. But in the days that followed, I spent hours on help lines (not Microsoft's—Gates makes you pay) in an attempt to get my system working properly again. Finally I had to hire a local techie to reformat the hard drive, at a cost of two hundred and fifty dollars and considerable time and aggravation.

The economy today is full of such unpaid labor. Much of the vaunted "productivity" of computers, I suspect, comes from the way they enable corporations to shift costs onto the invisible accounts of people like myself. But even that hardly begins to count the time that has been diverted into unacknowledged market work. Something still more basic is going on, something that concerns the nature of work itself. Not only have we become unpaid producers of the stuff we purchase, but more, the purchasing itself has become a form of work.

The New Factory of Need

Half a century ago, as America embarked on a war with Hitler and Japan, Franklin Roosevelt challenged Americans to produce more and consume less. Sacrifice in the war effort was a "privilege," FDR said, and he called upon all Americans to share this privilege equally. In 2001, by contrast, in the wake of the biggest attack upon this nation since Pearl Harbor, President George W. Bush (and some Democrats, as well) called upon Americans to go shopping. Shopping has become a patriotic duty—and duty implies work.

Quietly, step by step, the realm of consumption has become a mirror image of its supposed opposite, production. The economy doesn't really need what most of us produce. What it really needs is our belief that we need those things. Accordingly, the economy has become a kind of factory of need, producing consumption as ardently as it produces the stuff consumed. Not that long ago, for example, credit functioned primarily on the production side of the economy. For an ordinary person to go into debt was a sign of failure and a source of shame. Now "household" (i.e., consumer) credit totals some one-and-a-half trillion dollars. That's six thousand dollars of debt for every man, woman, and child.

There is a household shipping fleet of sports utility vehicles that enables people to carry truckloads from the mall. There's a warehousing system that holds stuff people schlep home but don't use—the ever-expanding closets and "Garage-Mahals," and a $12 billion self-storage industry on top of that. New homes today have three times the closet space of homes built in the 1950s. The average house size has grown by 50 percent even as families have gotten smaller. We live in warehouses as much as homes.

There are occupational illnesses in the factory of need, such as obesity and stress. There is child labor, as advertisers seize upon children as the path to their parents' wallets. Advertisers have even gotten into school classrooms via the infamous Channel One, which turns the compulsory school laws into a way to corral a captive audience of impressionable children. Advertising in schools is not just child labor, but a form of compulsory servitude as well.

A generation or two ago, children were important producers in the social commons. They would run errands for older people on the block, and look out for the younger children; they served a real purpose in the social ecology. Today, by contrast, that time has been commandeered by the factory of need, and older people are increasingly alone. A retired factory manager in Brooklyn once recalled for me how he used to look in on his grandmother every day after school. But times are different now he says. "My grandchildren would rather play Nintendo than come and visit me."

When kids spend four to five hours a day with television, video games, and the rest, that time has to come from somewhere. So too does the time we spend dealing with the deluge of decisions that the market brings daily to our door. Economists hail deregulation—of telephone service, banking, energy, etc.—for the "choices" that it offers. *But choices involve a hidden cost in the form of time.* Those hours we spend puzzling over the options of medical insurance, long distance, and investment plans—and then dealing with disputes over bills—are hours not available for other things.

Meanwhile, technology has quickened the pace in the factory of need, much as it has in the factory of production. Through computers, management can push more stuff at us to increase our output as consumers. The Web, moreover, combined with the credit card, has reduced the distance between the impulse and the buying act practically to zero. One click and the stuff is in the mail. This is steady-state consumption, and close to maximum efficiency in the factory of need.

And since the Web never sleeps, the computer has torn down the barrier of time as well. Shopping can slosh over into virtually every waking moment, including time at what is officially called "work." The majority of Web shopping is done from the office. People are browsing Expedia and the Gap when they are supposed to be working on spread sheets. "These days," a Wall Street Journal columnist observed, "checking morning e-mail is like taking a frenzied stroll through streets lined with hucksters."

Nothing so illustrates how buying has become a form of work as the way it has morphed into the workplace itself. The conventionally minded will point to this as evidence that people are working less. But in reality it shows how work, itself, is changing. An economy that needs our needing more than it needs our making will eventually realign the workplace to this new task. In the true office of the future, we will be paid to sit at our desks and shop. The most productive workers will be those who buy the most. On weekends and vacations, people will pay to do useful work (much as they pay to work on archeological digs now), to break the drudgery of all this buying.

The trend lines are going this way. The managers in the factory of need are contriving to get even more of our time. In his book "The Science of Shopping" (more accurately, the "Science of Seducing Shoppers"), Paco Underhill, a business consultant, lays out the guiding principle. "Our studies prove," Underhill writes, "that the longer a shopper remains in the store the more he or she will buy." Time is money, and the market wants more of it, as though it doesn't already have enough.

Reclaim the Time

In the American West, there is a growing movement to tear down dams so that water can flow back to its most beneficial uses. In much the same way, there's a need to release time back into the temporal commons. Given the pressing needs in the family, community, and civic spheres, we need a temporal reclamation project of major proportions.

To put it another way, more flexibility to the workday, and more time off, does not mean a slackening of work effort. To the contrary, it means a refocusing of work effort. The best thing Bill Clinton did as President may have been the Family and Medical Leave Act (now under attack from President Bush), which has enabled parents to spend up to four months with newborn children before returning to work. Business lobbyists predicted economic disaster. But instead, the nation had an economic boom, and parents got a few months to be real parents, instead of just purchasing agents for day care.

There is a need for more enclaves of time like that. We need to protect our time as much as we are trying to protect the nation's waters and wilderness. We need also new ways to activate time for community and civic work. To free up time is not enough; there must also be new channels by which it can flow into constructive uses. When the social commons is healthy, these are invisible. But with the commons in such disrepair, there is a need to put them consciously into place.

One such channel-building project is a new currency called Time Dollars, designed specifically for the community realm. In essence, Time Dollars are a service barter system. Help a neighbor, and you get time dollars. Somewhere down the line a neighbor will help you in return. The currency replicates the informal memory banks that used to operate naturally in small towns and inner city neighborhoods in which good deeds were remembered and returned. The dollars provide the etiquette for introduction to neighbors who have become strangers, and they help to revive the ethos of reciprocity and trust in settings in which it has declined.

Time Dollar networks are functioning throughout the country. An HMO for seniors in Brooklyn called Elderplan is using them to turn recipients of care into providers of that care for other members. The Baltimore Housing Authority is using them to turn public housing projects into functioning communities. "Social capital is something that government cannot provide," writes Edgar Cahn, of the Time Dollar Institute in Washington, D.C., in his book, *No More Throw-Away People.* He adds, "We have to create it ourselves. That happens in the space that we all share, in social settings that we create."

It happens in the time, moreover, that we ourselves have to reclaim. Time is the basic human resource. It is the starting point of freedom. To choose to use time for more worthy and important ends could be the next great freedom movement—the one that truly claims the promise of the Industrial Revolution. The reason to reduce the workweek is not just to gain more rest. It is also because there is so much important work that truly needs to be done.

CHAPTER 9

Time to Be a Citizen

PAUL LOEB

In 2002, President Bush, like his father before him, suggested that America needs more volunteers, but regretfully, he didn't say where already overworked citizens might find the time to pitch in. True, we spend a lot of time in front of the TV, but TV viewing is more an indicator of weariness than free time. International comparisons show that annual hours spent in front of the tube correlate strongly with annual hours worked. The more a country's people work, the more they watch TV. When you're exhausted, it's easier to curl up on the couch and grab the remote; it seems like considerably more effort to do something with friends or volunteer in the community. Active citizenship and real participation in our democratic political process requires time, as Paul Loeb, who has been studying citizen movements for many years, makes clear. —JdG

The ad in the airline magazine shows a young boy on a swing, the backdrop for an interactive pager held by a man's hands. "Maybe you don't have to send an e-mail right now," says BellSouth's ad for its interactive paging service. "But isn't it cool that you can?" The ad, with its headline of *work@lifespeed*, celebrates a world where our work can engulf our every waking moment.

The endless workweek, however, threatens not only to overwhelm family life. It also turns us away from addressing any of the major questions of our time, from the quality of the schools where our children and others will learn, to preserving our environment, building a just and equitable economy, and responding to the amorphous and shadowy threats of terrorism, which we're told will last our entire lives.

Along with the accelerated pace of global change, which I'll explore later, *endless work makes it harder to be an active citizen.*

People tell me this when I travel the country, speaking on citizen involvement. "I'd like to be more involved in my community and take a stand on important issues," they say. "But I just don't have the time." It's true for students beleaguered by outside jobs and debt, and for ordinary citizens stretched between the ever-escalating demands of their workplaces, commutes driven by steadily increasing sprawl, and trying to keep some time for their families.

It's true in every corner of the country, and for people working all kinds of jobs—though low-wage workers may be holding two jobs to make ends meet, while those more affluent see their single jobs spill over to fill all their waking hours.

Some citizens equally stretched do find ways to take important public stands. The barriers to community involvement are often as psychological as they are material and practical. However, the more time we spend at our jobs, the less we have not only for family and friends, but also for addressing the critical issues of our era. For more of us to act on any of them, we may have to take on one more issue—the length of the workweek itself.

We now inhabit an Alice-in-Wonderland world in which we have to scramble faster and faster just to stay in the same place. In a disturbing trend, employees in 28 states are now being forced to sue Wal-Mart, alleging that managers forced employees to punch out after an eight-hour workday, and then continue working for no pay.

The increase of work hours complements a more general politics of the whip, speeding up our working lives. Whatever our jobs, most of us now work longer and harder than we used to, do more in less time, and worry more about being downsized.

This is true whether we're on a factory assembly line, writing code for a software company constantly behind on the latest release, or teaching the kids of the poor in an underfunded school. We're told we need to become the salesmen of our own lives if we're going to have a decent future, and not become "losers" in an increasingly divided economy—wheeling and dealing self-promoters who make career advancement the center of our existence.

And that doesn't count the increased load of other activities related to economic survival. Not only do we spend more hours on the job, we receive fewer benefits, which continued to erode even during the Clinton-era boom. We spend more hours driving to and from our jobs, as urban sprawl, escalating housing prices, and lack of decent public transit options raise the stress of our commutes.

Once we could rely on employer-funded pensions and Social Security, confident that if we worked long enough, our old age would be provided for. Now, for most of us, saving for retirement has become an uncertain journey through treacherous shoals. We save what money we can, then try to parlay it into the maximum possible nest egg by spending hours studying investment-related articles, listening to financial talk shows, pouring over mailings from a hundred different mutual funds, and hoping we'll make the right choices for a future that seems increasingly precarious.

We may have no choice but to negotiate our individual passages through the time pressures we face. Making any significant dent in them will require changing the rules of the game, which means acting in common. We'll also need common action to reverse the manner in which immensely consequential national and global decisions are made that leaves no time for democracy.

Powerful corporate interests want unlimited speed to be able to conduct whatever activity they choose in an unrestricted global marketplace. Most promote a profoundly short-term concept of time—the next quarterly earnings report, the next cycle of the stock market, and for the politicians who back them, the next election.

This approach leaves little or no room for citizens to ask basic questions: Is a polluting plant good for the community? What's the impact of closing a factory and moving it to a low-wage state or nearly no-wage country? What kind of tax system will meet the needs of our society with fairness to all? How do we build an economy that treats people decently and respects our ties to the earth?

No company exemplified our hyperpaced world more than Enron. Enron successfully pushed the idea that energy could be delivered most efficiently without regulatory checks. Those who argued otherwise, they claimed, were obsolete dinosaurs. In arguments repeated often by the apostles of unchecked corporate dominance, they insisted: The future is here. Get used to it.

My own local utility, the publicly-owned Seattle City Light, made the mistake of buying the propaganda. Though they own dams sufficient to generate most of Seattle's needs, they switched from stable long-term contracts to buying energy on the spot. Then they hit a drought year, which dropped the water level behind the dams and left less available for generating electricity, and needed to buy more outside electricity than expected.

When Enron manipulated energy availability to drive the prices from $24 per kilowatt-hour to $450 to $500, they left the utility in a $600 million hole. City Light managers trusted that the market would be reasonable. They got outmaneuvered by a company built on speed, speculation, and the ability to work every possible angle to squeeze out the maximum possible dollars. They weren't used to energy politics being run like a Blitzkreig.

We've just had the briefest Congressional debate on immensely consequential national choices—like the tax cut that will transfer $1.2 trillion to the wealthiest one percent of all Americans, or the vote that gave President Bush unilateral power to go to war with Iraq

As powerful economic and political interests grease the wheels for corporations to act without public oversight, regulation, or check, it becomes harder for ordinary citizens to respond, much less to undertake the necessarily patient task of rebuilding grassroots democracy. We find ourselves constantly reacting, running to keep up, and trying to slow the juggernaut of change.

Yet we're also seeing the beginnings of a citizen activism that combines new approaches, like online organizing, with traditional grassroots outreach in a way that helps us keep up with the issues we face, even while living busy lives. E-mails can overload, as our inboxes pile up with disturbing news and urgent action calls. But movements, such as the challenge to runaway globalization, would be inconceivable without e-mail networks to pass on key information and bring people together to protest.

Cyber-activism has allowed us to respond to a variety of new issues as they emerge. In our hyperpaced political environment, we need these new approaches. But we also need more traditional forms of political outreach and connection, from vigils and protests to discussions of major public issues in churches, temples, PTAs, Rotary Clubs, and educational institutions, and with coworkers, neighbors, and friends. While electronic discussions can foster surprisingly productive dialogue, they work best as an adjunct to face-to-face conversation and community rather than a replacement for it.

People still need to gather, eat, joke, flirt, tell their stories, attach names to faces, and remind themselves why they joined their causes to begin with. "It's almost reassuring that we still have to do all the traditional things if we want people to respond," says a software editor who chairs her local Amnesty International chapter, "not just rely on the new technologies."

The increased pace of our lives has produced new campaigns to challenge workplace time pressures. After a long winter of focusing largely on the narrowest of demands, unions are again beginning to spearhead social justice movements, with work and time issues a core part of their vision.

Union-backed Living Wage laws, like those passed in Los Angeles, Detroit, Baltimore, New Orleans, and over 60 other municipalities, help ensure that city workers and contractors earn enough in a 40-hour week so they don't have to work extra jobs.

Recently, 87,000 Communications Workers of America members, who worked for the telecommunications giant, Verizon, went on strike against mandatory overtime and workplace speedups. They told of having to choose between keeping their jobs and picking up young children from day care, being disciplined for breaking to drink water or go to the bathroom, and being stressed to the point of physical illness. They won a slower pace and limits on workhours.

In an environment where workplace overload can have life-and-death consequences, nurses' unions have made clear that their members cannot treat their patients even adequately if they're exhausted from working forced overtime, including double shifts. When we frame these issues in terms of the quality of our work—and of our lives—our fellow citizens respond.

Reducing work hours gives us more leeway to act as citizens. In Michigan, United Auto Workers members wrote it into their contract to get Election Day off. Unlike most Europeans, whose voting participation is up to ninety percent, Americans have to work even on this critical day.

When those who didn't vote in the razor-thin 2000 election were surveyed, a fifth said it was because they were too busy. Although their response may be an excuse, it speaks to real barriers, which allow little time for citizen participation.

America's dominant culture makes speed an ultimate virtue, as if simply by moving faster we can overcome all obstacles, including our own mortality. Yet, as Milan Kundera writes, "there is a secret bond between slowness and memory, between speed and forgetting."

Challenging the increased pace of work and of change may require slowing down our own lives. Even in our activism we might remind ourselves that we're in it for the long haul, however difficult the times. We need time to play with our children, read a book, go to a movie, dance to good music, or soak in the bathtub and do nothing. If our causes call for more, and they always will, we can find other people to participate, or take on fewer projects.

One way or another we need to stop before we're so spent and bitter that we feel no choice but to withdraw permanently from the fray. "You can't solve all of the world's problems," longtime labor and environmental activist Hazel Wolf reminded me on the eve of her 100th birthday. "You have to guard against taking on more than you can do and burning out with frustration. But you can take on one project at a time, and then another. You can do that your entire life."

It's tempting to respond to the speed we all face with a short-term politics of our own, reacting on issue after issue, as we try to prevent further incursions on human dignity by a culture that would place every value on a global auction block. We can keep our eyes on the prize by drawing strength from what we fight to preserve, and thinking about the world we'd like to see.

We can tell the stories at the core of complex issues so that lives and communities aren't simply dismissed as expendable barriers to progress. We can raise

enough root questions so that we do more than challenge particular abuses of power, and instead offer broader alternatives. And we can remember the value of standing up for our beliefs.

As fisherman and environmental activist Pete Knutson says, "It takes energy to act. But it's more draining to bury your anger, convince yourself you're powerless, and swallow whatever's handed to you. When you get involved in something meaningful, you make your life count."

For most of us, our community involvement will inevitably be squeezed into whatever hours we have remaining after we earn what we need to get by. For nearly half a century, these leisure hours have been diminishing, as work takes over more and more of our lives. If we can begin reversing this, we'll have more time to heal the real wounds of our communities, of our nation, and of the world.

We fight for bread and roses, in the words of an old union song, not only for survival, but for the beauty and richness that makes life worthwhile. We fight as well for the right to be citizens, for the chance to create a democracy where all can participate.

CHAPTER 10

Time and Crime

CHARLES REASONS

It was in Chuck Reasons' sociology class at the University of Wisconsin, Superior that I first read futurists' predictions of a dramatically shortened workweek by the year 2000. That was back in 1968, just three years after the U.S. Senate estimated that we might be working only 14 hours a week by the turn of the twenty-first century. Chuck was a great teacher, one of the few whose class remains in my memory years later. I knew that he had gone on to an academic career as a criminologist and had studied law, as well. And though his published work focused at least as much on crime in the suites as on crime in the streets, I wondered whether his many years of research had turned up any links between overwork and crime, so I called him at Central Washington University, where he now teaches, to find out. This chapter is the result of our conversation. —JdG

Is there a link between overwork and crime? At first glance, such a connection isn't obvious; it might, in fact, be perceived as negative. After all, people who are working a lot don't have time for crime, do they? Idle hands do the Devil's work, or so the old saying goes. But a look at the facts and the trends shows the answer is not so simple. Overwork in America may indeed contribute to our crime rate, already rather high by developed nation standards.

Some years ago, the FBI started a "crime clock" to inform citizens of the United States about the frequency of crime. A crime clock comparison between 1995 and 1999 shows us that serious crime dropped during this period. For example, in 1995 an American was murdered every 24 minutes; by 1999 the rate had fallen to one murder every 34 minutes. Robberies decreased from one every 54 seconds to one a minute, while violent crimes went down from one every 18 seconds in 1995 to one every 22 seconds in 1999. Other crime categories showed similar declines. All of this was good news indeed.

But the above statistics don't tell us why the declines occurred. So how do we explain the drop in crime?

It's the Economy, Stupid

Work and the lack of it are very much related to crime rates, including violent crimes. Historically and contemporarily, as employment increases, crime goes down, while it rises with unemployment. During the boom of the 1990s, with its low unemployment rates, we saw violent crime rates fall to levels we had not seen since the '60s.

Increased employment helped to insulate us from crime. And, as we might have predicted, preliminary data indicates a slight increase in crime as our unemployment rate has risen during the current recession.

Increasing Employment and Reducing Stress to Fight Crime

By eliminating or reducing overtime, and by allowing for more permanent part-time positions, employers can create more jobs *and* reduce the criminal consequences of both unemployment and excessive stress.

For example, stress from time urgency and excessive working hours contributes to road rage. Reducing the stress generated by employment demands and overwork can also reduce child abuse, spousal abuse, suicide, homicide, and excessive drug abuse.

At the same time, creating more jobs through work sharing will help reduce unemployment, *and* the domestic violence, suicide, drug use, and homicide associated with being *out* of work. Overwork and unemployment are like two sides of the same coin in terms of their criminal consequences.

People who are idle, unemployed, and desperate to make ends meet are more likely to get involved in illegal activities of theft, excessive drug use, drug marketing, robbery, and other crimes of violence. There is tremendous stress on the unemployed to make ends meet for themselves and their families.

But, at the same time, the stress of overtime and excessive work to meet deadlines and productivity demands increases the potentiality of family violence, use of drugs, road rage, accidents on the job, and white-collar crime. For example, the higher the stress level in the workplace, the more accidents and deaths on the job and on the way to and from work, and the lower overall sense of security in our society.

Let's Really Support Family Values

While Americans pay a great deal of lip service to the significance of family values and the need for time spent with family members, our current structure of work decreases such possibilities and increases the likelihood of crime. Given the rampant consumer expectations and demands of our society, both partners in middle- and working-class couples feel compelled to work. Most families with both parents working do so out of perceived necessity, not because of career aspirations. Without a doubt, this makes child supervision more difficult.

In response to the enormous time demands on American workers, we have substituted the mantra "quality time" for the lack of "quantity time." Here, however, rhetoric and reality part company. Research shows that it is the *quantity* of supervised time, particularly after school, not the "quality time" we spend with our kids that keeps them out of trouble.

As a college professor, I am now fortunate enough to be able to schedule my classes/work so I can drop off my second grade son at school at 8:30 A.M. and pick

OCTOBER 24, 2003
www.timeday.org

It's TIME, for a change. You need some rest.

him up at 3 P.M. after school. But, given their work demands, most parents do not have the luxury of such close supervision. Typical working parents will both be gone from 8 A.M. until 5 or 6 P.M.; hence, the "latchkey" phenomenon—kids who are not under adult supervision from the time school ends until well into the evening. Not surprisingly, teens are most likely to commit crimes or become victims between 2:30 P.M. and 8:30 P.M.

But if, for example, employers reduced parents' working hours, provided more flexible schedules or more permanent part-time employment, among other options, those parents could be more available for their children.

Ironically, statistics show that high school students who have jobs get involved in more crime, not less, than those without jobs; the money they earn is often used for such recreation as illegal drugs, alcohol, and cars to evade parental control.

Add to this the temptations of stealing money and products from their employers and you have a volatile combination.

A Win-Win Situation

By taking back some of our working time and providing workers with more time away from the job, we can reduce the crime associated with the stress of excessive work demands *and* provide more supervision for our children, reducing the likelihood of youth crime. Sharing existing work, rather than laying-off thousands of workers and forcing thousands of others to work overtime, will create more jobs, and thus reduce criminal activities associated with unemployment.

In terms of crime prevention, shorter, more equitably distributed working hours offer a win-win situation. Business and social policies promoting better work/family/life balance will increase employment, promote family values, and reduce crime. An insecure America would do well to consider the link between time and crime.

PART FOUR

Health
Hazards

CHAPTER 11

An Hour a Day (Could Keep the Doctor Away)

SUZANNE SCHWEIKERT

While doing research for the film, Running Out of Time, *I visited the Meyer Friedman Clinic in San Francisco where the term, "Type A," was coined. I interviewed Dr. Friedman, himself, and an associate, Dr. Bart Sparagon, who now directs the clinic. In their view, the number one cause of premature heart disease in the United States was what they called "time urgency"—a continual sense of time pressure that has become more and more common in our overworked, over-scheduled society. Though not all doctors agree with this theory, there is little doubt that time pressure has a serious impact on Americans' health. In their recent book,* Joined At the Heart, *Al and Tipper Gore suggest that burnout and stress caused by overwork cost the U.S. economy as much as $344 billion a year. Since we launched* Take Back Your Time Day, *I've received many e-mails from doctors who all agree that overwork is a serious health problem. One of them was from Suzanne Schweikert, an obstetrician in San Diego, who is also doing research in public health. She sent along her reasons for concern. —JdG*

As a doctor, I've had plenty of opportunities to observe the many health consequences of our overworked, overscheduled, rush, rush, everyday lives. Among them, we can include hypertension, diabetes, heart disease, obesity, infertility, and many types of mental health disorders that are rising to nearly epidemic numbers. Of those, it is perhaps the mental health problems that deserve the most attention.

Three of the most common complaints in my medical office are unrelenting anxiety, chronic undiagnosed pain, and depression. While antidepressant medications may help with all three of these symptoms, they seldom provide a lasting cure. Unless patients eliminate some important stressors from their everyday lives, their resistance to anxiety and depression remains low, and even simple stressors will cause their symptoms to return.

Why are anxiety and depression so difficult to treat, and why are they epidemic? It is likely that people suffering from these disorders have exceeded the limits of their bodies' resistance. Anxiety is a natural state, occurring when one requires physiological resources to deal with stressors. However, when these resources are chronically called upon, one's system becomes depleted, and even simple stressors can become overwhelming.

The things that build up our reserves for dealing with stress are simple, *but they all take time.* For example, eating healthy takes more time than "fast food," exercise takes time, and proper rest and sleep take perhaps the most time of all. Stress reduction skills such as meditation and yoga also take time, but they can act together with diet and exercise to speed recovery.

Ultimately, it doesn't matter what triggers a person's anxiety or depression; the point is that their presence signals that the afflicted person has run out of fuel. It's time to restock, take a break, and wait out the storm. *But to do this takes time.*

When I ask my patients if they exercise, the number one excuse for not doing so is that they "just don't have enough time." When I then ask them what they could give up in order to exercise, I usually get a vague answer. The fact is, there are only 24 hours in the day, and we need to build in priority time for exercise, just as we do for any other important obligation.

I had one very obese patient who wrote an exercise appointment with herself on her calendar five times per week, and put three stars by it, meaning that it was the most important appointment of her day. She had discovered that exercise, unlike most of her other obligations, had a profound positive impact on her mood, and consequently, on other areas of her life.

Not only did she lose weight, but more importantly, she was getting along with her family, experiencing higher self-esteem, and no longer felt achy and stiff every morning when she got out of bed.

Obesity is inextricably linked to a lack of time and contributes not only to depression and anxiety, but also to a host of chronic diseases that will eventually make us sicker and less happy. This does not mean that we should all strive to be skinny. It simply means that a lack of exercise will catch up with us sooner or later—and probably sooner.

The Effects of Time Pressure on Pregnancy

One of the most troubling time-related problems in obstetrics is the trend towards "social induction" of labor. This tends to happen when a patient arranges for her husband to take time off work and for her relatives to be in town on her due date. If she doesn't naturally go into labor at the appointed time, she asks her physician to induce it. There is no medical reason to do so, and there are certain risks associated with it. But her desire to control the timing of her delivery weighs more than any other factors.

Her sense that "time is running out" for her family to be supportive pushes her to this decision. While some anxiety is normal, a healthy adult will choose the safest plan for her baby. Some, however, let their anxiety about the timing of the birth overwhelm them, and make decisions based on time pressures alone. This is but one symptom of the time shortage we suffer from in this country, and it brings some very difficult issues to the table—issues which need to be addressed long before we are about to give birth, and perhaps even before we plan a pregnancy.

Pregnant women are hit particularly hard by stress. While we can usually tolerate the normal stressors in our everyday lives, during pregnancy our bodies give us obvious signals to slow down. These range from minor fatigue and discomfort, to anxiety, depression, back pain, severe nausea and vomiting, and preterm labor.

It is common for pregnant women who are both working and taking care of children to tell me they feel weak and depressed, and that they do not have time to exercise or eat properly because of their job. Some women with gestational diabetes will not follow their diet or take insulin, because they state they are "too busy." This puts themselves and their baby at tremendous risk for complications.

It is understandable to want to earn as much money as possible before a baby is born, but people must begin to ask themselves at what cost? What other things could be done, besides working longer hours, to budget for a new baby?

When I asked one of my patients this question, she looked surprised, as if this had never occurred to her. She traveled for work, and often slept in hotels and ate airport food. She had been complaining about fatigue and back pain since her pregnancy began, but was still working long hours.

I told her there was nothing wrong with her or the baby yet, but that she should start listening to the signals she was getting. Her body was smart enough to know that she was pushing beyond her own limits. By her next visit, she had cut her hours at work, had stopped traveling, and was spending the extra time taking

walks. She and her husband had decided to buy a used car instead of a new one and to have a stay-at home vacation, which was less stressful with a new baby anyway.

It was clear to all of us that she was more ready to go through childbirth than if she had not taken this time to listen to her body. Indeed, unlike her first delivery experience, this one was happy and stress-free. She had sacrificed money for stress reduction and time, and the payoff was evident.

Another patient of mine had suffered from postpartum depression after her previous two pregnancies, and was terrified about getting it again. She was reluctant to take an antidepressant medication during pregnancy, even though she was already showing signs of depression. It seemed likely that the added stress of a new baby would be enough to push her into a deeper state of depression.

She was a stay-at-home mom and had a large number of family obligations. In addition, she felt the need to keep up with the clothes, cars, furnishings, and daily activities of her social group. Her husband was complaining that she was too tired to spend time with him, and the kids were unhappy about too many after-school activities. She was trying to be a supermom, and yet she was feeling like a failure. She eventually decided she would cut out all nonessential obligations except for the one she really enjoyed, a water aerobics class.

She spent her new free time making inexpensive decorations for the baby's room, and learning how to knit. She felt calmer than she had in years, and went through childbirth without any problems or medications. In the following weeks, she developed no signs of postpartum depression, and she told me at her six-week follow-up visit that she planned to keep her life this way permanently and to teach her children how to do the same.

The Health Insurance Conundrum

In both of these two cases, my patients realized that every responsibility and debt they accrued, from their home and car, to their kids' toys and clothes, took more time away from paying attention to their own health. They were lucky enough to recognize this and make a change. But why aren't the rest of us able to do the same?

For many of us, the problem is very simple but ironic: *our desire to keep our health insurance benefits ties us to jobs that are bad for our health.* Unless we are willing to give up the very benefits that might protect us in the event of illness or injury, we will be unlikely to make the one change that could dramatically improve our health and the quality of our lives.

Unfortunately, unless we change something, we will have little chance to enjoy the time we have left. The best solution is not for people to suddenly start giving up their health benefits and joining the ranks of the uninsured. Rather, the best solution is to make the part-time worker in America an insured one, and to allow all of us the freedom to move between full-time and part time work as we choose, without having our health benefits hang in the balance.

No discussion of the health effects of time is complete without some mention of the relationship between health insurance benefits and employment. The link between our jobs and our health benefits has come about as part of our strong work ethic, and the value Americans place on employment. However, while this would seem to promote a stronger economy, it does not always work that way.

For example, if they could work part time, many Americans would prefer to care for their elderly parents at home, rather than to place them in a nursing home. Instead, they choose full-time jobs in order to keep their health insurance benefits. In the long run, the elderly parents suffer, the children suffer, and the government or taxpayer carries the extra burden of the nursing home costs.

As the baby boomer generation reaches old age, the number of older Americans is expected to grow tremendously, and the costs of nursing care will continue to sap our economy. It would seem like a good time to take another look at the idea of providing health benefits to all part-time workers in this country.

Although this concept may sound like "socialized medicine," it doesn't have to work that way. If the 44 million currently uninsured Americans (the majority of which work one or more part time jobs) were given basic health insurance, they would no longer risk losing their jobs and savings due to illness or injury (which ends up burdening the tax system anyway). Indeed, it would provide an incentive for more people to work, and would give current full-time and over-time workers more flexibility in their jobs.

Many of us would consider doing jobs we *like* and working for smaller companies if we did not have to risk losing our health benefits. Others of us would continue to work full-time, but we would be able to leave a hostile or negative workplace without waiting three months or a year for our benefits to kick in at a new job. The opportunity to work part time during certain periods of our lives would bring us the ability to spend time with our families when needed, and would increase the time many adults spend with their children and elderly parents.

Thus, when I ask my patients who are obviously suffering from the stress of overwork why they don't cut back their hours, I am not surprised when their reason is "to keep my benefits." Ironically, the one thing they believe is there to protect their health is the same thing that hurts it in the longrun. It pays for visits to the doctor, but all we can tell our patients is that to decrease the stress in their lives, they may need to seek another job with shorter hours and no benefits.

Until we value the part time worker's decision to spend more time away from work, we are asking this vicious cycle to continue. We work in order to gain the benefits of health insurance, although the pressure resulting from overwork is making us sick.

In the end, we must each ask ourselves three important questions. First, is our physical health being affected by our lack of time? Secondly, is our emotional and psychological health being affected by our lack of time? And, finally, can our quality of life and our work ethic live side by side? The answer to all three questions is yes, and the solution lies in making some dramatic changes, both in the way we look at *and* in the way we pay for our health. This includes how much time we devote to it—briefly (as in popping pills) or longer (as in stress reduction and exercise)— and how we finance healthcare for all Americans (e.g. who gets insurance and who does not).

The right answers to these questions are not necessarily politically popular. But they will be, if enough of us begin to understand the impact of time, *and not having enough of it,* on our health.

Once we see the effects of time stress on ourselves, we may be willing to vote for a better way of doing things in the future. Considering long-term benefits to our quality of life, both as individuals and as a country, we may be able to budget money for the things that matter, and stop spending it on things that do not.

CHAPTER 12

The (Bigger) Picture of Health

STEPHEN BEZRUCHKA

The great conservationist, John Muir, once said, "Whenever you try to pick out anything by itself, you find it hitched to everything else in the universe." The view presented by this book is that shortening annual working hours and achieving greater time-balance in our lives will give Americans the chance to solve a host of problems. We may also see that overwork itself is a symptom of a deeper malaise—extreme inequality—that afflicts American society. The gap between rich and poor in the United States is now the greatest of any industrial nation.

Stephen Bezruchka, a physician and professor at the University of Washington School of Public Health, has been studying the key factors impacting national health performance for many years. He has arrived at a surprising conclusion: more than anything else, the health of nations is dependent on their relative levels of equality. One important reason is that income inequality leads to overwork, weakening family and community bonds that help to keep us healthy. —JdG

There is an old adage that "hard work never killed anybody." Whether that's true or not might be debated, but overwork certainly can harm our health in various ways. In the United States, overwork and its health consequences are part of a bigger picture—a *social structure* that in many ways makes it difficult for Americans to lead healthy lives.

The U.S. is not very healthy compared to other industrial countries, despite spending almost half of the world's health care budget. One useful measure of a country's health is its ranking in health indicators, such as infant mortality (deaths in the first year of life) or life expectancy (average number of years lived), compared to other countries. This comparison is often referred to as "The Health Olympics."

In the early 1950s, the U.S. was one of the healthiest countries in the world, but by 1960, it had sunk to the 13th healthiest, ranked by average number of years lived. Since then we have continued to fall, so that we are now 25th, *behind almost all other rich countries* and a few poor ones, as well. This health gap is large, for if we eradicated our number one killer, heart disease, we still wouldn't be the healthiest country.

More and more studies suggest that the hierarchical structure of society is the primary determinant of its overall health performance. Countries structured so that wealth and income are more equally shared are healthier than those where a "small privileged few" get the lion's share. The science demonstrating this is as good as that linking smoking and lung cancer. It is particularly well-documented in the recent book, *The Health of Nations: Why Inequality is Harmful to Your Health,* by Ichiro Kawachi and Bruce P. Kennedy.

One way to measure hierarchy in a society such as ours is to look at how much CEO's are paid compared to ordinary workers. In the U.S., they are paid about 500 times as much (up from a 40 to one ratio in 1980). In no other country today is the ratio bigger than 50 to one. In Western Europe, Canada, and Japan, CEOs make 20 to 30 times what the average worker makes, and often less. All do better in the Health Olympics than we do.

Health Care and Diet

Contrary to popular opinion, health care itself has little impact on the health of a population. Health care can be compared to the Army Medical Corps. The Corps doesn't decide whether to go to war, or the battle strategy, or the ordinance used, or the protective devices, or any critical factor that results in casualties. It just picks up the casualties and tries to revive them. Likewise, we can't expect much from medical care in producing health, despite the prominence given in the media to this resource and the fact that a third of our population lacks health insurance.

More surprisingly, perhaps, health-related behaviors such as smoking or diet are not the prime determinants of the health of a population either. The Japanese smoke twice as much as Americans, yet die from smoking half as often. It's not that smoking is good for you; it isn't. In any study, populations of smokers are less healthy than comparable populations of nonsmokers. But other factors are more important in determining overall health, and those factors relate to the hierarchical structure of society. Japan is a more cooperative society and far more egalitarian than the U.S.

Unhealthy Comparisons

How does inequality affect our health? First, the bigger the income or wealth gap, the more we feel left behind and the harder we work to try to catch up. We feel under pressure to prove ourselves against the measuring stick of self-worth, namely how much we earn and what it can buy us. The invidious comparisons we make with our neighbors (and increasingly with people paraded in front of us by our media) as the models of success, do us in.

Instead of getting what we want or really need, we want what the rich get! Those lower down in the hierarchy suffer more chronic stress from recognizing that they don't shape up to the standards. Relative to other income groups, poorer people have poorer health—the most well-documented finding in the field of public health. They secrete more cortisol (the chronic stress hormone), have higher blood pressure, possess poorer metabolisms with a greater propensity to diabetes, and have bigger waists, as they are unable to control their appetites.

If we are overworking because we are trying to catch up to the Joneses (or maybe even Bill Gates), we are very aware of being on a hierarchical ladder, and that alone, independent of any other factor, worsens our health. Most of us will never be able to catch up and consequently will feel shame and lose self-respect.

Working too much leaves us little time for other important aspects of our lives, including our children, and families, and social networks. Research makes clear that all of these relationships are good for our health; as they weaken, so do we. If we don't have time to form friendships and be seriously involved in organizations and our political process, our health will suffer. This fact, too, is well-established in the literature of public health.

Unattached Children

Doctors know that the most critical period for determining our health as adults occurs from the time we are but a gleam in our parents' eyes until we begin school. During that period, the first two years of life are the most important. Children who establish close parental contact (usually with a mother) in the first half year of life develop a secure style of attachment, and are later able to be separated from their parents in the second six months of life without displaying great anxiety.

Humans have always known this; in less-developed countries, mothers tend to wear their children, almost like a piece of clothing for the first year of life. Such intimate contact between a child and a mother is not just about receiving food, but also about promoting social development, so that a child can venture forth and explore, knowing he or she will be secure upon return.

Studies find that such securely attached children are healthier as they get older than are children who have had less prolonged or nurturing contact with their mothers. As they grow older, insecurely attached children are more likely to become anxious, aggressive, or depressed, or to develop difficulties in close interpersonal relations. Indeed we see this reflected in the huge increases in hyperactivity disorder among children, which is more common in poorer families where parents must work long hours simply to make ends meet.

Understanding this phenomenon, other industrial countries mandate extended maternal and paternal leave policies; the U.S., alone, does not.

The end result in the United States is a childhood where growing numbers of children do not socialize well, are preoccupied with various nonsocial or harmful social distractions, act out, do poorly in school, and later become emotionally unhealthy adults who do not cope well with stress and suffer from physical illness, too.

We're Not Number One

If we look at child welfare and educational attainment rankings among countries, we fare poorly there, too. We have the most child poverty of all rich nations, the most child neglect, the most homeless children, and arguably the worst outcomes on standardized tests of school achievement. All this occurs in the richest and most powerful country in history. We follow Benjamin's Law ("when all is said and done, more is said than done") when it comes to family values, whereas other rich countries walk their talk.

As adults, the poor also pay a higher *health* price for overwork. Many work two or more jobs, jobs that are usually temporary and insecure. They feel continually threatened by unemployment, and such anxiety itself is bad for health. For example, when a company announces that it will close in six months, workers and their families experience more illness right away, long before the jobs are gone.

Announcements of downsizing have the same effect on the nonpoor. Then, once the feared layoffs actually occur, we find that the unemployed have higher blood pressure, higher cholesterol levels, and a greater tendency toward obesity.

Overwork in the U.S. is exacerbated by the increasing gap between the haves and the have-nots. Our lives seem out of our control. Studies show that having a sense of control in the workplace and at home are critical for good health. This is difficult in our corporate environment, where we generally find hierarchical structures that leave most workers with little power.

The Roseto Effect

One way to offset the disadvantages of lower income and wealth is to feel a strong sense of belonging to a community. Studies show that communities of people who belong to hobby or special interest organizations, are active politically, work for causes that benefit society, belong to a spiritual community, or have strong cultural ties are healthier than are isolated families or individuals.

For example, in the 1950s, a group of poor immigrants from Italy who lived in Roseto, Pennsylvania, were the subject of study by doctors because they were so much healthier and long-lived than people in nearby communities, despite having the same risk factors (cigarette smoking, lack of exercise, obesity, diabetes and animal fat in their diet). What turned out to be the important factor was their community spirit; they way they cared for and helped one another; their solidarity.

They not only helped their friends, but friends of friends, and they displayed a strong sense of interdependence. Conspicuous consumption—keeping up with the Joneses (or the Giovannis), no matter who they were—was frowned upon.

But as time passed, their children became more like typical Americans—pursuing individual goals, becoming obsessed with watching their weight, taking expensive vacations, owning designer cars, and building expensive homes. The time they devoted to these pursuits left them less able to participate in activities that kept the community bonded together. These children weren't as healthy as their parents.

Experts in public health now call the health advantage that comes from having strong social bonds, despite lack of wealth, the Roseto Effect.

You get what you measure. Societies have goals and measure progress towards those goals. Some of us remember the goal in the United States in the 1960s— landing a human on the moon by the end of the decade. We measured and reported progress towards that goal and succeeded. By considering what we measure today, we can better understand our current society's goals.

The indices we revere don't track health; they track wealth creation, surely the preeminent goal in America today. Every minute of every business day, we follow and report the stock market indices, the Dow Jones and the NASDAQ, among others. Every quarter, we obsess over how much our GDP has risen. Ironically, the less healthy we are, the more GDP rises as expensive medical treatments add billions to the national cash register.

Instead of measuring wealth creation and GDP, we could measure health attainment using the most easily measured and comparative standard. What is our standing in the Health Olympics? Would we tolerate being ranked behind all other countries in track or skiing?

We ought to begin trying now to increase our health standing in the world. This would mean reversing the decline in relative health standards that began after World War II, i.e., giving up our obsession with creating wealth and its partner, inequality, and instead, sharing with and caring for each other. If we make these changes, we'd soon find ourselves with more time and more balanced lives, as well.

PART FIVE

Environmental Consequences

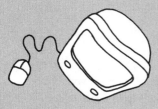
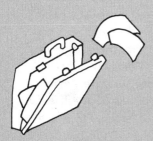

CHAPTER 13

Haste Makes Waste

DAVID WANN

In March of 2002, I addressed the Associated Recyclers of Wisconsin, a group of public and private waste management officials, at their annual state convention. The topic of my talk was "Haste Makes Waste," and I invited my listeners to consider a thought that at first may seem like a non sequitur. "If we want to reduce landfills," I suggested, "we should reduce working hours." I'm not sure how most of my audience reacted; a few came by to tell me they agreed, but most seemed skeptical. Nonetheless, as the following three chapters make clear, overwork and time pressure not only mean less recycling and more use of throwaway items, they also pose a threat to our fragile environment in other ways. When I was looking for possible contributors to this volume, I thought immediately of Dave Wann, an environmental scientist and former EPA official, who cowrote the book Affluenza with Thomas Naylor and me. Dave is an astute observer of the ways by which our daily activities endanger the earth. —JdG

Speed is irrelevant if you're traveling in the wrong direction.

—GANDHI

had an unsettling thought the other day as I wrestled—scissors in hand—with the fortress-like plastic packaging around a new electric razor. I wondered if anyone had accidentally taken his own life trying to unwrap a consumer item like this one. If a person's flustered grip on the package slipped, I thought, those sharp scissors could plunge into vital organs. Cause of death: thick, stubborn packaging.

I knew the packaging was as much for the manufacturers' and retailers' benefits as mine, and in a way, I resented that. They were making the money, I was spending the time—first the work-time to buy the expensive razor, then the fluster-time to penetrate its package.

I'd bought the electric unit because I was tired of buying and throwing out blades. I wanted something that lasts longer than refrigerator leftovers.

I hoped to do less damage to my checking account and to the environment with the electric razor, but considering all the electricity the razor would use and all the energy that had gone into its manufacture, I wasn't completely certain. Still, it did feel better than the prospect of tossing another five thousand blades (and all their packaging) before I die.

I thought about the man who got me into this shaving jam to begin with— King Gillette, who, at the end of the nineteenth century, pondered what sort of business he should launch. Why not sell an essential but flawed product, he reasoned, that would be thrown away after a few uses, providing a steady stream of profits? In a sense, Gillette and people like him were responsible not only for the disposable razor blade, but also for the calculated, costly, disposable culture we're tangled in.

To obtain the "convenience" of those throwaway blades, how many hours do we spend prowling supermarket aisles in search of new cartridges? How much "hidden" time do we spend in the car and at work? And of course, it's not just razor blades, but computer equipment, frozen dinners, paper towels, tape dispensers, batteries, even cars and houses, all of which typically have short and shoddy lifetimes.

Aren't we hurrying partly to overcome the hidden costs of these disposable, poorly designed products?

Frozen dinners, for example, seem to be quick and easy, but there's much more time involved than meets the eye. The packaging is programmed for a shelf life of maybe six months, a cook time of two minutes, and a landfill dead time of centuries. A surprisingly large percentage of the product's price is for packaging, and then we pay ongoing energy costs to keep it frozen and health costs from air pollution related to manufacture, distribution, and disposal.

Or take computers. They're incredibly fast, but their speed is sometimes a liability. For example, home computers not only enable workers to extend the workday into their personal lives, they also enable us to shop 'til we drop in the privacy of our own homes.

Unless we choose the often unavailable option of ground delivery, our Internet orders will be sent airmail, five times as energy-intensive as delivery by truck. When Amazon.com pledged to deliver copies of *Harry Potter and the Goblet of Fire* on the book's publication date, a squadron of airplanes distributed 250,000 packages to readers anxiously sitting by their mail chutes.

Computers have other hidden costs, which we pay for by working longer and longer hours. To take advantage of the computer's racehorse speed, we pamper it with the latest software, which takes time to download. We wait for it to boot up, and we wait as it steeplechases to a desired Web page. We "defrag" it, upgrade it, forgive its inopportune crashes that leave us helpless, and like a protective, anxious mother, we shelter it from viruses. These are some of the hidden *time* costs.

Then there are the many hidden ecological costs, well explained by Jim Fisher in a Web article titled "Poison PCs." "Along with the lead in its cathode ray tubes and circuit boards," he writes, "my computer was loaded with chemicals that have documented risks to public health and the environment: There was cadmium in its semiconductors, mercury in its switches and position sensors, chromium in its steel housing, brominated flame retardants in its circuit boards, nickel, lithium, cadmium, and other metals in its batteries. All that was missing was a 55-gallon drum."

It's not likely that computers will ever give way to index cards and typewriter ribbons again (that would be a return to the Dark Ages), but since they contain 700 different materials, computers must be designed for effortless recycling. And since they require so much energy to manufacture, our product strategy needs to change from obsolescence to durability.

The Faster They Produce, the Faster We Consume

As I fought with the electric razor's packaging, I wondered, has the industrialized, conveyor-belt pace that creates "planned obsolescence" become embedded in our daily routines? In effect, does *waste make haste,* which then creates even more waste in a vicious, accelerating cycle? If so, how do we break the cycle? To begin with, we need to acknowledge—as individuals and as a culture—that the best things in life really aren't things. The best things are bonds with people, contact with nature, and health—qualities that don't require us to be in a hurry.

To give ourselves time for these priceless forms of wealth, we need to reduce our junk intake, buying fewer but *better* things. More durable and environmentally-friendly things, like many Europeans do. We need to slow down to the speed of quality, rather than accelerating to the speed of quantity.

Make no mistake; this will require a change of historic proportions. There's good evidence that the high-speed chase we're in began centuries before the invention of the disposable razor blade, in the blacksmith shops, tanneries, and sawmills where the Industrial Revolution was born. When tinkers began perfecting technologies that could produce more goods than were necessary, they felt compelled to persuade buyers to consume the greatest number of products in the shortest period of time.

In the twentieth century, Henry Ford made speed an industrial requirement when he borrowed the idea of the assembly line from Chicago slaughterhouses to accelerate automobile output. The key elements of mass production, according to Ford, were power, accuracy, economy, system, continuity, and speed. The same techniques that he perfected for the car were soon adapted to the mass-production of houses.

Developers like William Levitt (who built Levittown in the late 1940s) erected 30 houses a day by dividing the construction process into 27 different steps. Every piece of lumber was numbered, every nail accounted for, every task in the house-building process given to a different team. The houses were built at remarkable speed, and when the dust settled and the first families moved in, an army of salesmen were there to greet them, hawking everything from milk delivery to curtains.

What postwar economists loved about the accelerated pace of house construction was that each new home was a ready market for stuff. And a market for stuff was what they thought the economy needed more than anything else.

Wrote marketing analyst, Victor Lebow, in 1950, "Our enormously productive economy demands that we make consumption a way of life, that we convert the buying and use of goods into rituals, that we seek our spiritual satisfaction, our ego satisfaction, in consumption . . . *We need things consumed, burned up, worn out, replaced, and discarded at an ever-increasing rate.*"

Manufacturers, smelling spoils, ramped up the speed of their conveyors. As Alvin and Heidi Toffler point out in *Creating a New Civilization,* "In the new hypercompetitive marketplace, being first to market allows companies to command higher prices and profit margins. Even a few months of lead time over competitors can mean the difference between success and failure."

Observe the Tofflers, "The interval between desire and gratification is quickly approaching simultaneity as consumers come to expect a greater array of novel products and services at near breakneck speed."

Speed Kills

The problem is that speed kills. When production systems are in a hurry, care falls by the wayside, along with mountains of waste. To give just one example among many, production capacity and consumer demand have combined to deplete about one-fourth of the world's fisheries, according to the World Resources Institute, with another 44 percent currently being fished at the biological limit.

Sonar technology tracks large schools of fish; trawling nets—the bulldozers of the ocean floor—gather them in, and refrigerated processing ships bring them back to market. In the process, a third of the global catch (30 million tons a year) is killed and tossed overboard because it's unmarketable.

Much of that fish catch is fed to America's 60 million cats, and the beat goes on.

The pace of industry strikes every inch of the globe, dicing habitats into fragments and smothering them under mine tailings, stripe-shorted tourists, logging slash, and pavement. For example, since each of America's 215 million automobiles requires a fifth of an acre for roads and parking spaces, every additional five cars smother another football field–sized chunk of America. Ponder this image for a moment: 38 *million* football fields, already covered with pavement, and many more to come.

Even the essential nutrients of life—nitrogen, sulfur, carbon, and phosphorus—have become hyperactive, far surpassing the natural cycle rates that remained constant for eons. An overdose of nitrogen causes rain to be acid and lakes to become clogged with algae. Too much carbon, too fast, and the world's glaciers begin to melt.

In 1991, hikers in the Alps came upon a startling time capsule: an intact human mummy protruding from a melting glacier. Apparently trapped in a snowstorm more than 5,000 years ago, he returned with a symbolic message for us, notes environmentalist Lester Brown: the Earth is getting warmer, quickly. Ask residents of Alaska, where the average temperature has risen more than five degrees in the last 30 years. Engineers are frantically shoring up sections of the Trans-Alaska pipeline threatened by melting permafrost. Meanwhile, every single day the world economy burns as much fossil fuel as it took nature 10,000 days to produce, warming the earth even faster.

The Faster We Consume, the Faster They Produce . . .

The message we get every day is hurry up and consume. But many scientists now agree that overconsumption is the world's most serious environmental threat, because for every product we consume, an average of 20 times its weight in raw materials was consumed to make it. The raw materials that go into a gadget or article of clothing may have disrupted biological habitats at the mine site, farm field, or chemical plant. Then, product manufacture, distribution, advertising, and packaging take their toll. At the end of the line, our use of the product may contribute further impacts to health, air, water, and land.

Every day, each American consumes 120 pounds of stuff, figuring in all the natural resources used in the making of our products. Stone and cement, coal, farm products, minerals, oil, wood, and so on flow at increasingly faster rates from sacrificial sites, as if the speed was turned up on a conveyor belt smorgasbord that runs through field and forest and right into our neighborhoods.

The Faster We Consume, the Faster They Produce, the Faster We Consume . . .

The average American now requires roughly 24 football fields (or acres) of natural resources to maintain his or her standard of living, despite the arithmetic fact that there are only five acres available for each person on the planet. And five acres per capita must also meet the needs of millions of other species that support us and share the planet with us. As countries like China strive to raise their levels of consumption, where will four or five more planets come from?

No Time to Care

The commercial need for speed often results in faster, more destructive extraction, quick and sometimes shoddy manufacture, and blitzkriegs of advertising (for which each average American spends more than $500 annually). All these impacts are costly and require us to pick up the pace. One poignant example is the beef industry, in which cows are bulked and slaughtered at younger and younger ages to increase the volume and velocity of marketable product. At the slaughterhouse, the assembly line moves so fast that cows are sometimes butchered alive.

In recent years our household budgets have skyrocketed for day care, elder care, health care, lawn care, house cleaners, psychiatrists, chiropractors, herbalists, party entertainers, and online vendors—in direct proportion to our quest to be "carefree."

Court reporters document that we talk faster than we did in the '60s. Visitors from other countries comment that we appear to be walking in fast-forward, and graphologists note that our writing is progressively degenerating into scribble.

We sleep less, cook and eat faster, and even have sex faster. The best-selling book, *Five Minutes to Orgasm Every Time you Make Love: Female Orgasm Made Simple,* is a great indicator of our perceived need for speed. But is there really anything "simple" about orgasm, or any other biological event?

To the rest of life on earth, time is something to be savored. Biological and physiological rhythms and cycles define and celebrate time in a clock-free world—things like the temperature of the soil in spring, mating rituals, and phases of the moon. Other animal species eat when they're hungry, not when our clocks tell them to. The critical factor for other species is fitting in with the timeless patterns of evolution. In short, time is synonymous with life itself. Yet, for many Americans, "time is money."

We used to "slow down and smell the roses," but now we only have time to "wake up and smell the coffee." We schedule our lives to fit abstract time rather than natural time, forfeiting opportunities to understand how nature works, and be part of it.

WORK LESS WASTE LESS

Are you working so much you don't even have time to recycle? You're not alone. Surveys show that Americans who work long hours use more convenience items, recycle less, and have a bigger negative impact on the environment.   www.timeday.org

Average time spent on one of the country's most awesome outdoor experiences, the Grand Canyon? Twenty-two minutes!

We're finding out that consumption is itself time-consuming, carving away opportunities to experience nature directly. Instead, we regard it as a commodity to be snacked-on like animal crackers. American Wilderness Mall exhibits, for example, enable weary shoppers to get a breath of natural fragrance in a stage set wilderness. For about the price of a pair of good hiking socks, tourists are led through six different wilderness settings. How many different simulated species can *you* spot?

No Time to Recycle

Maybe you're wondering about the fate of the electric razor packaging I finally wrestled to the ground. I assure you it went into the recycling container. But what about the several Super Bowl stadiums of waste the country generates every day? Are Americans taking the time to recycle it?

About a decade ago, Jerry Powell, editor of *Resource Recycling* magazine, observed that more people took part in recycling than voted. "Recycling is more popular than democracy," he concluded.

I called him to see if he stood by that statement now, and was relieved to hear him say, "Absolutely. There are 140 million homes with curbside recycling available, and about 70 percent take part. When you add in drop-off centers, office recycling of paper, telephone book recycling, and so on, you easily surpass our low levels of voter turnout." (A dubious benchmark, when you think about it.)

But Jerry is only half right. We may have recycling systems in place, but we're using them less, partly because we're in a hurry. For example, in Seattle, once the national leader in recycling, city waste management officials recently announced that the amount of the city's waste that is being recycled has dropped from 52 percent to 38 percent (and that's below voter turnout!) over the past few years. The drop off in recycling occurred precisely at a time when working hours were rising. Many people say they are just too busy, too tired and too overworked to recycle.

Another problem, as Jerry Powell points out, "is out-of-home consumption." "For example," he adds, "at work, it used to be standard to bring your lunch in reusable containers. These days, haste makes waste when we rush into a convenience store or a take-out restaurant, where burgers and pizza come in throwaway packaging. We take garbage out with us, and a large percentage of that kind of waste ends up in landfills."

The less we recycle, the faster we'll churn through natural resources, and the harder we'll have to work.

Slow Down and Take Care

Picture the typical American family—2.6 people—at home on a weekend. Marty, the Mom, wears a casual designer sweatshirt with a thumbs-up on it. "I'm a confident consumer," it says. Yet she's also constantly in a hurry, as if her life was a race. To keep up, she gulps her fourth cup of coffee, a beverage that induces symptoms doctors compare with a stress-induced panic attack—elevated heartbeat, increased blood pressure and respiration, and gastric secretion. It's life in America's fast lane, but unfortunately, many of the finer things, such as nature, are reduced to a blur. We can only hope that Marty and millions of Americans like her put the brakes on before it's too late.

When the phrase "Haste makes Waste" was first uttered, back in the fourteenth century (also when the mechanical clock was invented), it meant, "Go slowly, take care. Do it well, so you don't have to do it again." That advice is even more compelling today, at a time when haste and time pressure are contributing to growing mountains of waste and growing threats to ecological systems. And when it comes to megachallenges like species extinction, global warming, and the contamination of global water supplies, we may not get a chance to do it again. The sobering—and let's hope rallying—fact is, we're running out of time.

CHAPTER 14

The Speed Trap

ROBERT BERNSTEIN

Robert Bernstein has been involved with both shorter work time and alternative transportation—issues he sees as closely connected—for many years. He's the coordinator of a list serve for the national shorter work-time movement (www.swt.org) and he's been involved as a transportation planner in his hometown of Santa Barbara, California. When I called to ask him to write this chapter, he was in the process of a long and painful recovery from a terrible accident—he'd been hit by a car while riding his bicycle to work. The accident had been nearly fatal and Robert is still healing from his many injuries. Despite his condition, Robert readily agreed to write the chapter. —JdG

> "The cities will be part of the country; I shall live 30 miles from my office in one direction, under a pine tree; my secretary will live another 30 miles away from it too, in the other direction, under another pine tree. We shall both have our own car. "We shall use up tires, wear out road surfaces and gears, consume oil and gasoline. All of which will necessitate a great deal of work . . . enough for all."
>
> —ARCHITECT, LE CORBUSIER, *THE RADIANT CITY* (1967)

When we think of transportation-caused pollution, we usually think of air pollution, noise pollution, or perhaps water pollution caused by roadway runoff. But geographer John Whitelegg uses the term "Time Pollution" to describe a far more pernicious transportation effluent.

The causal arrow of transportation and time demands points both ways. If we have more time, we can choose slower less energy-intensive modes of transport. But, conversely, a poor transportation system forces us to spend more time in transit or spend more time earning the money for transport, or to do both.

Imagine being back at the early part of the last century and being the first person on your block to own a motor vehicle. What freedom and mobility you suddenly have! What sex appeal if you are a young man! You are literally the king of the road as you cruise along at 25 mph, almost ten times the speed of a typical pedestrian.

But what happens as more of your neighbors acquire this amazing new technology? First, there's a traffic jam and a search for parking. Suddenly, having a car does not seem to be quite as much of an advantage. Yet civic leaders realize they must respond to the demands of the new elite of motorists, especially since they are the ones with the most money, power, and campaign contributions.

Public money is spent to "improve" the roads. Streets are paved with tougher surfaces. Corners are rounded to allow these vehicles to make turns without having to slow down as much. And, most importantly, streets are widened not only to accommodate the increase in traffic, but also to accommodate the increased demand for places to store these vehicles.

Storage is not only needed at home. It is also needed at work, at the market, and at the ballpark. The entire landscape changes as porches give way to wider roads and garages. Who wants to sit out and read on a front porch anyway when noisy, polluting traffic rushes past?

Those rounded street corners make crossing the street on foot riskier and more time-consuming. Walking feels frightening at times and the rest of the time it is just less pleasant with the noise and fumes of the motor cars. It also feels slower and almost pointless compared with the rush of activity in the road.

Doubly Deprived

As roads are "improved" and vehicles get faster, cheaper, and more common, something else begins to happen: neighborhood shops and markets give way to more distant "supermarkets."

This is the *big* turning point. Walking was already becoming less pleasant and more dangerous. But it was still possible to take care of all daily needs without a car. With the loss of neighborhood suppliers, however, a car becomes a necessity.

Work less, Waste less

www.timeday.org

What is the alternative? Long walks or long waits for public transit to get to ever-more-distant places of daily business. If you don't have a car, you are not only at a disadvantage relative to those who do; you're actually at a disadvantage relative to your own situation when no one had a private motor vehicle.

This is what is meant by "time pollution." The speed and mobility of the motorists actually force nonmotorists to spend more of their day in transit. The nonmotorist has no more choice in the matter of time pollution than she does to avoid breathing automobile-polluted air or listening to automobile-created noise.

How many of us are affected by this? Even in the prosperous car-oriented United States, about one-third of all people do not drive. While some choose this lifestyle, most are too young, too old, too disabled, or too poor to drive.

Even one generation ago, half of all children walked or bicycled to school. Today, the figure is just one in ten. Children lose autonomy, self-confidence, and the ability to make new friends from just being out and about. The Centers for Disease Control have targeted this as a prime cause of childhood obesity and the consequent rise of what used to be called "adult onset" diabetes, heart disease, and other diseases of inactivity.

In terms of time, this means parents must become chauffeurs to their children, and women bear the brunt of this forced labor. Women are also more likely not to own a car and are more vulnerable when walking or waiting for transit on sidewalks becoming ever more deserted.

Slower Than We Think

Motor vehicles average much lower speeds than commonly assumed. Over all driving conditions, average speed is only 25 mph. By AAA estimates, it costs about 50 cents per mile to own and operate an economy car. At a median wage of $15 per hour, this means the average American spends an extra two minutes to earn the money to go each mile.

But, as the late social critic Ivan Illich pointed out, this only tells part of the story. The average American motorist drives over 12,000 miles per year. We spend 850 hours per year either driving or earning the money for driving. And where does all of that movement get us? To exciting new vistas and experiences? Only a tiny fraction of our time is spent in such activities. Every new technology is hyped as saving time and expanding horizons. The car ads show scenes of smiling drivers zooming along scenic mountains or coastal roads, or open highways.

Rarely do we see the reality of daily motoring as we sit in traffic jams on the way to the job that pays off the car loans. Or driving to the shopping center to get the aging vegetables that have replaced the fresh ones from the local grocer. And where did those vegetables come from? The local farms have all been paved-over to make room for the shopping malls and their vast parking lots. Now our food comes from hundreds or thousands of miles away and most children grow up with no idea of where it was grown.

Changing Land Use

There is a dynamic relationship between time spent on transportation and land use. For thousands of years in human history, land use patterns were relatively unchanged. People lived within a few minutes of their daily needs. Farms, shops, parks and later schools, factories, and medical facilities were all near home.

Relatively dense cities were surrounded by satellite towns and villages, and had forests and farms in between. There were obvious corridors of transportation between the satellite towns and the main cities.

When railroads began to develop, they were built along those obvious corridors, and land use patterns were not significantly changed. In Europe today, railroads still connect the centers of most mid to large towns and cities. Travelers and business people arrive by rail close to where they do business, see cultural and historic sites, and find lodging.

Not so in most of the U.S. today. Why is the U.S. so different? We are told that Americans have a "love affair" with the automobile. Perhaps. But this is not the whole story.

Historian Ashleigh Brilliant traces the interesting history of the only U.S. city designed originally around high-speed rail. Surprisingly, that city is Los Angeles. High-speed rail allowed far-flung cities to be in easy commuting time from downtown. This made the Los Angeles area effectively very large.

But development was all clustered along those rail lines in traditional cities with walkable downtown areas and surrounding citrus groves and orchards. It was with the introduction of private motor vehicles that this changed. Motor vehicles can go at equal speed in any direction. They are not confined to rails. And private cars are not confined to historical corridors between satellite towns and central cities; they can go every which way. That leads to a land use that never existed in all of human history: suburban sprawl. Suburban sprawl fills in all of the open space between satellite towns and central cities.

Obvious corridors of transit disappear and it becomes impossible to get to most needs without a private car. The result is a vicious circle of cars creating sprawl and sprawl creating forced dependence on cars.

Suburban Nation

Since the 1950s, 86 percent of U.S. population growth has occurred in the suburbs. Two-thirds of jobs created from 1960 to 1980 were in the suburbs. While 10 percent of all motor vehicle trips are suburbanites commuting into a city to work, 40 percent of trips are suburbanites commuting across the sprawl to jobs in suburbia.

How did this happen in America? Thanks to the popular movie, *Roger Rabbit,* many Americans know the story of the destruction of the Los Angeles commuter rail system by a real-life conspiracy of auto, tire, bus, paving, and oil interests.

But that does not explain most of what has happened, anymore than the Civil War explains the end of slavery in the United States. In both cases, larger economic forces were at work. While most Americans are aware of subsidies for Amtrak and for urban buses and subways, few are aware of the far greater subsidies for private motor vehicle use.

Autos On Welfare

While fuel taxes have historically been used to pay for paving certain roads, most of the infrastructure that serves motorists is not paid for through motoring user fees. Here are some examples of these externalized costs that effectively subsidize private motor vehicle use:

- "Free" parking on public streets, at places of work and shopping.

- Mortgage tax deductions for suburban homeowners with no such benefit for urban renters.

- Highway patrols and roadway fire and rescue operations.

- The cost of providing military force to secure the flow of oil. Half of all oil consumed in the U.S. is used to move vehicles on trips of three miles or less.

Noise, vibration, air, water, and soil pollution are not only objectionable, but they are also expensive. They reduce productivity of farmland, increase maintenance costs for structures, create large health impacts, and lower property values.

But the biggest externalized cost of motor vehicles is the land they use. Motor vehicles require ten times the space of people on foot and substantially more than that of people on bicycles or on transit; almost all of that land is paid for through general funds and tax credits from general funds.

The Sierra Club Web site includes a page in its Sprawl section called "America's Autos on Welfare." It cites eight different studies with estimates of 300 billion dollars to over one trillion dollars per year in subsidies for private U.S. motor vehicles.

Overworking For Cars

These subsidies have at least three major effects on work time. The immediate effect is the 100 to 300 extra hours per year that each American needs to work to pay for them. But the subsidies also make it impossible for other transportation modes to compete, thereby eliminating transportation choices. This in turn has two other effects.

It forces Americans to work another 400 or more hours per year to pay for the immediate nonsubsidized costs of driving. And it leads most Americans to spend another 450 hours or so a year in traffic generated by the unique sprawl created by subsidized motor vehicle use.

Freedom of Choice

Americans are proud of their freedom and independence. Yet, if most Americans are asked why they drive to work, they generally give one of two answers. Either they say there is no alternative available, or they say it is unsafe to walk or bike to work through the traffic of all the other motorists. Neither is a matter of free choice.

Both are the result of the vicious circle of sprawling land use and forced automobile dependency. And both are the result of American economics that reward those who drive and penalize those who do not.

Many Americans have moved to suburban areas to escape urban crime. Yet a study in the Pacific Northwest, by Alan Durning of Northwest Environment Watch, showed this safety to be an illusion. Suburban dwellers avoided some death and injury from slightly reduced crime. But this was far outweighed by the increase in traffic deaths and injuries resulting from their need for more driving!

One attempt to mitigate the problem of time spent in suburban commutes has been to change to more flexible work hours. This has meant staggered start and end times for work or for some, working four longer days each week. While this has reduced peak demand of road capacity, it has broadened the peak so that in much of America, "rush hour" now includes most of the day.

Work time flexibility alone seems to provide little advantage to offset the damaging time demands of a society that is overly dependent on private motor vehicles. Shorter work time might help here—more people would choose to walk, bike, or use public transit if they had more time—but the gains would be even greater if they were combined with a reduction of our dependence on the automobile.

It is no coincidence that Europeans have far more free time than Americans, and that Europeans are not so dependent on automobiles. Europeans drive less than half as much as we do, and that gives them more time directly and indirectly.

Having free time allows one to walk, bike, or take the bus, and to travel at a more leisurely pace. But a society designed around walking, biking, and transit is also one that ends up with more free time!

CHAPTER 15

On Time, Happiness, and Ecological Footprints

TIM KASSER AND KIRK WARREN BROWN

Common sense ought to make clear that our rush, rush lifestyle leads us to use throwaway products, recycle less, and, in general, pay less attention to the impacts of our consumer practices on the environment. Nonetheless, data confirming this is hard to come by. Considering the importance of these issues, remarkably few studies explore the connections between time pressure and overwork with environmental behaviors. Psychologists Tim Kasser and Kirk Warren Brown recently conducted one such study and their findings are outlined in this chapter. Although preliminary, their data tend to confirm what we already suspect. Both our environment and our far-too-frantic lives call out for more studies like this one and for a national commitment to act on the information they provide. It's my hope that Take Back Your Time Day *can be the catalyst for far more research on the social and ecological impacts of our American obsession with work and consumption. —JdG*

A s suggested elsewhere in this book, Americans today are working and consuming more than ever. Are they doing so to the detriment of their health, their happiness, society's cohesion, and the sustainability of our ecology? We hope to contribute to the answer to that question by presenting new scientific evidence, which demonstrates that the amount of time people work does indeed have important associations with both their personal well-being and their impact on the Earth's natural resources.

For the last three years we have been surveying individuals from across the United States about their lifestyles, levels of personal happiness, and environmentally relevant behavior.[1] We also asked these individuals how many hours per week they typically work at their job(s) and how much they are paid (i.e., their income). These data allow us to test two questions important to the themes of Take Back Your Time Day.

First, is it the case that working less really could make people happier? In other words, is the number of hours one works associated with one's psychological well-being?

Second, is there evidence that working fewer hours might help people live a less ecologically damaging lifestyle? In other words, does working many hours decrease the likelihood that people will spend the time it takes to act in ecologically sustainable ways?

We also examined how people's income relates to their personal well-being and their ecologically relevant behavior. People usually work long hours in order to make more money, and so income is an important factor to examine. But does trading "material affluence" for "time affluence" really improve our personal and collective quality of life?

Our Sample

To explore these questions, we recruited a sample of 308 people from 48 U.S. states. They included men and women who worked anywhere from 0 to 95 hours per week and who had personal incomes ranging between $0 and $250,000 per year. Participants in the study had expressed an interest in completing our survey (having read about it in the media) or were contacted directly through mailings to their homes.

To measure people's personal well-being, we assessed participants' satisfaction with their lives. Everyone in the study completed a well-validated survey that asks how much they agree with statements like "I would change nothing about my current life" and "The current conditions of my life are excellent."[2]

To measure people's ecological behavior, we used two different questionnaires. First, participants were presented with a list of 40 environmentally beneficial activities and were asked how often they performed each of them. For example, participants reported how often they "buy certified organic food when I shop,"

---

1. This research was supported by generous grants from the Society for the Psychological Study of Social Issues, and from the Simplicity Forum.
2. Pavot, W., E. Diener, and E. Suh. "The Temporal Satisfaction with Life Scale." *Journal of Personality Assessment* 70 (1998): 340–354.

"rent things I need rather than buying them," "turn off lights when not in use," and "recycle nondeposit aluminum cans."

Second, we assessed the "ecological footprints" of our participants by asking questions such as "How often do you eat animal-based products?" "How many miles per gallon does your car get?" and "How big is your home?" [3]

Based on answers to these and other questions, we were able to estimate the number of acres of natural resources necessary to sustain each participant's lifestyle. A person who eats a lot of meat, lives in a big house, and drives many miles in a large car, for example, has a bigger ecological impact, or footprint, than a vegetarian who lives in a small, energy-efficient house, and who regularly uses public (or foot-powered) transportation. According to studies done by Mathis Wackernagel of Redefining Progress, and other environmental scientists, to be ecologically sustainable, our personal ecological footprint should be less than five acres. Instead, the average American footprint is about 24 acres.

The Overwork Blues

We began our statistical analyses by examining the relation between work hours and personal well-being. The data revealed a significant association between the number of hours that people work and their satisfaction with life: *People who worked fewer hours reported being more satisfied than those who worked many hours.*

As can be seen in Figure 1, as people's weekly work hours increased, their life satisfaction decreased. Not surprisingly, we found that people who worked more hours also made more money, but personal income was unrelated to life satisfaction;[4] that is, how satisfied one was with life did not depend on one's wealth.

These results suggest that being time affluent (i.e., working fewer hours) seems to support happiness, whereas being materially affluent (i.e., having a higher income) does not, at least among citizens of the U.S. The old adage that "money does not buy happiness" has been widely supported by other research, including ours, but these data are among the first to show that working fewer hours might reap benefits in terms of one's satisfaction with life.[5]

---

3. The environmental behaviors measure was adapted from the following source: Green-Demers, I., L.G. Pelletier, and S. Menard. "The impact of behavioural difficulty on the saliency of the association between self-determined motivation and environmental behaviours." *Canadian Journal of Behavioural Science* 29 (1997): 157–166. The ecological footprint measure comes from the following source: Dholakia, R., and M. Wackernagel. *The Ecological Footprint Questionnaire.* San Francisco: Redefining Progress, 1999.
4. Life satisfaction correlated $r = -.14$ ($p < .05$) with work hours and $r = .04$ ($p > .50$) with income.
5. Diener, E., and R. Biswas-Diener. "Will money increase subjective well-being?" *Social Indicators Research* 57 (2002): 119–169.

Smaller Footprints

We next explored how material and time affluence relate to ecologically relevant behaviors. The results showed that people who spent fewer hours at work reported behaving in more ecologically sustainable ways, as indexed by both their smaller ecological footprints *and* their higher levels of environmentally sustainable behavior.[6] People with higher personal incomes, however, were less likely to behave in environmentally beneficial ways; they also had bigger ecological footprints.[7]

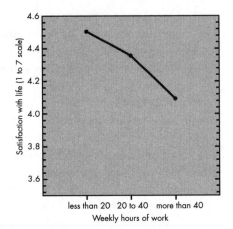

Figure 1. Life satisfaction according to weekly hours of employment.

Figures 2 and 3 graphically represent the results for the ecological footprint measure; as can be seen there, *the number of acres necessary to support one's lifestyle increases as the number of work hours increases* and as level of income increases. In sum, whereas material wealth appears to work against ecological sustainability, working fewer hours can support the well-being of the Earth, upon which, of course, our quality of life ultimately depends.

Although these data support the idea that working fewer hours can reap both personal and ecological benefits, we must remind readers of the maxim that "correlation does not imply causation." In other words, just because we have found statistically significant associations between fewer work hours, on the one hand, and both happiness and ecological well-being, on the other hand, we cannot conclude that working fewer hours actually *produces* these benefits.

For example, we do not know if working fewer hours really makes people happier, or if unhappy people work more to escape their personal difficulties. Similarly, we do not know if working fewer hours provides people the opportunity to live a more ecologically sustainable lifestyle, or if the environment is so important to them that they work fewer hours so they have time to behave in an environmentally friendly fashion.

More research is necessary to better understand the processes through which material and time affluence relate to differences in personal happiness and eco-

6. Work hours correlated $r = -.20$ ($p < .001$) with environmental behaviors and $r = .23$ ($p < .001$) with ecological footprint.
7. Income correlated $r = -.25$ ($p < .0001$) with environmental behaviors and $r = .32$ ($p < .0001$) with ecological footprint.

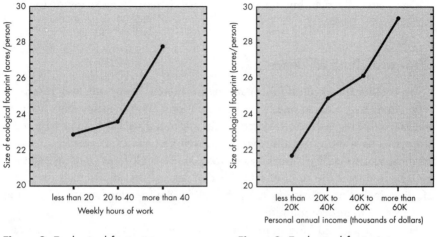

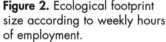

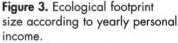

Figure 2. Ecological footprint size according to weekly hours of employment.

Figure 3. Ecological footprint size according to yearly personal income.

logically relevant behavior. For now, all we can say is that the results presented here are preliminary and suggestive. But what they suggest is quite provocative.

Off Course

One conclusion that can be drawn is that our culture is clearly on the wrong path towards happiness and sustainability. The trend over the last few decades in the United States (and Great Britain) has been towards increased time at work.[8] One result has been unprecedented increases in economic wealth. But as demonstrated by past research and current data, such increases in wealth, at least in more economically developed nations, have generally done nothing to improve citizens' quality of life or feelings of life satisfaction, even though we have more "toys" and luxury.[9]

In fact, we pay a high price for "buying into" the materialistic values and goals propounded by consumer culture. Individuals with such an orientation to life report lower personal happiness and life satisfaction; more anxiety, depression, and physical health symptoms; poorer quality interpersonal relationships; decreased contributions to one's community; and more damaging ecological behavior.[10]

8. Schor, J., *The Overworked American: The Unexpected Decline of Leisure.* New York: Basic Books, 1992.

9. Myers, D.G., The American Paradox: Spiritual hunger in an age of plenty. New Haven, CT: Yale University Press, 2000.

10. Kasser, T., The High Price of Materialism. Cambridge, MA: MIT Press, 2002.

Our materially rich, but time-poor lifestyle is destroying many of the best things in life.

Towards Time Affluence

We could feel locked into this pattern, but there is a way out, and Take Back Your Time Day points to one of the best solutions: choosing time affluence over material affluence. As these research results suggest, if we chose to give up some income to have more free time, we could well be happier. We could disengage from the vicious cycle of "work→earn→consume→work more" and instead have the time to pursue the kinds of activities that research has shown truly bring satisfaction, including nourishing our personal development and relationships, and contributing to our communities.[11]

Further, we would have more time to pursue ecologically sustainable practices instead of the quick, "throwaway" lifestyle habits that often accompany being too busy.

Enjoying the benefits of time affluence may thus lead both to a greater sense of satisfaction with our lives and to a greater likelihood that we will create a healthier planetary home for ourselves, our children, and generations to come.

11. Kasser, T., The High Price of Materialism. Cambridge, MA: MIT Press, 2002.

PART SIX

Historical and Cultural Perspectives

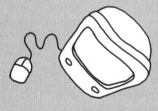

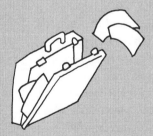

CHAPTER 16

When We Had the Time

BENJAMIN HUNNICUTT

Along with Juliet Schor and a handful of others, Benjamin Hunnicutt has been one of the intellectual pillars of the shorter work-time movement. His writings bring to life powerful moments in American history, stories that ought to be part of every student's education, but sadly have been forgotten. It was from Ben that I first learned the wonderful story of the Black-Connery Bill, recounted again in this chapter. We launched Take Back Your Time Day *on April 6, 2003, the 70th anniversary of the passage of the Black-Connery Bill, which would have made 30 hours the official U.S. workweek (anything more would have been overtime) by the U.S. Senate. I met Ben Hunnicutt while producing the special,* Running Out of Time, *for PBS. I'll never forget the trip my coproducer, Vivia Boe, and I made with Ben to Battle Creek, Michigan, where together we interviewed veterans of the Kellogg Company's 30-hour workweek (also recounted in this chapter). It was amazing to learn that such an experiment had actually occurred in the United States, and to hear how much it meant to the people who had lived it.*
—JdG

teach in one of the last remaining leisure studies departments in America. Who, after all, needs to know what to do with leisure when we don't have any? But one question comes up frequently when I talk about how overworked Americans are: *Maybe we have to struggle hard to live these days, but at least we have it a lot better that most other people in the world and throughout history, don't we?* Technology has twice blessed us. We are much wealthier and we don't have to work nearly as hard. Right?

Wrong!

Most of us assume that preindustrial folk had to work like slaves virtually all the time to keep from starving or being eaten by wolves, or whatever. The anthropologists' discovery that the "Original Affluent Society" was the "primitive" hunter-gatherer is, therefore, something of a shock to modern prejudice.

Original Affluence

For years, I have relished the surprise and occasional dismay among my audiences when I reveal that our industrial society is poverty-stricken in the time we have to live as compared to most of the rest of humanity throughout history. Even the majority of slaves in the ancient world and serfs during the Middle Ages did not work as hard, as regularly, or as long as we do.

From our point of view, hunter-gatherers "work" little or not at all. We might recognize what they are doing as "work" during only a few hours of activity a day. They are "affluent" because most of the time they have "enough" and can spend the majority of their lives as they wish: playing, sitting around, performing rituals, and doing things (gossiping, arguing, nurturing, flirting, telling stories . . .) with family and social groups. For these people, "enough is as good as a feast." They are rich in time to live.

Standard anthropology texts typically point out that, "Another common misconception concerning industrial and preindustrial modes of production is that industrial workers have more leisure than their preindustrial ancestors. The reverse seems to be true, however . . . this leads to the question of why the great labor-saving potential of technology has [not resulted in] an ever greater amount of leisure." [1]

Why, indeed!

Our daily grind was virtually unknown until modern times. It may well be that our way of constantly working is unique. While we dash from place to place, meeting to meeting, frantically jabbing elevator buttons, desperately fighting traffic, the so-called "primitive" people of the world have a quiet breakfast with family, stroll around their gardens—perhaps taking a swim and planning for the delights of the coming afternoon hunt and evening feast.

---

1. Harris, Marvin. *Culture, Man, and Nature: An Introduction to General Anthropology.* Cambridge: Harper and Row, 1985: 218–220.

Not only is the pace of our lives accelerating, as James Gleick has shown us in his splendid book, *Faster: The Acceleration of Just About Everything,* we have become virtually full-time workers. Out technology has allowed our jobs to follow us everywhere. We have become long-distance runners, plunging headlong at a sprinter's pace. No end seems in sight, except the grave or exhausted retirement. What happened?

Dreams of Leisure

After the "Neolithic Revolution" when we began domesticating food crops, farmers and city dwellers found it necessary to work a good deal longer than tribal societies and subject themselves to a more regular routine. Periodically, they have had to work very long and very hard indeed with harvesting, planting, etc. Even so, they were never as devoted to work, or so absorbed by it, as we.

Moreover, throughout history, humans dreamed of less, never more work. Through the ages, *leisure* was seen as the "basis of culture," the human condition yearned for, the hope expressed in legend and myth, the promise of heaven. At its very best, paid work was a subordinate value understood as a *means* to other, better things.

Aristotle is often quoted on this point, and rightly so. He wrote, "We work in order to have leisure," a sentiment the modern reader finds hard to understand.

This view continued well into the modern age. For over a century, prior to the 1930s, laborers throughout the industrial nations successfully reduced their working hours, cutting them virtually in half, and fully expecting their victories to continue.

Led by the United States, peoples of the industrial nations believed that industry and capitalism would continue to provide humans with more and more of the good things of life; more money *and* more time. This was how most people defined "progress" for centuries—higher wages *and* shorter hours. This is why they submitted to the rigors of work's new discipline and to the stress of living in a capitalist world driven by greed and envy. These two demands were the essence of the Labor Movement.

The American Federation of Labor's 1926 recommitment to the "progressive shortening of the hours of labor" celebrated labor's achievements to date—the eight-hour day and five-day week—and called for continuing action. The six-hour day was next on the agenda, then the four-day week and the four-hour day were soon to follow.

The original vision that persisted throughout the nineteenth century, that work would be reduced to a subordinate role in life, and the peoples of the industrial world would be able to work more to live, and live less to work, seemed about to come true, nearly eighty years ago.

The Old Economic Wisdom

Economists agreed. Describing the hundred-year-long work reduction process around the turn of the twentieth century, most confidently predicted that this decline would continue well into the future. There was no reason to expect it to stop. Indeed, this was arguably *the longest and most influential social and economic movement in modern times.*

What other movement had lasted so long and involved so many people throughout the industrial world? Stacked up against other "social movements" and "economic trends," this one was gigantic. Moreover, unlike other more abstract, hard-to-see "movements," this was close to home, involving the way in which ordinary people lived their lives and spent their time everyday.

Hundreds of books and articles were written predicting that work would soon become a subordinate part of life, and rightly so. Speaking before the Young Men's Hebrew Association in New York in the mid-1920s, Julian Huxley called the two day workweek "inevitable" because of the simple fact that "the human being can consume so much and no more. . . . [2]

John Maynard Keynes, the best known economist of the century, wrote in the early '30s that, "when we reach the point when the world produces all the goods that it needs in two days, as it inevitably will . . . we must turn our attention to the great problem of what to do with our leisure." Indeed the time was rapidly approaching when "three hours [work] a day [will be] quite enough to satisfy the old Adam in most of us!" [3] Keynes and Huxley agreed, as so many had maintained at the time, that leisure would overtake work well before the century ended.

Enlightened Owners

This view of progress spread even to conservative business people. Walter Gifford, president of AT&T, the largest corporation in the United States in the 1920s, was one of several business leaders who recognized that "industry . . . has gained a new and astonishing vision." The final, best achievement of business and the free market need not be perpetual economic growth and everlasting consumerism, he argued, but "a new type of civilization," in which "how to make a living becomes less important than how to live." [4] As it had been doing for a century . . .

"[m]achinery will increasingly take the load off men's shoulders . . . Every one of us will have more chance to do what he wills, which means greater opportunity, both materially and spiritually. . . . [Steadily decreasing work hours] will give us

---

2. "Professor Huxley Predicts 2-Day Working-Week," *New York Times* (Nov. 17, 1930): 41:1.
3. Keynes, John Maynard. *Essays in Persuasion.* New York: Harcourt Brace and Company, 1932: 369.

time to cultivate the art of living, give us a better opportunity for . . . the arts, enlarge the comforts and satisfaction of the mind and spirit, as material well-being feeds the comforts of the body."

"Liberation Capitalists" such as Gifford, W.K. Kellogg (Kellogg's Corn Flakes®), and Lord Leverhulm (one of the Lever Brothers—the British soap kings) expected to perfect work by subordinating it. Good jobs were still possible, even in the midst of the tightly controlled, specialized, and frenzied environment of the modern office and factory, so long as the center of life was shifting; so long as people "worked more to live and lived less to work."

They believed that work would soon be put in its rightful place, becoming the servant of people's larger concerns with living, and modern jobs, despite their shortcomings, would be redeemed. The culmination of industrial capitalism was not to be perpetual economic expansion and eternally more consumption. Mass leisure would become progress' final, grand achievement.

The Best to You Each Morning

In the 1920s and 1930s, people in the United States began to live this new freedom; experimenting with new kinds of activities, hobbies, fads and fashions. Some recovered vital parts of life lost to industrial progress, such as starting creative projects around the house (the do-it-yourself phenomena), reinvigorating neglected communities, spending more time with family, friends, and nature, or reading.

For example, W.K. Kellogg put the rhetoric of his fellow "Liberation Capitalists" into practice in Battle Creek, Michigan. In December 1930, he and his CEO, Lewis Brown, began the six-hour day in his cereal factories. Even in the midst of the Great Depression, the experiment was a grand success, paying for itself in short order as productivity increased, and giving workers two additional free hours a day. As one woman put it, life in Battle Creek became something very much like "summer camp."

We have excellent records of what people at Kellogg thought about and did with the "extra time." The Women's Bureau of the Department of Labor did a thorough empirical study, and newspapers, magazines, radio, and scholarly journals reported in detail about what most people at the time simply assumed was "the coming thing"—business's next "great initiative."

Family and community were the two main beneficiaries. Kellogg workers spent most of their "extra time" at home and around the neighborhood, strengthening and improving those places. Workers continue to tell stories about the six-hour

---

4. Gwinn, Sherman. "Days of Drudgery Will Soon Be Over: An Interview with Walter S. Gifford." *American Magazine* (November 1928). See also "Address Before the General Election Board." *Addresses, Papers, and Interviews,* 4 (September 1931): 108.

day; how parents had time to lavish on children, how life seemed quieter and more peaceful then, how the neighborhood seemed more like a community.

One of the workers cautioned a young interviewer, "If you remember anything I tell you, take as much time as you can with your children when they come. Play with them. Read to them. It's as good for you as it is for them, maybe better. It don't get no better in this world, and if you miss those days, working all the time, you don't get a second chance."

Leisure infrastructures began to form. Private commercial recreation enjoyed the new business—skating rinks, movies, etc.—and survived in the town. New firms opened even in the dark days of the depression.

However, since money was tight all around, it was public facilities (parks, community centers), private voluntary nonprofit organizations (YMCA, fraternal orders), and traditional institutions (churches, synagogues) that flourished, supported not by increased revenues, but by the extra time people had to spend.

The Balanced Life

Schools became involved, opening their doors to a community rich in time to live. Teachers began to instruct students in the "the arts of living," preparing them not only for work, but also for the reality of leisure. Liberal arts and sciences were reinvigorated. "Extra curricular" activities burgeoned. Parent involvement expanded. "Room mothers" (parents—including some men—who volunteered to help teachers in the classroom) appeared. Librarians saw a new opportunity opening. Libraries would emerge at last as a vital community institution.

Workers spoke often about how the "balance" of their lives shifted. Instead of organizing their days around the job, they found that concerns about how to spend their lives away from work gained prominence. The economic equation seemed to shift as well. Economic concerns waned somewhat as extra-pecuniary interests waxed strong. "What shall I do" competed with "what shall I buy."

Those who became used to six-hour days, and to the expansion of their lives that the "extra time" provided, frequently looked back on the eight-hour day as a kind of barbaric slavery, saying things like "I wouldn't go back to eight hours for anything. I wouldn't have any time to do anything but work and eat."

Beyond Business

Meanwhile, President Herbert Hoover, with strong conservative and business support, began the national task of repairing the damage caused by the 1920's orgy of consumerism and the Great Depression that followed. Realizing, as William Green, president of the American Federation of Labor said, that "free time will come, the only choice is unemployment or leisure," Hoover began a national campaign to share the work, relying on business and labor's voluntary cooperation. The campaign was successful; other businesses across the country, in addition to Kellogg's, voluntarily reduced work hours and either maintained their labor force or expanded it. Hoover's administration claimed that 25 percent of "all employees" were working fewer hours and sharing their jobs. A national commission estimated between three and five million new jobs created.

The Democrats responded with their own scheme after the 1932 election-legislated work sharing. Initially, President Roosevelt and Francis Perkins, his Secretary of Labor, had endorsed the conservative, voluntary approach. But they soon turned to labor's thirty-hour legislation, introduced in congress as the Black-Connery bill and known for a while as the Black-Perkins bill, because of the administration's strong support. This bill initially set the workweek at thirty hours, with substantial overtime "penalties."

Seventy years ago, on April 6, 1933, the Senate passed the bill, and the House was on the verge of adopting it. Newspapers and magazines across the nation predicted that the six-hour day, thirty-hour week was within days of becoming a national reality.

But the Roosevelt administration got cold feet and encouraged government job programs instead of work sharing to increase employment. Still, even in the dark days of the Depression, discussion began about a new dawn of freedom. Americans began to realize in unexpected ways that the nation's founding values, Freedom and Liberty, were expanding beyond the political realm into the economics of daily life.

Liberty seemed to be manifesting itself as a Pursuit of Happiness, transcending economic concerns, going beyond the controls of bosses and the rigors of modern jobs, opening up in a new public arena of freedom in leisure. Abundant free time would compliment and balance abundant material blessings. Indeed the belief was widespread that work's reduction was necessary to stabilize the economy so that the nation's material blessings might return as well.

This was the high-water mark of the politics of work reduction, the apogee of the expression of Liberty as the "Pursuit of Happiness."

Recently, historians have been speculating about "history as if"; about what might have happened if things had gone just a little differently. Surely, American history would have altered in a dramatic way if the thirty-hour week had become law. We might not be as materially "wealthy" as we are now as a nation. As one Kellogg worker noticed about her life, "what to do" might have come to compete with "what to buy."

Perhaps, as was certainly the case in Battle Creek, the public and private infrastructures of leisure would have grown. When set in place, such resources might have enlivened family and community life. A democratic culture may have grown in a world where most of us did our own music, drama, conversation, history, and storytelling, instead of buying these essential human activities from "professionals" as we do now.

Perhaps the idea of Liberty could have been realized in new ways, rivaling Liberty's other "New Births" in such dramatic periods as the Civil War and The Civil Rights struggle.

Renewing the Dream

Given the overwork that we are now experiencing, and given the fact that other industrial nations are far outpacing the U.S. in expanding leisure, should we not look to our own past for guidance and for a model of another kind of American dream? Might we not profit by recalling a dream more noble and practical than perpetually escalating consumerism and eternally expanding "need," the very antitheses of expanding Liberty?

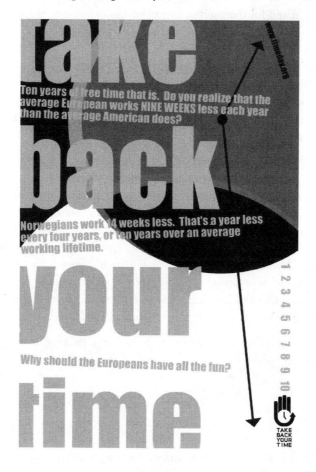

If our forefathers and mothers who lived during the Great Depression, and the ordinary people in Battle Creek living ordinary Midwestern lives, could dream of a richer life based on shorter hours, why are we unable to imagine such things and, instead, continue to work harder and faster? Why do we continue to allow our technology to enslave us, instead of seeing machines primarily as Labor Saving Devices, as workers certainly did for a century and a half?

Perhaps it is unfashionable to hold up the past as a guide to present action. But if ever there were a case in which history can provide us with a lively alternative to our own overworked reality and our present dull dreams of "more, always more," it is the history of work reduction in the U.S.A.

We might also reconsider how people throughout history valued leisure as the center of their lives, how they built their cultures up from that center and worked to support that base. We might find in the historical record inspiring examples of how the people of the world struggled with leisure's challenge, finding things worth doing in and for themselves, caring less for expanding wealth, domination, and the satisfaction of new "needs" and manufactured pleasures.

We might find in the historical record, models of the value of expanding time—freedom for family, community, learning, health, nature, history, play and joy, spiritual awareness and practice.

Monsignor John Ryan was a leader during the Depression-era struggle for shorter working hours. In a society obsessed with work and consumerism, we would do well to consider his advice:

> *Just why a people should spend its time in turning out and consuming a hundred kinds of luxuries which minister only to material wants, instead of obtaining leisure for the enjoyment of the higher goods of life is not easily perceptible. . . . One of the most baneful assumptions of our materialistic industrial society is that all men should spend at least one-third of the twenty-four hour day in some productive occupation. . . . Human life is primarily qualitative. It consists in thinking, knowing, communing, loving, serving, and giving rather than in having or enjoying. Its supreme demand is that we should know more and love more, and that we should strive to know the best that is to be known and to love the best that is to be loved.*[5]

Is it too much to ask again for the right to live in balance, something the U.S. already believed possible seventy years ago?

---

5. Ryan, J. A. "High Wages and Unemployment," *Commonweal* 13 (January 7, 1931): 359–260. Also see *Questions of the Day*. New York: 1931: 242.

CHAPTER 17

Can America Learn from Shabbat?

RABBI ARTHUR WASKOW

Thirty years ago, I saw a film about the life of Francis of Assisi, perhaps the most beloved of Christian saints. Franco Zeffirelli's Brother Sun, Sister Moon *was full of Hollywood sentimentality and probably, in many ways, far from reality. In every scene, Lady Claire looked as though she'd just stepped from the set of a Lady Clairol commercial. Nonetheless, the movie contained a powerful message. Francis spoke sharply to those who, in his day, had become possessed with possessing, obsessed with producing and consuming. Francis reminded them to remember what Christ said about the lilies of the field and the birds of the air "who do not toil and yet are more beautiful than Solomon in all his glory." The film's music, sung by the rock star, Donovan, was a bit sappy for my taste, yet one song remains in my mind:*

"If you want your dreams to grow, take your time, go slowly,
Do few things but do them well, simple gifts are holy."

Our great religious traditions, as Rabbi Arthur Waskow makes clear in this chapter, have always reminded us to take time for rest and contemplation, time to consider what is really important to us and to others with whom we share creation. Rabbi Waskow has been active for many years in the movement for shorter work time. I became aware of his work when I visited his Free Time/Free People Web site. It's my hope that religious leaders of all faiths will consider Rabbi Waskow's message carefully, and talk with their congregations on the weekend of Take Back Your Time Day, *or before, about slowing down, observing the Sabbath, and thinking more deeply about what is most important in our lives. —JdG* everal years ago, I went to a folk song festival in Philadelphia. Many of the singers sang labor songs of the 1930s, civil rights songs of the 1960s, and peace songs of many decades. The audience sang along, nostalgia strong in the air. Then Charlie King began singing a song with the refrain, "What ever happened to the eight-hour day? When did they take it away? . . . When did we give it away?"

The audience roared with passion, not nostalgia. This was about our own lives, not something from the past. I was startled. Suddenly I saw that my own sense of hyper-overwork, of teetering on the edge of burnout, was not mine alone. And suddenly I saw that everything I had learned about the joys of Sabbath were not just for lighting private Jewish candles at the dinner table and chanting private Torah in the synagogue.

I began to talk with others, especially with scholars who have studied overwork as a growing pressure in American society, and people whose religious and spiritual traditions call for time to reflect, to be calm, to refrain from Doing and Making in order to Be and to Love.

Out of those discussions came an effort that brought Christians, Muslims, Buddhists, Jews, Unitarians, and spiritually rooted "secular" intellectuals together to redress the rhythms of work time and time for family, community, the Spirit. By freeing time, we thought, we could help free people.

Free time. Not just through the ancient practice of the Sabbath, but also through new ways—befitting an industrial/informational economy—of pausing from overwork and overstress.

But that gets ahead of the story. What did we find when we began exploring America from this angle of vision?

Juliet Schor's book, *The Overworked American,* showed that the promise made to us thirty years before had been betrayed: The new computer technology did *not* give us more leisure time. Most Americans were working longer hours, under more tension, than they had a generation before.

Not Just a Personal Choice

Other studies followed. Some of them pointed out the increase in temporary workers and part-time workers, suggesting Schor was mistaken. But it has become clear that "underwork" and "overwork" are in fact closely related. Corporations that seek to keep workers "part time" and "temporary" (so as to pay them less and avoid providing medical or pension benefits) drive these "part-time" workers into finding extra jobs just to keep hanging on by their fingertips to a barely adequate income. Underwork *breeds* overwork.

Some blue-collar workers are shanghaied into compulsory overtime—a seventy-hour week, sometimes. Their bosses would rather pay them extra than add new workers with medical benefits and Social Security. The workers lose touch with their kids, but they can't say no. In many cases, "downsizing" (that neat euphemism for dis-employing workers) leaves fewer workers to carry out the same amount of work. The numbers of the dis-employed, the jobless, climb; and so do the numbers of the overworked since the remaining jobholders work longer under pressure to get the job done. The fear that they will be the next workers "downsized" helps spur them into overwork.

Conversely, the overwork of some—12-hour days, 60-hour weeks—reduces the numbers and the quality of jobs that are available to others. Overwork breeds dis-employment.

It is not just poor people or blue-collar workers on wage/hour status who get forced into overwork. Myriad are the middle-class social workers trying desperately to keep up with growing caseloads by working twelve-hour days. Many are the wealthy lawyers whose law firms expect them to bill 60 or 70 hours a week or get shuffled away.

Indeed, the overwork/overstress reality runs across class lines. From wealthy brain surgeons to single mothers making minimum wages at fast-food stop-ins, tens of millions of Americans are overworked.

But who is to say it's "overwork" if people *choose* to do it? Those who really feel burnt out can just slow down, can't they? Any malaise that people feel is just a result of their own choices and of their refusal to face the consequences of their own choices, isn't it?

No. It isn't.

Treating overwork as a private, personal life choice, treating burnout as if it's the result of internal confusion and incompetence is like—very like—saying that women who felt discomforted, disempowered, and ill at ease in the 1950s were simply choosing their lifestyle and their discomfort. Most of those women felt themselves to blame for their unease. For many, it took Betty Friedan to show that they were being treated unequally and that they could do something about it.

I think we are in much the same situation today. There are deep human needs for rest and reflection, for family time and community time. But economic and cultural pressures are grinding those deep human needs under foot.

Who says there are such human needs?

● The Scriptures Say . . .

For all the religious traditions that take the Hebrew Scriptures seriously, there is a teaching we call Shabbat. (The word is usually translated into English as "Sabbath," and comes from the Hebrew verb for pausing or ceasing.)

In Exodus 20: 8–11, the reason given for the Sabbath is to recall Creation; in Deuteronomy 5: 12–15, it is to free all of us from slavery. In the Jewish mystical tradition, it is taught that these seemingly two separate meanings are in fact one. Meditate on them, and we can see them that way.

And we are taught not only the seventh day Shabbat; there are also the seventh year and the seven-times-seven plus one year, the fiftieth year, the Jubilee.

In the seventh year, the land must be allowed to catch its breath and rest, to make a Shabbat for God, the Breath of Life. Since nearly everyone in ancient Israel was a shepherd or a farmer, this meant that almost the whole society rested. Since no one was giving orders and no one was obeying them, hierarchies of bosses and workers vanished.

In this year-long Shabbat, even debt—the frozen form of stored-up hierarchy— was annulled. Those who, because of poverty, had been forced to borrow money were released from the need to repay; those who, out of wealth, had been pressed into lending were released from the need to collect.

And in the fiftieth year, the land could breathe freely once again and not be worked. All land was redistributed in equally productive shares, clan by clan, as it had originally been held. (Lev. 25 and 26: 34–35, 43–45; Deut. 15: 1–18). This year was called "yovel," usually rendered in English as the "Jubilee."

These year-long Jubilee observances that the Bible calls "shabbat shabbaton," "Sabbath to the Sabbatical power," or "deeply restful rest" are times of enacting social justice, and times of freeing the earth from human exploitation. They are times of release from attachments and habits, addictions and idolatries.

Indeed, in these socially revolutionary passages of Torah, the text never uses the word "tzedek"(justice), but instead the words "shmitah" and "dror," which mean "release." It is what Buddhists today call "nonattachment." The deepest root of social justice, according to these biblical passages, is the profoundly restful experience of abandoning control over others and over the earth. And, conversely, the deepest meditation intended to free us from our egos cannot be experienced as long as we are egotistically bossing other human beings or the planet.

Balance

The tradition of Shabbat did not teach that this restfulness and utter nonattachment was the only worthy path to walk. Rather, the tradition was rooted in an earthy sense of sacred work as well as sacred rest. Indeed, the tradition taught a rhythm, a spiral of Doing and Being in which the next stage of Doing would always be higher and deeper, because a time of Being had preceded it, and in which we could bring a fuller, more whole self to the Being because we had Done more in the meantime, and in which both Doing and Being were more holy because we had *integrated* them into a balanced life-path.

According to Evan Eisenberg's book *The Ecology of Eden,* this rhythm of Shabbat may have emerged from an effort of Western Semitic communities to cope with the emergence of monocrop agriculture in the Sumerian empire. Semitic small hill-farmers, shepherds, and nomads had to face the new high-efficiency agriculture with its emphasis on population growth, ownership, and armies.

The question was what should the communities of Canaan do? They could ignore the new efficiency and go under. They could imitate it and disappear. Or they could learn what was valuable and Godly within it and absorb that into their own lives in ways that kept their culture both sacred and distinctive.

So, one year every seven, they pretended to become hunters and gatherers again. They would eat only what grew freely from an uncultivated land. They reaffirmed their age-old teaching that God alone, and no human being, owned the land. They came through this crisis of profound challenge to their sacred life path changed, but intact as a people whose Sabbatical restfulness was precisely a sign of their covenant with God.

The Crisis of Modernity

In the last century, all traditional communities on Planet Earth have been living through an analogous crisis. The great leap in economic efficiency and military mastery that came with Modernity played the same role in shattering Rabbinic Judaism, Christianity, Islam, and Buddhism that Sumerian efficiency and power played in the Western Semitic communities.

Thus it is not surprising that just as we realize we are being swamped by the new Global Gobble of human communities and the earth itself, just as the Nazi Holocaust and the H-Bomb and sweatshops and the burning of the Amazon basin and the privatization of water supplies and global warming come to pass, the need for rest, reflection, and calm comes back into our consciousness.

ADULT PLAYGROUND RULES

NO LAPTOP OR CELL PHONE USE ALLOWED.

NO WORRYING ABOUT DEADLINES.

NO BUSINESS SUITS ALLOWED.

NO BUSINESS MEETINGS.

TAKE BACK YOUR TIME

RECESS ISN'T ONLY FOR KIDS
WWW.TIMEDAY.ORG

Already in 1951, in the aftermath of those grotesque mockeries of Making—the Holocaust and Hiroshima—Rabbi Abraham Joshua Heschel (who later marched alongside Martin Luther King against racism and the Vietnam War) wrote in his book, *The Sabbath:*

> To set apart one day a week for freedom, a day on which we would not use the instruments which have been so easily turned into weapons of destruction, a day for being with ourselves, a day of detachment from the vulgar, of independence of external obligations, a day on which we stop worshipping the idols of technical civilization, a day on which we use no money . . . on which [humanity] avows [its] independence of that which is the world's chief idol . . . a day of armistice in the economic struggle with our fellow [humans] and the forces of nature—is there any institution that holds out a greater hope for [humanity's] progress than the Sabbath?

Christianity, Islam, and Rabbinic Judaism all reinterpreted these biblical teachings in their own ways. But all of them, as well as Buddhism and perhaps all the world's other spiritual traditions, taught the necessity of periodically, rhythmically calming one's self for inward reflection, for time to Love and time to Be.

Who Will Lead the Change?

Who can—and will—do something about the denial of these needs, the subjugation of human beings and the earth to the pharaonic (and our modern American) notion that Shabbat is a waste of time, that tireless work is the real proof of one's worth?

You might think that the labor movement would do something about it. After all, the eight-hour day that now seems lost to many of us was the result of labor struggles beginning in the 1880s: "Eight hours for work, eight hours for sleep, eight hours for what we will!" Similar in meaning was the slogan of women garment workers who were members of the Industrial Workers of the World: "We want bread—and roses too!"

There have indeed been some recent stirrings of interest in the American labor movement toward curtailing overtime, often in the hope of opening up more jobs for the dis-employed. But anxieties among workers about making more money in the short run have so far drowned out most of these wistful desires for more rest.

The connection between overwork and undercitizenship was also made by Ralph Nader during his 2000 presidential campaign. Nader said that today it's harder to be a citizen because people are working 160 hours more each year than they did twenty years ago. Nader, wrote one reporter, "gets the most rapt attention from his middle- and working-class audiences when he talks about their shrinking leisure time."

What about Business?

Some studies are beginning to show the costs of compulsory overwork. Reg Williams and Patricia Strasser, professors of nursing at the University of Michigan, estimated in the *Journal of the American Association of Occupational Health Nurses* that the total cost of depression at work is as high as $44 billion. They pointed out that health care workers have focused much attention on the workplace risk factors for heart disease, cancer, obesity, and other illnesses, but little emphasis on the risk factors for depression, stress, negative changes in personal life, negative changes in the work environment, and difficulties in interpersonal relationships.

Similarly, studies at Cornell University's School of Industrial and Labor Relations found that workers who put in more than fifty hours per week are more likely to experience "severe" work/family conflicts, and workers who are pressured into working overtime by their supervisors suffer significantly higher rates of alcohol use, stress, and absenteeism.

A Role for Religious Communities

As businesses become aware of these costs, they may become willing to adopt policies that give workers more free time, but in many cases it will take vigorous struggle to win these changes. And here is where the religious communities could, out of their own values and commitments, become important.

What would it mean for the different religious communities to undertake the effort that their own traditions teach?

Over the past few years, a network of Jews, Christians, Muslims, and Buddhists, initially brought together by The Shalom Center, have been examining these questions. We have been developing a statement called "Free Time/Free People," and circulating it among a broader group of religious leaders and activists.

Among the signers were such well-known spiritual and intellectual leaders as Gar Alperovitz, Rabbi Bradley Shavit Artson, the Rev. Tony Campolo, Sr. Joan Chitister, Harvey Cox, the Rev. Bob Edgar, Roshi Bernard Glassman, Maria Harris, Susannah Heschel, Msgr. George Higgins, the Rev. Jesse Jackson, Rabbi Michael Lerner, Rabbi Richard Levy, Marcus Raskin, Sharon Ringe, Juliet Schor, Alan Slifka, Rabbi Sheila Peltz Weinberg, Dr. Cornel West, and the Rev. Walter Wink.

They have been joined by key organizers and institutional activists, including Imam Feisal Abdul-Rauf (president, American Muslim Sufi Assn.), Fred Azcarate (executive director, Jobs with Justice), Kim Bobo (executive director, National Interfaith Committee for Workers Justice), Heather Booth (founder of the Midwest Academy), Rev. David Dyson (Chairperson, People of Faith Network), Paul Gorman (executive director, National Religious Partnership for the Environment), Rabbi Mordechai Liebling (The Shefa Fund), Sensei Pat Enkyo O'Hara

(Zen Peacemaker Order), Mark Pelavin (assistant director, Religious Action Center of Reform Judaism), Meg Riley (director, Washington office of the Unitarian Universalist Association), Sr. Christine Vladimiroff (prioress, Order of St. Benedict), and key editors of the important Christian magazines *Sojourners, The Other Side,* and *Witness.*

The religious communities are in a position to do two things at once:

- Reawaken in their own members the wisdom of restfulness, willingness to open more of their own time for Being and Loving, and the richness of prayer, meditation, chant, and ceremony that can make this real; and

- Take action in the world of public policy to free more time for spiritual search, for family, and for community; and to create a real full-employment society in which "jobs" carry with them a decent income, access to health care, dignity, and self-direction—jobs secure enough and decent enough to let workers loose their grip on fear and seek Free Time.

For the sake of this second sphere, there is every reason for the religious communities to reach out to the labor movement, the environmental movement, groups that seek to nurture the family and "family values," and women's organizations.

The Free Time/Free People statement urges American political, economic, and cultural leaders as follows:

- To reduce the hours of work imposed on individuals without reducing their income;

- To strongly encourage the use of more free time in the service of family, community, and spiritual growth; and

- To make work itself sacred by securing full employment in jobs with decent income, health care, dignity, and self-direction.

Some New Ideas

As our Free Time discussions continued, the religious leaders agreed that while it was important to encourage restful observance of the Sabbath, the sabbatical principle needed to be explored and shaped into new practices and policies, as well as old ones. This approach, they realized, would make possible an alliance that has been sorely lacking in American society and politics for the last twenty years: an alliance between blue-collar wage/hour workers and white-collar salaried professionals.

What is more, the alliance would not be a merely mechanical coalition, but would be rooted in the deep human sharing of a soul-need held in common.

Thus, a common effort to win Free Time would guide each of these groups to see the shared humanness in "the other," as well as "the self."

What specific actions in the public and communal spheres might give reality to Freeing Time?

Imagine setting aside two Fridays every year in mosques, two Friday evenings/ Saturdays for synagogues, and two Sundays for churches to explore the meaning and the life-giving practice of these times for pausing. In many congregations there are now "Sabbaths for the environment," "Sabbaths for labor," etc. In very few is there a "Sabbath for the Sabbath," examining the very intention and practice of a restful day.

Imagine limiting compulsory overtime to no more than five hours a week.

Imagine turning Fridays, or Friday afternoons, into free time, with commitments not to reduce weekly incomes or salaries.

Imagine businesses setting aside seven minutes every morning and every afternoon in the midst of work as Quiet Time. No work, no telephone, no conversation. Time to sit quietly, to meditate, to drowse, to dream.

Imagine setting aside one week every year as Neighbor Time, for neighborhoods to celebrate folk festivals of their own and share stories, songs, and conversations. What's more, imagine for this week shutting down not only factories and offices, but also highways and airlines, television and hotels.

Imagine offering one "sabbatical" year of paid Social Security between ages 45 and 55 to everyone in exchange for one year's delay of Social Security retirement pay.

Imagine working with businesses to make paid leave time for family and community service available to all workers.

This last possibility deserves fuller examination because it could make a growing difference in the world. As matters stand now, many businesses encourage their high executives to use paid work time to volunteer their services to museum or university boards or similar civic enterprises. But very few businesses offer all their workers the same possibility of volunteering for the local PTA, synagogue, or Sierra Club as part of their paid work time.

Is this a utopian idea? Not at all. Like some of the other approaches sketched above, it might be adopted by some businesses out of a sense that, in the long run, it would be economically worthwhile—reducing absenteeism from mental and physical illness, reducing anger, friction, and sabotage at work, and building better business/community relations.

Other businesses might well respond to quiet persuasion or public economic pressure from religious communities, labor unions, and civic organizations by encouraging this kind of family and community service. Since more and more high schools are making community service part of education, it might not be too difficult to define it as part of the work sphere, as well.

Still other businesses might respond to the carrot of governmental contracts (local, state, and ultimately national) conditioned on offering workers paid family and community leave time. (This kind of contractual carrot has already been used in affirmative action and "living wage" ordinances.)

Imagine, finally, *a living wage, with livable hours!*

All these approaches might help our society renew families, neighborhoods, grassroots communities and institutions, like our congregations themselves. They would make possible more grassroots effort to achieve Free Time. And they would give new breathing time to many overworked and many ill-worked people to once more meet their neighbors, renew themselves, and rediscover their deepest visions of a sacred world.

PART SEVEN

Taking Back Your Time

CHAPTER 18

Enough—
the Time Cost of Stuff

VICKI ROBIN

One argument often used as an objection to shorter working hours is that the average American needs to work long hours "just to make ends meet." But what is missed in this argument is that the ends themselves are all too often the result of time pressure and overwork. "Convenience" products do save time—on cooking, for example—but they usually cost more and thus increase the amount of time we have to work to pay for them. This sort of thing can reach absurd heights. Take, for example, a new product I saw recently—microwavable pre-scrambled eggs. Since all you do is heat them in the microwave, you save about five minutes in time over what you would have spent if you'd broken some real eggs and scrambled them yourself. But the pre-scrambled eggs cost about 20 times as much as plain old eggs do, about 12 minutes in working time for someone making an average salary. So where is the time savings here? Vicki Robin's popular book, Your Money or Your Life, *has helped millions of people around the world reassess their spending habits and decrease their personal spending by an average of 25 percent, thus, at the same time, reducing their need for long working hours. Vicki is an acknowledged international leader of the simplicity movement, founder of the Simplicity Forum and one who walks her talk, living simply and joyfully and inspiring others to do the same.* —JdG magine *Time* magazine. No, not the one with the red border and the predictable news. This is a magazine *about time*. Articles range from black holes to boredom, from cosmological beginnings to untimely endings. It's informative, reflective, provocative, and political. Flipping through the pages, you dip into one fascinating story after another. Then you come across an ad that catches your eye.

The picture couldn't be tackier. Looking penetratingly right at you is a fortune teller with all the classic features—dark brows, full lips, gaudy rings, a flowing paisley scarf around an unruly tangle of long black hair and red-tipped fingers embracing a misty, glowing ball. The headline is even worse: I See A Short Life, But It Could Be Different If You . . .

Yet you can't help but read on. "Bring your lunch to work and add a year to your life. Cut up your credit cards and add ten years or more. Save 20 percent of every paycheck and double your years on earth."

Okay, you think. This is either a big hoax or there's something to it, so you check out the Web site and find there's a book, a tape course, and a free lecture in your hometown. Even though you are a charter member of Skeptics Coalition Against Mendacity (SCAM), you follow the instructions and indeed, all the promises come true.

Reverie over . . . Back to reality.

Your Real Hourly Wage

What happened in this fantasy scenario? You learned the "time cost of stuff." For example, look at your salary. Let's say that when you landed your job you were promised $20 an hour. Supposing you are young and single, that should be plenty for a decent existence. Yet you can't seem to make ends meet. There is always more month than money.

Follow along with this very approximate calculation to find out why. Twenty dollars an hour for a 40-hour workweek would be $800 a week. But your transportation cost (imagine a middling choice of carpooling with another worker in your office) is $20 a week. Half of your car payment should be thrown in, because you upgraded autos to suit your new profession, adding $25 a week more. Restaurant lunches run $30 a week over what you'd pay for a sandwich at home. Whatever duds you buy to look right at work (suits, dresses, uniforms) are part of the weekly cost—conservatively about $25 a week for most people. About once a month, you go to a seminar to improve your chances for advancement—another $50 a week. Oh, and then there are taxes for another $125 a week. You're down to $525 a week.

But it gets worse. Your commute time adds 10 hours a week to your job hours. Just getting dressed, fed and out the door in the morning and at night, relaxed back into a semblance of sanity, adds another 10 hours. The one-day a month trainings add another three hours a week. The bits and drabs of uncompensated overtime (the extra half hour at your desk, the calls on the weekend, the e-mails and pagers that stalk you mercilessly) could add another 10 hours easily. The books you read for your profession (just ask, would you take this book to bed if you didn't have this job?) add another seven hours a week. Leaving it there, we get an 80-hour workweek.

Do your own math here. Divide the $525 you've got left (your actual salary) by 80 actual hours and your real hourly wage comes out to just over $6.50 an hour. That was a very fast trip from median to minimum wage. With that $6.50 an hour you need to pay rent, basic clothing and food costs, phone, utilities, and the baseline cost of your car. Now, if you want to go to the movies, out to dinner, or on vacation . . . well, think again.

But most Americans don't think again. They spend as if they actually made that $20 an hour. Which is why debt is epidemic and ends never meet. *Your Money or Your Life* (the book that introduced the 'real hourly wage' to America) reveals how unconscious purchasing actually drives you back again and again into the workplace to support your buying habits. A new car at $6.50 an hour becomes over 3000 hours—a year and a half on the job. A daily "double tall skinny" latte ends up costing over 100 hours a year—that's over two weeks of work.

The Fullfillment Curve

Once you really *get* the time cost of stuff (if you do the real hourly wage calculation yourself you'll get it *very profoundly*), your willingness to waste your "life energy" (the time it costs to make a dollar) undergoes a profound shift. Every potential purchase must merit your valuable time. A $6.50 item must be worth more than an hour with a friend or a good book.

And it must be worth one hour of an all too short life. Stuff may multiply by ignoring mounting debt, but time cannot. Even the most sophisticated medical techniques and anti-aging strategies don't add that many years to your four score on earth. Nearly a third of your life-hours are spent sleeping (or should be), and another third or more are spent in school or on the job. Of the remaining third, a third of those are spent just maintaining your physical existence. Now what do you want to do with what's left? Those hours don't number in the millions or even hundreds of thousands. They are precious. "What," as Mary Oliver asks, "do you want to do with your one wild and precious life?" Shop?

As you live with the implications of this real hourly wage calculation, you will slowly discern what belongs in your life and what doesn't. Consider what I call "the fulfillment curve." Some purchases add to well-being. Some are just clutter. Some material items are necessary for survival. Basic food, clothing, and shelter fit here. The little money spent on survival goes a long way to an experience of fulfillment. Being hungry, cold, and tired is sheer misery, and meeting those needs is

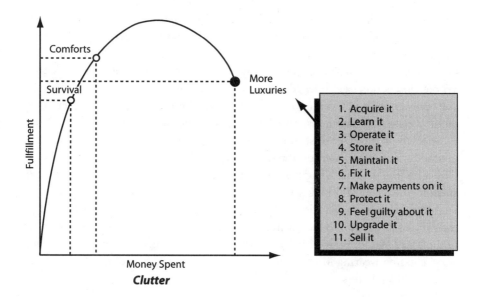

Clutter

joy indeed. Other purchases add comfort, like a better bed, a more secure home, a greater variety of food, nicer clothes.

Beyond comforts are luxuries, things that still add to quality of life, but are likely simply upgrades of what you already have that works perfectly well. The problem with luxuries is that they cost a lot of life energy, and often you don't notice when acquisition has stopped bringing happiness and started adding to misery again. How so?

Take a kitchen gadget. Or a boat. Or a bigger house. Or whatever. There is a time cost of searching for it, selecting it, and bringing it home. Then, of course, you have to read the manual—any gadget could come with a 50-page booklet. Using it mightn't seem like such a trial, but if you don't really need it then every use just fills up your time . . . uselessly.

Do you have a storage locker where these things end up? Or a moorage? Or just an attic where you keep the box? Then storage itself costs you time. And what modern item doesn't cost you time to take care of it and fix it when it breaks. Up to the attic to get the box, down to the dining table to pack it up, and then off to the post office to ship it back to Kalamazoo or somewhere else in the vast Midwest. Of course, if you buy anything "on-time" there's the work-time cost of the interest charges. You work half your life it seems to just pay off *the interest* on your debt. Not to mention extra "late fees" because with so much work to do and other things to take care of, you often fail to send in your bills on time.

Insurance, of course, has gotten out of hand these days. Cars, houses, lives, airline tickets, jewelry, health—everything you own seems to come with a surcharge to protect it. And that surcharge costs you time on the job. If you think at all (and doesn't modern life conspire to limit that reflective function?), then you realize that a lot of your stuff is not so necessary. It also costs the earth a whack of resources. It probably costs a $3-a-day worker elsewhere in the world a week of her life. Other people would give their eye teeth to have it if they even *had* your measly salary. Whole closets don't get opened lest the sheer embarrassment of riches confront you. But the guilt is there, and it worms its way into odd minutes of every day, eroding your stuff happiness. Ahh, best to just get rid of it all.

So the final time cost of stuff is the cleaning out and getting rid. Out comes the digital camera to photograph the high-end stuff for an on-line auction on eBay. Out come the stickers to tag the remaining 200 odd items for a yard sale. Forget spending that Saturday hiking in the mountains.

And thus ends the sad tale of American stuff. Well, not quite. What isn't sold in the garage sale goes off to the Thrift Store. What isn't sold there is bundled and sent to the Third World. Which is why you can now go to indigenous villages and find small children wearing Mickey Mouse T-shirts instead of homespun and stitched clothing. But I digress . . .

Enough.

If this cycle isn't interrupted by a bit of self-preservation (What! Waste my life on that cr-p!), you consign yourself to being a wage slave unto death in support of your stuff. So here's the real secret of the Fortune Teller. It's what's at the peak of the Fulfillment Curve. A simple word that makes a profound difference in the quality of your life. ENOUGH.

When you have Enough, you have everything you need. There's nothing extra to weigh you down, distract, or distress you; nothing you've bought on time, never used, and are slaving to pay off. Enough is a fearless place. A trusting place. An honest and self-observant place. It's appreciating and fully enjoying what money brings into one's life and yet never (or almost never) purchasing anything that isn't needed and wanted.

All that stuff beyond enough—beyond the peak, where the Fulfillment Curve begins to go down—is simply clutter. Clutter is anything that is excess *for you*. It's whatever you have that doesn't serve you, yet takes up space in your world. To let go of clutter, then, is not deprivation; it's lightening up and opening up space and time for something new and wonderful to happen.

You have a choice, at every moment, with every purchase, to ask, "Does this item add to my experience of fulfillment or is it just clutter?" "Is it worth my 'life energy', the work time I've invested in earning the money to buy it?" "Is having this taking my life in the direction I want it to go?" Many things will pass the test. But many won't, and letting go of them will lead not to deprivation but to the vast joy of having 'enough.'

Remember, the Fortune Teller says, "Enough is freedom, and clutter is a fate worse than dearth." Every time you shop—in person or on-line, with money or credit cards—ask, "Is this stuff worth the time of my life?"

CHAPTER 19

The Simple Solution

CECILE ANDREWS

Cecile Andrews is the founder of the Voluntary Simplicity Study Circles movement. Thousands of Americans now participate in these study circles, meeting with friends, coworkers, or neighbors to see how they can help each other reduce spending, debt, and stress while building community and finding more balance in their lives. Reducing overwork, overscheduling, and overstress in American life is not just a personal matter, but also a personal matter. As people meet to talk about their personal lives in simplicity study circles, they begin to talk about larger, more systemic problems. Many people are finding that by simplifying their lives they not only reduce their need to work so much, they also find the energy to help change the political and economic structures that keep us overworking. In changing their own lives, they begin to change society as well. —JdG

I went to the woods because I wished to live deliberately. To front only the essential facts of life and see if I could not learn what it had to teach. And not, when I came to die, discover that I had not lived. I did not wish to live what was not life, living is so dear; I wanted to live deep and suck out all the marrow.

—THOREAU

ʃimplicity. That time-honored, venerable concept has reemerged in the last several years. People are cutting back so that they can live more fully. They are asking how much is enough and finding that less is often more, and they are challenging our competitive, commercialized, consumerist definition of success.

Throughout history there have always been the few who have tried to live more simply—particularly for spiritual reasons. But, today there is a surging interest among the general public, because too many people just feel pushed to the edge.

I've discovered that the idea of simplicity creates a yearning in people's hearts, but at the same time, fearfulness. They sense that living more simply brings a more centered, balanced life, but they also worry that it means deprivation. They fear they won't have any fun in their already joy-starved lives.

But the opposite is true. People aren't enjoying themselves now, because there's no time for fun. When you greet friends they tell you how busy they are. (I always feel that I should move on quickly so as not to take up too much of their time!)

Cancel Something

In fact, I've come to feel that the nicest thing you can do for people these days is to cancel something. Try it. Announce a party and then cancel it. You'll hear people breathe a sigh of relief. A free night! Or cancel a meeting at work. Pure joy! (Of course, many people will probably use the extra time to catch up on some other work.)

In my talks with people about simplicity, I've come to feel that one of my primary purposes is to help people learn to enjoy themselves more—to help them take back pleasure. Studies have found that enjoying ourselves with neighbors and family is one of the best things we can do for our health.

But what's stopping us from experiencing this sense of joy? Too much to do! It seems as if the high point in people's days is to cross something off the to-do list. This is as good as it gets. (Maybe Simplicity is crossing things off your list even if you haven't done them.)

Of course we're talking about the art of living. The South African poet, Breyton Breytonbach, said that Americans have mastered the art of *living with the unacceptable.* Gradually we've adjusted to unacceptable levels of work hours and having less time for the important things in life.

The simplicity movement is a response to this. We're the small child who says that Emperor Overwork has no clothes. We, in the movement, are saying that life as we're living it is not right. People used to move through their lives in a leisurely manner with time to enjoy themselves—hanging out, taking time to talk with friends, absorbing nature, or just sitting and thinking about life. Instead of enjoyment, people now pursue escapism—watching television or going to the mall.

But true enjoyment—savoring life—takes time. When you're exhausted from working all day, all you can perform are the brainless activities of television viewing and shopping. In fact, international studies show that the longer an industrial country's annual work hours, the more time its citizens spend watching television.

It's hard to switch to a more leisurely life with the constant pressure to hurry up. I went to a copy shop one day and there was a huge poster on the wall that said "Do More!" At first I was startled, because I didn't know if the sign was aimed at me or at the employees. Then I realized that it's the basic American creed—it's the message we get all the time.

And we certainly fall into line. Obsessive multitasking has taken over. Think of the things you've seen people do while they're driving—putting on makeup, changing clothes, eating cereal, nursing a baby, reading the newspaper, and of course, jabbering on cell phones. Cell phones. Cell phones. Cell phones. Ring. Ring. Ring. Ring. Ring. Let's not waste a minute!

But since we're told all the time that we have the highest standard of living in the world, we think we're having fun. We need to help people see that this is not a happy country. The World Health Organization says that one of the biggest issues for employers in the coming years will be depression, with the resulting problems of absenteeism, larger health costs, and employee turnover.

We know why people are depressed at work. They're frantic and hopeless. As layoffs continue, the work piles up. When I speak to employee groups, I always ask them whether they feel they can do anything about their situation. They just sit there and shake their heads. "Isn't it strange," I comment, "that the people in the most powerful country of the world have no control over their work lives?"

The Attractions of Simplicity

And so, the simplicity movement continues to grow. People are attracted for different reasons. As I travel around giving workshops and talking with people, here's what I hear:

Family. Although lots of people are worried about money, what I hear most about is concern about family. I like to ask people if they know how much time married couples spend talking with each other each day. Some young unmarried people in the audience guess one, maybe two, hours. But the married people know better. Almost everyone guesses somewhere in the vicinity of the correct answer: 12 minutes! (And to think that academics are still trying to figure out the cause of divorce.)

Clutter. A lot of people have come to see the Simplicity movement as the answer to clearing out clutter! Although it's certainly much more than that, a concern for clutter gets people to think about their lives. Just why do they have so much stuff? Why are they overwhelmed by piles? There's just not enough time to sort

America Needs a Break

We're working longer hours than do the citizens of any other industrial country. Overtime work should be voluntary.

check out our website: www.timeday.org

through things! People come to realize that to have order in their homes, they need more time.

Community. People have less and less time with friends in a community. Harvard professor Robert Putnam, in his book, *Bowling Alone,* has shown how human interactions have declined over the last forty years. Not only do people see friends less often, they are less involved in civic activities such as PTA or the League of Women Voters.

Work. This may be the primary impediment to a simpler life. But it's not only our long hours, it's our massive insecurity—the worry that we might be laid off. Because many people are so in debt from our egregious consumerism, they're fearful about speaking up and demanding change.

Health—physical and mental. The diseases of stress and the diseases of loneliness are sapping our energy and vitality. Lack of sleep is linked to all sorts of life threatening issues, from accidents to cancer.

Spirituality. At the core of all of this is people's desire to experience life with depth and connectedness, to feel that they are a part of a greater whole. But there's no time for reflection, contemplation, or meditation, the age-old routes to a life of Spirit. (At one time in my life I found myself saying, "I'd better hurry up and meditate! Can I work a half hour of meditation into ten minutes?")

Solutions

All these issues come down to *time,* of course. We need time for our friends and family, time for creativity, time to reflect, time to commune with the universe. A lot of people are rebelling by turning to Simplicity.

The exciting thing about this movement is that it is bubbling up from the people. It is the people saying that things must change. I've come to see myself as sort of a courier in this grass roots movement, carrying messages from group to group, telling people what others have said and what they're doing.

Again, here's what I'm hearing:

People are slowing down; they're cutting back; they're downscaling and down shifting.

In particular, *they're trying to live on less so they'll be able to work less.* They monitor their consumption habits and discover that much of their spending is unconscious, and that there's just too much stuff that brings them no satisfaction.

So, they start to spend less. They start buying second hand; they rent, they barter, they borrow. They "use it up, wear it out, make it do, or do without." They find that the best way to save is to stay out of the malls, and that certainly saves them a lot of time, as well.

And they discover that it's not a life of deprivation! Their lives become a creative challenge. An adventure! Instead of just running out to buy something—as we're been hypnotized to do—we're assisting in the rebirth of ingenuity.

People begin to find new, creative ways of living, like renting out part of their house, or getting rid of a car. They start growing their own vegetables and returning to simple, inexpensive, pleasures like potlucks and neighborhood cookouts. They don't worry about remodeling kitchens and bathrooms or buying the latest fashions.

And they discover all sorts of unexpected benefits. Limiting their consumption means they have less clutter, so they spend less time cleaning and maintaining stuff. Driving less means they get more exercise and have more time for reflection and long conversations. Eating lower on the food chain means they lose less time to sickness and fatigue.

And, most of all, they discover a new self respect because they are clear about their values. They're living lives of integrity because they know that their new consumption habits are good for the planet and even help to undermine corporate injustices. (Simplicity is the ultimate boycott!) This new sense of self worth saves people the time that's often spent in self doubt and recrimination.

It's amazing how it all comes back to *time.* As people realize this, they begin to use their time deliberately, and they begin to live with more depth and exhilaration. They discover their particular passion and take time to pursue it. They begin to create community and quit wasting time with people they don't enjoy. There's no regret about how they're using their time because they've learned to live life to the fullest.

The Obstacles

Now, the truth be told, all of this isn't necessarily easy. Our culture has made it very difficult to swim against the stream. It's hard to move slowly when everyone around you is frantic and fragmented. And sometimes people feel that they have no right to question things. Because Americans are so affluent compared to the rest of the world, we think, "Who am I to complain about my life? Look at all we have."

But we're now realizing that we're poor in many ways: in terms of community, friends, security, an inner life, and of course, *time.*

Some people shy away from Simplicity because they believe it's an elitist movement. People often tell me that this movement is just a bunch of middle-class whiners. I always say, "Of course it's a middle-class movement. We're the ones who have experienced affluence and found it wanting."

We are 5 percent of the world's population but we use 25 to 30 percent of the world's resources. Our consumerism contributes to pollution and global warming. Our need for oil leads us into war and exploitation of other cultures. So, this is important to more of us than just the middle class. As Gandhi said, "Live simply so that others may simply live."

Unfortunately, as more people are drawn to Simplicity, there is greater confusion. In part, it's because Madison Avenue has "discovered" Simplicity and is using it to sell things. "Simplify your life—Buy a Toyota! Simplify your life—use our checking system."

But people are also confused because Simplicity isn't simple. It takes more time to walk or ride your bike than to drive to the store. Recycling and composting aren't as "easy" as throwing everything into the trash. Simple does not mean easy! Simplicity is a complex idea dealing with perennial human questions. "Who am I?" (A corporate robot?) "What is my purpose?" (Accumulating as much money and fame as I can?) "How shall I live?"(Like the advertisers want me to?)

Ultimately, we're asking people to stop and reflect, to question themselves about *what's important and what matters*. We're urging people to look at the consequences of their behaviors and evaluate them, asking, "Is this the way I want to live? What are the consequences of my behaviors for the well-being of people and the planet?"

Simplicity is "the examined life," a life in which we live *deliberately.* It's the art of "discernment," trying to see clearly what's important. It's freedom to make your own choices. Some will embrace Simplicity in the city, some in the country or the small town. Some will stay in their jobs and work to change things from the inside; others will leave and start new efforts within the community. Some will cook all their meals from scratch; others will embrace the café society.

We're trying to find *balance* in life, and we're out of balance in so many ways— between an inner and an outer life, time in nature and time in artificial surroundings, time for solitude and time in community, time with creativity and time with physical labor, and time at work *and* time with family. It all comes back to time.

Ultimately it's about how we're using the time of our lives. Are we living fully? Are we wasting our time? No one put it better than Thoreau when he talked about why he went to Walden. He wanted to live deliberately, "and not, when I came to die, discover that I had not lived."

And so, through Simplicity, we're taking time to live fully and joyfully. We're taking back our lives.

PART EIGHT

Workplace Solutions

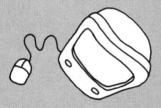

CHAPTER 20

Jobs to Share

CAROL OSTROM

This chapter is the first of several about changes in the workplace that could lead to shorter working hours and more time for American workers. If you've tried some of the ideas put forth by Vicki Robin and Cecile Andrews and actually find you could live with less money, some of these suggestions may also be for you, and you may be able to make them work for you through patient and intelligent conversation with your employer. As the next two chapters make clear, you'll need to convince that employer that the change you propose will benefit the company, as well. And it probably won't be easy, though when I read the engaging writing of a skilled reporter like Carol Ostrom, I can't imagine why her employer wouldn't agree to almost anything just to keep her words coming. —JdG

The first time we made a pitch for a job share—three of us would-be sharers perched nervously in the city editor's little office at the edge of the newsroom—it didn't go well.

What I remember most now, more than a decade later, was one of my colleagues kicking me under the table, hard. I was in the midst of an impassioned speech to the editor about why I needed to share my job.

I was saying—quite eloquently, I imagined at the moment—how much I loved writing, loved journalism, but that other parts of my life were demanding attention, and they were parts I could no longer put "on hold." My elderly aunt needed help, my elderly mother was getting too old to provide it and needed her own help, my partner wanted to have a life with me, and I just couldn't put it all together.

I remember saying I was the kind of person who was compelled to go full steam ahead on stories, that I was simply constitutionally unable to do the half-baked job that perhaps would have let me "coast" through this demanding period. A shared job, I enthused, would let me really work when I worked, and still attend to my other responsibilities. Otherwise, I feared I would have to make dire choices.

Eloise, my coworker, was kicking me in the shin because she had suddenly realized that our editor was not getting it. *So* not getting it. While I was caught up in the rapture of seeing my life as a coherent whole instead of a frantic dash from one disjointed deadline to another, Eloise had noticed the editor staring at me with an incredulous look. Eloise knew, as I did not, that our editor was about to end our little pipe dream with a rocky reentry to reality.

That was more than a decade ago, and I wasn't taking notes. My selective and subjective memory cells imprinted only the meaning of the message. It went like this: "I can't imagine *why* you want to do this. I just can't understand why *anyone* would not want to give 150 percent to their work, *all the time!*" Her tone suggested, not too subtly, that we had all lost our minds, if we'd ever had any.

Needless to say, she turned us down. Years later, after a regime change had installed a different editor, we made the pitch again. Times had changed. We had learned a few things. And we got the job share—a three-way, time-on, time-off share in which three of us shared two jobs, each working four months on, two months off. We agreed to always have two of us there to cover one another's very different beats, to be willing to leap back into full-time work if one of us went on leave for pregnancy or other reasons, and to be enthusiastically available.

We also agreed to forgo a fair chunk of benefits, including some health and dental insurance premiums, which we each paid out-of-pocket for two months a year.

Over the next decade, the job share morphed, temporarily disappeared, reappeared, and finally was transformed into an entirely different animal we didn't even know existed: the "temporarily reduced work year."

During those times, I coordinated care for my aunt, kept my elderly mother from collapse, shouldered some complex family business, and even had time to read. Eloise and Susan, my job-sharing colleagues, found they could work and be moms and have a life, as well.

Susan, for example, formerly fatigued from juggling high-pressure beats with the demands of being a wife and mother of two, then three, suddenly found time for herself. She painted the inside of her home, began exercising, read voraciously, and still had time to volunteer at her children's schools, helping with projects such as the yearly Halloween pumpkin patch visit. She and the kids romped at the beach, and she reveled in spending time with them while they were still young enough to want to do that.

Over the years, we job sharers earned kudos from bosses for our creativity and hard work. We earned prizes, accomplished projects, and helped earn our newspaper some national recognition as a good place for working women.

In the process, we learned—sometimes the hard way—hard lessons about job shares. Maybe they were lessons about how companies work. Or about how people think. Or all of the above.

Lesson Number One: Getting a job share is not about you. It's never about you, no matter what your company says. It's about your company's needs.

Two: To get one, you'll need to figure out what the job share *is* about, from your company's perspective.

Three: Once you get the job share, the real work, especially the PR work, will begin.

Four: It's not going to be easy to teach those you work with to appreciate the benefits of your job share.

Among the memories I have from our halcyon days is an exchange between a couple of editors, somewhere in the midst of one of those wild weeks of honest-to-God actual news. Dammit, was Susan here or on leave, someone demanded to know.

"Who the hell knows?" snapped the other editor. "(The editor who gave us the . . . job share) is the only one who understood their schedule, and he's . . . (not here any more)." (This comment has been edited for taste, libel, and respect for former editors.)

Let's start with what I said before about how a job share is not about you.

At the beginning, we pitched the idea from our perspective. We would be better people. We would be able to take care of our lives. We were smart enough to say that we would be able to do more reading, more talking to people, more living in the world, and that would, of course, make us better reporters. We would come back armed with Great Ideas. And with the energy to shape them into Great Stories.

Editors nodded. Yes, yes, um hum, okay, righto. All Very Important Stuff. Um hum. What we didn't know then, and finally gleaned the hard way over the years, was that these things don't sell job shares, at least not at our workplace.

We learned that some managers think employees are spoiled brats, whiners who want their company to "solve all their personal problems." (As Dave Barry would say, I am not making this up.) We learned that managers who grant a job share or a request to go part time put themselves on the line. Very likely, they're going to face a barrage of questions at budget time. They can hardly argue that they're desperately shorthanded if they've allowed someone to work less than full time, can they? And what manager thinks he or she has more than enough resources to get the job done?

We learned that some managers, like our first city editor, will see any attempt to work less than full time as a sign that an employee is not committed to the company, i.e., entering the "mommy track" that goes around and around, but never climbs the hill toward bigger and better jobs. After we got the job share, one manager hardly spoke to us for years.

And we learned that the notion of a job share can transform even the most understanding, wonderful editor, one who really does want you to be happy, into a formidable opponent, simply because she imagines that her job will become immeasurably harder if you're vanishing from view.

In her imagination, terrifying scenarios popped up like mushrooms in a damp Northwest fall: *What if*, say, you finish a story—a cover profile she has scheduled to run while you're gone—and quickly escape to the wilds of Borneo, where your cell phone is eaten by a crazed orangutan? Meanwhile, the subject of your story is arrested for the axe murder of his teenage lover, who happens to be the mayor's love child from a youthful affair with Tina Turner. And you're the only one he'll talk to.

Some parts of her fears were realistic, of course. *What if* she couldn't find a reporter or an artist to make changes to a story or an illustration? A lot depends, she found out over the years, on an individual job sharer's commitment to be available, even off the clock.

We got our job share, finally, because newsroom managers wanted desperately to hire someone with specific skills for a particular position. The money wasn't in the budget, and managers didn't see any coming down the pike. But the job share, we noted repeatedly, after we finally caught the drift, would be a way to "gain" a position. Some Pollyanna might say it was a "win-win." Okay, whatever.

The point is that it might have gone a lot more smoothly for us if we'd figured out earlier that it wasn't about us. We finally had a major realization: While there might be some high-level murmurings about employee satisfaction and family time, when it ultimately came down to the squinty-eyed view of someone trying to actually run a department—in this case, someone charged with squeezing the makings of a daily newspaper out of a bunch of prickly, independent, sensitive journalists—there was nothing like plain, old-fashioned self-interest to get someone's attention.

As in: "We can help you get what you need."

When you do the thinking about that, think about it not only from the company's perspective, but from an individual manager's perspective. Either can be your ally. In our off-again, on-again job shares, we had it both ways. Sometimes it was the upper-level folks, seeing an opportunity, who pushed the idea through. Other times, it was a frontline manager, who saw a way to get what he needed to run his little fiefdom smoothly. These days, a company or a manager could very well see a job share as a way to trim the budget while keeping valued employees around until the economy perks up.

I should mention the third person whose motivations, strengths, and weaknesses you need to understand: That would be you.

We asked for a three-way, months-on, months-off share, instead of the more traditional days-on, days-off share, in part because our beats demanded long-term, enterprise-type stories that could be planned and executed better with sustained periods of work. We also knew that when we did do breaking news, a days-on, days-off share wouldn't cut it. Any editor who heard, "Oh, I'm off tomorrow. I'll finish up next week," would make it their business to become Job Share Enemy No. 1. We'd heard that the local Public Defender had offered a months-on, months-off work arrangement, and the two-month leave periods gave lawyers time to really take a break from their intense, demanding, difficult work life. We could relate.

But the most important reason we opted for that type of share was that two of the three of us correctly identified ourselves as a particular kind of person. We hesitated to put a negative label on it, but we both agreed about our symptoms. You could call it "somewhat undisciplined," or perhaps "Type A." One editor, on one of my reviews, phrased it nicely: "You're conscientious to a fault; you always want to do more."

But what sounded almost like a strength, my colleague and I knew, would quickly turn into a deal breaker on a job share. We both knew that if we started a story on Monday, thinking we could finish it up on Wednesday, but actually had more reporting to do by the time we were supposed to be "off" on Thursday, we just wouldn't say "Bye!" and leave. We'd stay there and finish it. On our "off" time. Worse, if we knew we could only reach someone on one of our days off, a phone interview from home, say, we'd do that, too. Ultimately, if we tried to share days-on, days-off, what we'd end up doing, we predicted, would be to work full-time and get paid for two-thirds.

That's probably a good segue into the "proving yourself" part.

For the first round of our job share, we *did* work nearly full-time. At home, my partner was initially underwhelmed by the deal, since I worked a good two weeks into my first month off, finishing a long project. And because we job sharers were taking over another person's beat, we had to do a good deal of learning from one another. It's a long way from covering the Hanford Nuclear Reservation to covering Religion or Polling/Demographics. Those of us who felt confident sketching the inner workings of a fuel rod on a paper napkin stumbled when it came to rattling-off the changes wrought by Vatican II, and vice versa. And nobody but Susan was a natural at interpreting cross-tabulations on surveys.

But by the time we got the job share we knew one thing for sure: If we didn't make this easy—seamless, even—for our editors, our job share would be history

Are you working so much you don't even have time to recycle? You're not alone. Surveys show that Americans who work long hours use more throwaways and convenience items, recycle less, and in general, have a bigger negative impact on the environment than those who work less. Every environmentalist knows that on a finite planet we can't keep producing more and more stuff forever. It's time to trade productivity increases for time instead of things.

TAKE BACK YOUR TIME

WORK LESS, WASTE LESS

before I learned what numbers to call at the Department of Energy when the radioactive waste cleanup went awry.

Fortunately, we were all pretty good sharers in our hearts, meaning we didn't try to keep the "good stories" for ourselves or somehow arrange things so that the next person up had to do all the drudge work. Real turfy, me-first types should probably reconsider sharing a job, because it will ultimately sabotage the deal.

I think that brings me to No. 4. Envy. Resentment. Confusion.

Let's do confusion first. Despite our constructing giant charts, plastering them everywhere and peppering our various editors with them, there always seemed to be confusion about who was where when. And what they were covering. Which inevitably led to the 5th "W:" "Why?" As in, "Why the hell are they doing this????!!!!"

What we found worked best was to just keep working. Focus on what you do best, and try to do it as much as possible.

Then there's envy and resentment. You're between a rock and a hard place if you come back from two months off and someone asks how it was. If you say "Glorious! I feel like a new woman! Check out the Palm trees I painted on my toe-

Time

is a family value

We Americans talk a lot about family values, but our long working hours, the longest in the modern industrial world, mean families seldom see each other.   Only 25% of American families share dinner together.   If we want to strengthen American families, there's no substitute for quantity time; time together keeps marriages and families together.

Take Back Your Time Day • October 24, 2003

nails!" the reaction of the harried wage slave you left behind may be less than wholeheartedly glad for you. On the other hand, you hardly want to say, "Oh, Gawd, it was *awful!* I sprained my back in aerobics, and spent the entire two months lying on the floor moaning in pain!" After all, this share is supposed to bring you back full of enthusiasm and new-found energy, right?

We opted for telling people about the "things we got done." Stuff that didn't sound particularly attractive but was necessary. Spending time with Mom. Visiting Auntie in the Home. Attending PTA meetings. Painting the house.

And we made a point of reminding people: This wasn't free. Not only did we take two-thirds pay, we lost benefits. And we gave up a lot to get that reduced pay and benefits: We learned new, strange stuff, we coached our colleagues, we worked on our time off when required. None of us was driving a new car or going on shopping sprees.

But for all of us, having the job share then, when we needed it, let us breathe. It kept us from having to make an awful choice between family and work, a choice that leads to resentment, guilt, or poverty—or all of the above.

When we worked, we really worked. And when we were on leave, we had time for the things you don't even know you don't have time for when you are working as hard as we were. You have time to listen. I noticed, perhaps for the first time, and for sure, for the first time without being resentful because I was so rushed, that old folks sometimes don't get to the point in a straight-line fashion.

Sometimes they talk a while before you can figure out what's going on. Sometimes they're telling you important stuff, but it takes a while to get there: I'm afraid I'll run out of money. I don't feel so steady on my feet any more. If I give up driving I'll be dependent, and that scares me. I stopped going to the condo board meetings because I can't hear what people are saying anymore.

Some of those things I could do something about. And not only did I have time to hear them, I had time to find some solutions.

I'm not sure people are meant to work full-time. I think life is more complicated than that. From the beginning of my working life—a part-time college job at "Auto Lane," a used car lot owned by a wild and crazy guy—I have believed that we human beings need time to think, make music, weave baskets, play with kids and dogs, bond with one another, and care for friends and family. We need time to dance, draw, write letters, and learn Italian. Those of us with demanding jobs, jobs that continually spill over into our personal lives, jobs that consume a lot of energy and space and brain waves, often don't have the time for those things while we work full-time.

I'm not sure exactly how full-time work came to be so dominant, but I know I think it's a bad idea. But there it is, and if we want a life, we have to somehow configure ourselves into that 8 to 10 hours-a-day slot. A job share is a way to do that. Taking back time. Taking back your life.

Remember that first editor who shot down our job share? She ended up taking early retirement and moving to a small town in Idaho.

And the editor who conjured up Borneo and orangutans whenever she thought about her reporters working part-time? One day she got so stressed and busy she forgot to pick up her little kid after summer school. He sat on the step, lonesome and scared, waiting. When she finally remembered to pick him up, he got in the car and burst into the biggest tears she'd ever seen.

She was so horrified at what she'd done, she changed her life, her job, her hours. First, she took a leave. Then, she came back part-time—in a job share—working a three-day week of night and weekend shifts. Sometimes we kid her now about her earlier opposition. She knows we understand.

CHAPTER 21

A New Bottom Line

**IRENE MYERS, LARRY GAFFIN,
AND BARBARA SCHRAMM**

If there's any group of people I talk to who immediately get what Take Back Your Time is all about, it's career counselors and coaches. They see in their clients the toll that overwork (and choosing work for the money instead of the meaning it brings) takes in stress, burnout, and depression. From all around the country, many of them have volunteered to help make Take Back Your Time Day a powerful event, and several have asked if they might write about their experiences for this handbook, offering free advice to thousands of weary souls they might never meet in person. Among them are Larry Gaffin and Irene Myers, one a career counselor and the other a coach, who are my neighbors in a co-op apartment building in Seattle. Both told me that, whatever career counseling conferences they attend throughout the country, the problem of overwork is high on the agenda for discussion. —JdG

There is a half-conscious struggle going on in the hearts and minds of American workers. As career counselors and coaches who help people every day with key pieces of the life/work puzzle, we have become all too aware of the dimensions of this struggle. The current climate of overwork and overconsumption that prevails in this country has persuaded people to stay on the familiar treadmill, with their lives inextricably linked to a bottom line of credit card payments, bank accounts, and mortgages, believing that there is little latitude for change.

But amidst the clamor of this persistent mindset there is another voice that seeks to be heard, another bottom line—one of inner wealth rather than outer wealth. It is the bottom line of a life well lived.

This richer bottom line is linked to clear alignment between personal choices and deeply held values as well as satisfying relationships with self, family, friends, community, and environment. It encourages sound wellness practices that nurture mind, body, and spirit and acknowledges natural rhythms. It recognizes that what we do best and enjoy doing most provide the best guidelines for finding optimum job fit. It can lead to a deeper sense of purpose, which in turn adds energy to life.

Boston Globe syndicated columnist Ellen Goodman has succinctly summed up life according to the predominant vision held by our culture: Normal is getting dressed in clothes that you buy for work, driving through traffic in a car that you are still paying for, in order to get to the job that you need so you can pay for the clothes, car, and the house that you leave empty all day in order to afford to live in it.

Reorienting Our Vision

If we are to reorient our lives around the other bottom line of inner wealth, we need first to develop a more desirable and compelling vision to replace the prevailing one. People's primary frame of reference—way of thinking, belief system, or life vision—largely determines what they see and value, and how they act. This explains why it is difficult to release ourselves from the grip of the status quo and inevitable overwork. But it also suggests that vision-setting is a resource for creating what we would prefer, namely, a future that keeps work in balance with the rest of life.

Purposely reorienting clients to a compelling and sustainable vision for the future is central to the coaching profession and that of holistic career counseling and mentoring. A vision, as defined in *Co-Active Coaching*, is, "a multifaceted mental image and set of goals that personally define and inspire a client to take action to create that picture in his or her actual life." This preferred picture is "constantly attracting the client's desire to bring the image to fruition." According to prominent Bay Area coach Leslie Lupinsky, "Planning one's life and taking actions without a conscious vision of a desired future is like driving a car while looking in the rear view mirror."

Each of us already holds a vision for our own life, whether or not it is conscious or healthy for ourselves, our family, and our planet. If you can change the vision individually, you help change the system collectively.

There are predictable obstacles to initiating change. The old bottom-line thinking speaks with many familiar voices: *"Working fewer hours in my current job might not give me enough to live on." "If I try to get my hours reduced, my boss might question my commitment and I might lose my job altogether." "My spouse wouldn't go along with it." "You can't rock the boat. You just have to find a way to cope. Be realistic." "It takes a lot to go against the status quo. I'm not sure I can take that on."*

Cultural anthropologist Jennifer James says that we would rather settle for a known hell than an unknown heaven. Underlying the perceived obstacles is fear, but we must recognize that fear will always be a companion when making any change. It takes powerful clarity and motivation to give credence to our dreams and to our half-conscious yearnings and desires. Dreams speak to us in symbolic language that few take time to understand in our waking lives. Dreams are a reservoir of deep knowing, waiting for us in stillness.

In our rush to produce, provide, and perform, to be perfect and to please, we've lost sight, individually and collectively, of essential spiritual truths expressed through the centuries by wisdom traditions. Capitalism and the warrior archetype have served us for many years, but every behavior pattern has its dark side and when taken to an unexamined extreme, will eventually snap back and hurt us.

One of our recent clients was determined to focus solely on creating the perfect resume. When asked about her relationships at home she burst into tears. She was caught up in trying to succeed in terms defined by our current workaholic norms and it was costing her a rewarding intimacy with those closest to her. For her the old bottom line thinking was bankrupt, but still held mythic power.

What do individuals need to do to create better life/work balance? To begin with, they must make the commitment to change things for the better, even if their first steps are small. With stories of giants falling—giants such as Enron, who symbolize the priorities of the old order—maybe it will become easier to stop and question those priorities. But how can we speak for ourselves with an authentic and persuasive voice when we don't know who we are and what we really want?

If the answers are to come at all, consistent uninterrupted quiet time, alone, is one first step to knowing our authentic self. "If we want our world to be different, our first act needs to be reclaiming time to think. Nothing will change for the better until we do," says seasoned organizational consultant Margaret Wheatley.

Making a request for change can be like stepping to the edge of darkness and into the unknown. Nevertheless, the three of us agree that there is no other way forward, except to learn who we are and what we want for our lives and then to go after it with determination, in a spirit of generosity and caring toward those we meet along the path.

Preparing to Act

Along with commitment to a compelling vision, those who seek a balanced life need to develop a realistic plan of action. There are essentially four options:

1. Stay where we are and cope with conditions as they are;

2. Commit to a vision of finding the ideal job fit somewhere else altogether;

3. Act through a bargaining unit if that structure is available;

4. Determine the specific type of work schedule change that we would like to see, examine the pros and cons from our employer's perspective, and in that light, prepare a plan for negotiating a change.

Let us suggest a negotiation process you can use for almost any worker-management, employee-employer concern. For example, let's assume you are asking for a more flexible schedule. How might your employer benefit? Such flexibility could reduce absenteeism, day-care costs, and commute stress. It could increase morale, retention of employees, and productivity.

Let us assume for the purpose of this example that no one at your organization has ever asked for a flexible schedule. This usually means the boss is likely to say no. He or she might say something like, "Our business has profited for 25 years on a 9 to 5 schedule, so why change?" Assume initial resistance to your idea. Then . . .

1. Outline a clear goal in terms of what you want to request. Develop a one- or two-sentence statement of your request. Be specific. "Tom, I am here today to request a change in my work schedule from 9:00 to 5:30 to 7:00 to 3:30. I'd like to discuss the details of this with you."

2. Do your homework. Collect facts, figures, and comparable examples/precedents in your industry, position, and organizational culture. Employers appreciate employees who help them do their work. Come prepared with a presentation and solutions that will also benefit your employer and make his or her job easier. Develop answers to all the objections to your request that you can anticipate. Figure out:

   a. What you need/can afford.

   b. The ideal plan/compromise/minimum you will accept.

   c. The advantages/disadvantages for you.

   d. The advantages/disadvantages for your company/organization.

3. Mobilize support. Gather evidence of others in your organization who might desire the same benefit.

4. Rehearse. *Develop and practice a script.* The script will increase your resolve to make your request, instill confidence, and keep you on track during the presentation when and if your nerves start to get the upper hand.

5. Present your plan. If you assume your employer will say no or be resistant, you could lead with the following: "Tom, I've given my request some thought. I would like to let you know that I believe my productivity and commitment to our organization will increase, because I'll have shorter and less stressful commutes, as well as fewer interruptions and distractions from colleagues between 7:00 and 8:00. My concentration will increase.

Also, I've tried to think about concerns you might have about my proposal. I'd like an opportunity to speak to any you might have."

If "Tom" does raise questions you haven't anticipated, ask for a week or two to research possible resolutions, asking to meet again later. If he flatly rejects your request you might try the following: Let him know that you understand his position and that this request is a departure for him and the organization. Would he be willing to think about it and meet again in two weeks? Would he be willing to try it for one month, and then, if it doesn't work, go back to the traditional work schedule?

If he says yes to this, you need to ask for some specific measures of success/failure in the experiment. If he says no, you can thank him for the time, tuck your idea away and try again with a different manager/boss at a later date, or seek employment at an organization willing to accommodate your request. If you take this latter approach, negotiate for the desired flexible schedule after you've been offered the job, but *before* you start working.

6. Thank your employer and follow up. Do whatever you need to do to reach closure with your employer or to keep the idea moving forward.

Finding Courage

One hurdle to overcome may well be the employer, but another might be your own fears. We find that employees are reluctant to claim their own voice and power to ask for something new. They are often resistant to doing the hard work and necessary preparation that must come before proposing changes to their employers. Acclaimed organizational development consultant Geoffrey Bellman points out that employees often do have power and can be a major resource in influencing existing patterns of work. In Bellman's opinion, the current situation is not likely to improve without employees' championing the personal and societal values that would be served by reducing hours worked. There is much room for taking personal responsibility for changing business-as-usual. Sometimes, it is a matter of communicating the need for better balance with our employers in a spirit of mutual respect so that we might truly be heard.

Even with commitment and a realistic plan of action, people often still need help finding the courage to take the necessary steps. Getting inspiration, structure, and support from working with a coach, career counselor, mentor, or group of peers can be the needed catalyst for initiating and following through to achieve the desired vision of work-in-balance.

Joan was a highly committed but overly stressed elementary school music teacher when she sought out coaching to help her reevaluate and then consider alternative fields. She had come to a crossroads when she realized that the stress and intensity of her work schedule was having a detrimental effect on her health. It was clear that her old schedule, which allowed her only a few minutes of break during the day, was not sustainable.

During the coaching process she engaged in while on a leave of absence, she took stock of her past successes and identified her top strengths and values. She clarified for herself what was most important in the context of her whole life and the investment she had made so far in teaching. In other words, she came to know herself more completely, so that her final choice did not leave her with the nagging thought that "I wonder if I should really have switched over to clothing design instead."

Toward the end of her leave she confidently negotiated with her principal and school district an arrangement allowing

her to continue the teaching she loves. She now works four days a week but only two days in a row, with Wednesdays off. And her principal readily acknowledged that the number of special programs she had been used to directing during the year extended much beyond a normal load. Also, hiring a former substitute for Wednesdays has provided another teacher with part-time employment. Joan is finding the new schedule a very workable solution that allows her to devote more energy to her family, her music, and other creative pursuits.

Sheryl, another client, was afraid that working a three-quarter-time position would not provide enough to live on. After much counseling work, she became able to entertain the vision of what she might gain in devoting one quarter of her work week to her pent-up creative inclinations. Once released from her self-imposed fears related to the lost one-quarter-time income, she produced a long dreamed of CD of her original compositions, expanded her photographic portfolio, and acquired the energy and time to regularly practice her music and compose.

The thirteenth century poet, Rumi, makes a suggestion still relevant today:

Sit down and be quiet.
You are drunk, and this is the
edge of the roof.

Our current drunkenness comes from overconsumptive lifestyles fed by overwork. Heeding the other bottom line requires making a commitment, refocusing on life-sustaining values and practices, and allowing an individually crafted vision of a balanced life to inspire us forward to make it reality.

CHAPTER 22

Working Retired

BEVERLY GOLDBERG

Not long ago, I was speaking with a relative who happens to be on the Republican staff of the U.S. Senate Special Committee on Aging. She asked what I was doing and I mentioned Take Back Your Time Day. She agreed that overwork was a problem for many Americans but had no sympathy for my suggestions that working hours should be reduced. After all, she pointed out, millions of baby boomers would soon be retiring and getting Social Security and pensions. We would all have to work even more to pay for these retirees and keep the retirement system going. Having studied these issues for some time as part of her job, she was well-informed about them. I suggested an idea I saw as a way out, fully expecting her to have already considered and rejected it.

What if, I asked, we implemented a phased retirement program based on one already in effect in Sweden that could ease the transition for baby boom retirees and actually keep more of them working part time, thereby also reducing the burden on pension systems? For example, what if at age 55, workers cut back their hours to 32 a week (or gained two extra months of vacation) and received 20 percent of their pensions? Then at 60, they might cut back to 24 hours (or work only 60 percent of the year); at 65, to 16 hours, with the amount received in pensions rising commensurately. At 70, they might choose to retire completely or continue working part time.

In my view, such a program would have several benefits. It would reduce immediate fiscal pressure on retirement systems. It would open up space in companies for new workers while assuring that older workers remained as mentors within the companies. It would also allow workers to phase into retirement and begin to find other avocations and hobbies they hadn't had time for previously. This is extremely important because many workers, upon going from a 40-hour workweek to full retirement, find they don't know what to do with so much leisure time, deeply regret their total loss of contact with their workplaces and former co-workers, and experience serious depression as a result.

Were the Social Security system to take the lead in encouraging such a change, companies could well follow without a phased retirement law, though legislation might be needed for the idea to function most effectively. I was surprised when my relative actually seemed intrigued by the idea and offered to test the political waters with it if she were given a concrete proposal as to how it might work.

But phased retirement, in whatever form, is only one way to encourage older Americans to continue to work productively, as Beverly Goldberg makes clear in this chapter. —JdG

Have you noticed the growing media fascination with the so-called working retired?

Who, you may wonder, are these people? The picture you get depends on the slant of the journalist doing the reporting. Sometimes the stories tell of those over sixty-five who, after a few years of leisure, have returned to some sort of employment because of boredom, loneliness, or increasingly, finances—the economic woes afflicting our nation having adversely affected savings and pensions.

At other times, the stories are about those who have not left the workforce after reaching retirement age because of the pleasure or satisfaction they get from working, or because their employer wants them to stay in order not to lose skills in short supply or, again, because they simply can't afford to retire completely.

At the other end of the spectrum are the stories about people who took early retirement packages when their companies were downsizing and found that they just did not like staying at home or found the amount on which they had to live inadequate. They have taken part-time jobs to keep connected and to supplement what income they have. And, of course, there are those who, when in their fifties, found themselves victims of collapsing companies. They then spent a long time unemployed because no one in their field would hire someone over fifty. They now work at anything they can find to keep bread on the table.

Although the stories of those working retired treat it as an unusual occurrence, in reality it is a growing trend. There always were some people who remained in the workforce after they had reached the "official" retirement age of sixty-five, but they did not attract the kind of attention that made them an important category,

www.timeday.org

Recess Isn't Only For Kids
Take Back Your Time Day

one worthy of its own name. The difference is that as the baby boomers—that huge population of children born after World War II—near retirement age, they are redefining the meaning of retirement.

After all, just as we entered the new millennium, about 10,000 boomers a day started turning fifty. Boomers make up about one-third of the population of the United States. Today, there are more than 14 million boomers over fifty years old, and many are looking at very early retirement. At any rate, they are planning retirement from the jobs they now have.

Those who are planning to "retire" include "Norman," fifty-five, a Court Officer in New York City for some twenty-four years. (The people whose stories appear here asked me not to use their real names and to change some facts in order to avoid problems that might result if their employers learned of their plans.)

Norman had been planning to stay on the job a few more years, but because of all the mandatory overtime since the events of September 11, 2001, he will leave the minute he hits the twenty-five year mark, which will allow him to begin collecting his pension. He already has bought a house in Las Vegas, his chosen new community. Ah, you are saying to yourself, a life of leisure, a bit of gambling, warm weather all year round. Not quite.

Norman chose Las Vegas because it is one of the fastest growing cities in the nation, and it needs teachers. He always wanted to teach, but by the time he earned his degree in education, the baby bust had begun, and the market for teachers had dried up. Norman used his vacation this year to make arrangements to work as a substitute teacher when he retires. He says that while he feels guilty about leaving New York when the city is facing so many early retirements, he just can't take doing so many extra shifts anymore.

Another person with plans to "retire" is Sally, a sixty-one-year-old controller at a college, who intends to leave her current position (which, over the years, has become a sixty-hour-a-week marathon) as soon as she can. She wants to retire so she will have time to travel and work with adult illiterates, but she keeps being persuaded to stay on "a little longer" to get the school past one more hurdle.

Though exhausted, she has agreed to stay an additional year, but only after the school accepted her demand that she be allowed to work from home two days a week. She believes this will lessen their dependence on her and increase their trust in the person she has trained to replace her, thus making it possible for her to leave without feeling guilty.

Norman and Sally will be joined in five years by John and Miranda, a couple who just turned fifty, but decided a few years ago that they wanted to "retire" as soon as possible to run a weekend bed and breakfast. They came to that decision after spending a few long weekends in such places. John and Miranda both work at large corporations (he in marketing, she in communications), and they say that they rarely have time to "enjoy each other and life." Now they spend the occasional weekends when both are free looking for a place to buy and begin fixing up. It is not that they hate what they do, they explain, but rather they hate that it is *all* that they do, and that the only vacations they have managed to take together because of their work have been long weekends.

Longer, Healthier Lives

Why is this idea of retiring in order to work at something new and different yet another phenomenon attributable to the boomers? The answer lies, in large part, in longer life expectancies. Many of today's retirees, especially early retirees, can look forward to some thirty to forty years of life after retirement. In part, it also is a result of the fact that the boomers are often healthier than retirees in the past, because of medical advances and the care they take of themselves. They also have more education, and many are eager to acquire still more in order to develop skills that they can use for a new career, often involving a business of their own.

For example, Daryl, who has had a successful mid-level management career in banking, says he can't wait until his youngest daughter finishes college, so he can begin to pursue his dream. A father at twenty, he had to put aside his plans to become a lawyer, but he did complete his bachelor's degree while working to support his growing family.

Now fifty, he plans to go to law school at night, then once he has his degree, he will "retire" and open a law office in his old neighborhood, where he believes he can make a difference by providing affordable legal services. He says that "with any luck I'll be able to be a lawyer as long as I was a banker, but I'll love it, and I'll work only when I want to."

Note the similarities in all these stories of retirement: the desire for *more free time* and the drive to do something more interesting and more rewarding.

Dissatisfied Workers

There is another set of stories, those of the people who will work retired because they have to. These are the people who suddenly discover that the amount they have saved and their pensions are just not going to be enough for thirty or forty years of possible retirement. These are the people who either never thought through the implications of all those stories about how much life expectancy has increased or did not think those stories applied to them because their relatives "didn't live that long."

Wondering how they could have had so little foresight is pointless. Their short-term thinking is similar to that of senior management in most companies. Although human resource directors have been trying to explain the coming demographic realities about aging to management for ten years now, they have met with little success. Indeed, they complain that the recent economic downturn has cost them a lot of ground in their efforts to get management to address the implications of the aging of the population and the dissatisfaction employees express about their jobs.

In fact, according to a summer 2002 survey by the Conference Board, less than half of workers are satisfied with their jobs. More important, the percentage of satisfied workers thirty-five to forty-four years old has fallen from 61 percent to less than 48 percent over the past seven years. These numbers clearly signal a problem ahead for corporate America. As the huge baby boom generation reaches retirement age, corporations will need these workers to replace them.

If we combine those findings with one of the points raised by the Organisation for Economic Co-operation and Development (OECD) on the demographic analyses of the workforce of the future, the difficulties ahead for corporate America are staggering. The OECD warns that labor force participation by those over fifty-five will have to increase by about 25 percent to maintain a constant total employment-to-population ratio from 2005 onward, so the problems companies are facing will multiply.

New Ways to Work

The problems that result from a desire on the part of so many to retire early, however, can be alleviated to a degree by putting in place step-by-step retirement plans that would allow older employees to begin to find a balance between work and leisure that suits their needs as they draw closer to retirement. Managers also may find that some of these ideas (which are sometimes in place already, primarily for women with young children) can be adapted to workers at different stages of the life cycle, helping them to achieve work/life balance and regain enthusiasm and energy. Of course, these alternatives to full-time work will be accompanied by lower salaries and, in some cases, reduced or prorated benefits:

- Phased retirement. This involves approaching workers who are nearing retirement to discuss their plans and, if they are interested, to make arrangements that allow them to reduce the number of days they work each week slowly over a set period. For example, someone sixty-four may want to work four days a week for six months, then three for the next six months. Upon reaching retirement, they may be willing to stay on half-time, or continue to phase out slowly. Such an arrangement would allow the company to keep these workers' skill sets for a few years past retirement.

- Flexible time arrangements. Perhaps an employee is finding commuting in heavy traffic too much of a burden. Would working from, say, ten to four make a difference? Would being allowed to work at home a couple of days a week do the trick?

- Job sharing. In a department that has a number of people nearing retirement, a job sharing arrangement could help reduce turnover. Such turnover could create havoc, as too many new people come in at once without company or job specific experience. Job sharing that is well-structured but flexible works well. For example, if each person involved not only is willing to work two-and-a-half days each week or every morning or afternoon, but also to occasionally do a full week in return for an important week off, say, for a cruise or the birth of a grandchild.

- Temporary work. Setting up an in-house temporary services agency can be invaluable. Employees who want to stop working full-time but keep their hands in and earn some extra income register with the agency at retirement. Because these "temps" are former employees, they do not need to learn the corporate culture and procedures; they can jump right into the assignment. This works particularly well when the agency can tap a temp who worked in a given area to fill in for someone who is leaving for a long vacation or out because of illness. It is also useful at times when the workload is larger than usual, say, in accounting firms around tax time or in retail at Christmas.

- Consulting arrangements. Retirees who want to travel are often open to taking an assignment in a different region for a time. Some would be interested in consulting work part of the year, especially in areas where weather is a factor. In such cases, the company could plan to do projects that require more workers during favorable weather periods.

It is time to be inventive, to try new approaches. Human resources' managers can develop many other plans for older workers, ranging from mentoring programs to on-call work arrangements. More important though may be a rethinking of a lot of the managerial ideas that result in people wanting to leave their jobs to join the working retired.

Creative Judgement

For example, it may be time to judge workers not by how many hours they spend in the office but by what they produce. It may be time to stop mandating long hours—and for many workers who fall in the managerial category, long unpaid hours—instead of hiring additional workers. It may be time to ensure that workers actually can take vacation time just because they need a break (somehow there is always a way to arrange for a vacation that is deemed important enough, such as a honeymoon). And it may be time to start offering greater opportunities for growth, including time for courses, or the chance to take on new assignments.

Remember the five people you just met who are planning to retire early and become part of the growing population of working retired? Would they be making the same decisions if America followed a different model—one that acknowledges the fact that people have lives outside work?

CHAPTER 23

A Case for Sabbaticals

BOB SESSIONS AND LORI ERICKSON

As a documentary television producer, I have a job that often allows me to take the equivalent of sabbaticals even while I'm working. I travel widely on stories and these breaks from everyday routine, while officially qualifying as work, take me out of the everyday and its persistent demands and allow time for greater reflection and comparison between lifestyles and the relative happiness they bring. For example, I recently traveled both to Mexico and Africa, working on a film about world hunger. I was essentially away from all but emergency phone and e-mail contact for several weeks. I worried about disasters happening at the office, but in fact, that world and my colleagues got along fine without me. And without the everyday stresses of the office to deal with, I felt calmer than I had in a long time. I also learned again that we have much to learn from other cultures.

During my travel, I witnessed poverty and deprivation, but also a joy and a comfort with daily life that seems far removed from contemporary America. The poor people I met were always able to make time to talk with me and visit with friends and relatives, and they took obvious pleasure from such connections. I learned again the value of the siesta and the long meal, especially at Kenyan restaurants where, after ordering dinner, one waited for the chicken to be killed, plucked, and cooked before it was served. Those were times for slow beers and long talks. With our short vacations, we have little time for such things. But with sabbaticals . . . —JdG

Not long ago, we took a month-long sojourn amid the spectacular peaks of the Canadian Rockies. For four weeks we traded schedules full of activities, meetings, deadlines, and commitments for long hikes through mountain valleys, picnics by rushing waterfalls, and nights spent camping underneath a canopy of brilliant stars.

Being away for a month helped us regain our balance, our sense of who we are, and our commitment to what is most important to us. We had time to connect with each other and our two sons in ways that are difficult to achieve in our normal routines. Through the long twilights of the northern latitudes, our hearts opened to thoughts and dreams that are normally hidden below the busyness of our lives.

One way of looking at our time away is that we have been on sabbatical. Not in the official sense of the word, for Bob teaches at a community college that doesn't offer sabbaticals, and as a freelance writer, Lori has never had an employer sponsor a paid leave of absence. But, in a deeper sense, our time away brought us the rewards that a true sabbatical should provide—rest and a new perspective.

Our belief in the importance of these extended times away has evolved gradually during our twenty years together. Bob spent the first half of his adult life working relentlessly before realizing the harmfulness of such a schedule. Both of us have seen friends burn out on careers that were fulfilling but overwhelming. Most of all, we have seen the rejuvenation that can come from extended time off from a job.

We are convinced that everyone needs a sabbatical. Not just academics at four-year colleges and universities, but also factory workers, mothers, waitresses, store clerks, bankers, physicians, farmers, and nannies. Not just time off to vacation (though relaxing is certainly an essential part of a sabbatical). Not just time off to do another form of work (though a sabbatical often involves labor of some sort). A sabbatical is an amalgam of work and leisure that lets us loosen the grip of the everyday on our lives and rediscover what brings us joy. Sabbaticals provide a time to question priorities, gain perspective, and figure out what's next.

The word "sabbatical" reflects its religious origins. Its root comes from Sabbath, the Biblical injunction that humans should rest every seventh day. Sabbath was given as a blessing to humans, a divinely ordained rest from labor. Wayne Muller, in his book *Sabbath: Finding Rest, Renewal and Delight in Our Busy Lives,* says that the main purpose of Sabbath is to "create a marker for ourselves so, if we are lost, we can find our way back to our center." Spiritual masters from Buddha to Jesus have advocated a rhythm between work and rest, stressing the necessity of time away from ordinary tasks for meditation, prayer, and rejuvenation.

Universities later secularized the idea of Sabbath as a way of encouraging academics to do sustained research in an area of study. Generally granted every seven years, sabbaticals offer professors leave with pay to pursue a project that advances both their individual interests and those of the university.

Sabbaticals for Everyone

Within the past decade some businesses have picked up on the idea of sabbaticals as well, though generally they are reserved only for upper levels of management. Such sabbaticals tend to be more varied than academic ones in their duration, frequency, and composition. Many employees take extended trips, some do service or volunteer projects, others go back to school to learn a new skill, and some choose to spend more time with their families.

If saints, mystics, scholars, and highly paid executives need substantial time away from their usual routines in order to do their work well, aren't sabbaticals even more important for ordinary people?

In order for sabbaticals to become a more common feature in American work life, we need to be more flexible in how we think of them. One lesson we can learn from academia is the importance of going into a sabbatical with a thoughtful plan. Professors must apply for a sabbatical, and not just because the institution wants its money spent wisely. Schools have found that asking faculty members to write a proposal for their time off helps them make their sabbaticals more valuable.

The process of applying for a leave can enhance the experience even if people don't keep entirely to their plan. Because Americans have worked long hours for so many years, many of them—whether executives or line workers—wouldn't know how to truly benefit from a sabbatical.

One recent study indicated that increasing numbers of Americans find their jobs to be by far the most interesting aspect of their lives. Many of us have forgotten (or never learned) how to find meaning outside of the comfortable structure of a job. Perhaps we need sabbatical counselors or discussion groups that could help people clarify what they desire and need from their time off, and to help them think creatively about what they might do.

What if you have an employer who's unwilling to pay for your sabbatical, no matter how good your proposal? As the idea of sabbaticals spreads, people are finding innovative ways of taking them, even if they work in jobs that typically don't grant extended time off.

Some employees save money and live frugally for several years so they can take six months or more off without pay. Others trade raises for more vacation time, or work out a plan with their employer that includes a combination of vacation, sick days, personal leave, and unpaid time off. While many take their leave in intervals ranging from a month to a year, some have negotiated "periodic sabbaticals" such as a week off every month for a year.

Our own experience shows how even an institution that doesn't grant sabbaticals can offer its employees many of the benefits of them. Two years ago Bob was able to arrange an exchange with a teacher at a comparable school in Yorkshire,

England. The two institutions agreed to pay each professor's regular salary and benefits, and our two families saved a great deal of money by swapping houses and cars.

While Bob was still teaching, he had the revitalizing experience of doing so in a very different system. Even better, our five-month stay gave us the chance to explore the British Isles in a way we never could have done on a two-week vacation.

As workers become more efficient, the rising wealth they produce can—and should—be returned to them in temporal as well as financial remuneration. Workers of all kinds and levels should enjoy the benefits of improved productivity. One of the basic promises of the great modern transformation to industrial capitalism is that everyone would be increasingly better off as the benefits of mass production accrued. In many ways this "promissory note" has been paid.

Time for the Spirit

However, as the steady decline in happiness among American workers since the 1950s attests, there is more to happiness than an increased standard of living. One way to understand the pleas of too-busy Americans is that they are asking for more time to actually enjoy what they have.

Fundamentally, Americans need schedules that allow them to explore and express more aspects of themselves than even good work can provide. Many of us are fortunate to have jobs we enjoy a great deal. But we could be more productive in them if we had more time off to nourish our spirits and develop other parts of our lives.

This assumption underlies the university sabbatical system. Academic sabbaticals serve two main purposes. They reinvigorate scholars and give them time for in-depth research work. In return the institution granting this "expensive" leave gains in two ways: the school's status rests, in large measure, on the quantity and quality of its faculty's scholarly output, and professors' students and colleagues benefit from their new knowledge and vitality. It is not surprising to find many college faculty members still full of energy, enthusiasm, and creativity in their 70s and even 80s.

Almost every employer could reap similar benefits from granting sabbaticals. The literature about "downshifters"—people who have given up highly paid, high-powered jobs for less stressful employment—is filled with testimonials from workers who would have stayed with their former jobs if they could have had more time off. They made the hard choice to leave work they loved because the time required by the job had turned their love into a nightmare. When they leave, their employers lose valuable and highly trained employees who are difficult to replace.

Thus sabbaticals are a win-win situation. On sabbatical we can nourish our souls, enrich our communities, and improve our health by reducing our stress—

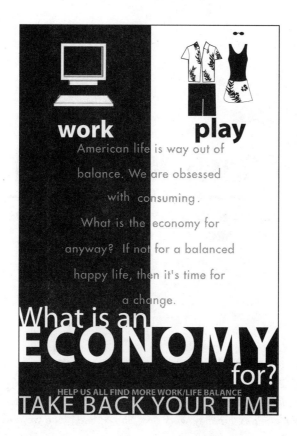

work   play

American life is way out of balance. We are obsessed with consuming. What is the economy for anyway? If not for a balanced happy life, then it's time for a change.

What is an ECONOMY for?

HELP US ALL FIND MORE WORK/LIFE BALANCE

TAKE BACK YOUR TIME

and employers benefit as well from having employees who return to work invigorated and refreshed.

Taking a sabbatical isn't often easy. It typically requires creativity, hard work, and a significant financial commitment. But those who have taken them say that these life-changing experiences are more than worth the effort.

When we led a course on voluntary simplicity at our church several years ago, we were surprised when nearly 50 people turned out on four different evenings to discuss how they might simplify their lives. We listened as one person after another, in a group full of highly educated, successful people, expressed deep emotional and physical weariness at lives that seemed hopelessly rushed and frenetic.

What we need, clearly, is a better balance between work and rest. As Wayne Muller says, "If certain plant species . . . do not lie dormant for winter, they will not bear fruit in the spring. If this continues for more than a season, the plant begins to die. If dormancy continues to be prevented, the entire species will die. A period of rest—in which nutrition and fertility most readily coalesce—is not simply a human psychological convenience; it is a spiritual and biological necessity."

We remain convinced: everyone needs a sabbatical.

CHAPTER 24

America Needs a Break

**KAREN NUSSBAUM, CHRISTINE OWENS,
AND CAROL EICKERT**

I first met and interviewed Karen Nussbaum in 1991. At the time, she was President of 925, SEIU, a union for office workers. I found her perspective enlightening and a little chilling, especially her observation that "26 million Americans are monitored by the machines that they work on." She added, "one woman recently told me her computer screen often flashed "You're not working as fast as the person next to you!"

I turned to Karen again in the fall of 2002 to ask her to support Take Back Your Time Day. By that time, after a stint as director of the Women's Division of the U.S. Department of Labor, she'd become the assistant to AFL-CIO President John Sweeney. I was delighted to hear that Karen still felt the issue was essential to the labor movement and that she was eager to help. She'd seen the chapter outline for this book and had a suggestion: "You talk about labor in this book, but none of your chapters are written by organized labor in its own words." I agreed that this was a serious failing. Karen recommended correcting it by getting representatives of the AFL-CIO, including herself, to write a chapter. "Would they do that?" I asked. "We'd be happy to," she answered. Soon afterwards, Karen Nussbaum joined the national steering committee for Take Back Your Time Day. —JdG

In 1996, working families were struggling with the consequences of the longest sustained decline in wages and benefits during the longest sustained recovery in history. Newly-elected AFL-CIO president John Sweeney barnstormed across the country holding "America Needs A Raise" rallies.

Wages did finally rise a bit, but the other key problem plaguing working families—time—has only gotten worse. Now we believe that America needs a break! Work hours have generally been increasing for Americans while the ability to control hours has declined. In response, unions have fought to gain control over hours through high profile work actions, bringing to light the crisis that long and unpredictable hours create for working families, along with other consequences, such as risks to patient safety in hospitals.

This essay highlights the dilemma faced by workers confronting long hours they cannot control, and it provides examples of union efforts to win work and family reforms that help workers meet their obligations at home *and* on the job.

The Battle Over Work Hours: An Enduring Struggle for Workers and Their Unions

From the earliest days of unions, setting limits on work hours was a key demand. "I work from can't see to can't see" was a common refrain for nineteenth and early twentieth century workers. Those who labored in turn-of-the-century industrial factories—making garments, processing meat, producing steel—worked as many as 80 hours a week, losing life and limb to fatigue-induced injuries and rarely seeing their families.

Eventually, the deplorable working conditions of Sinclair Lewis' "The Jungle" and factories like the Triangle Shirtwaist Company gave way to the reforms of the 1920s and 1930s and the prosperity of the 1950s and 1960s. By the 1970s, sociologists were speculating about a future problem for Americans—too much leisure time.

But economic and workforce changes beginning in the late 1970s, and accelerating since then, took care of that problem. Part-time and temporary positions with low wages and no benefits proliferated, forcing many to piece together several jobs to get by. The minimum wage was frozen (thus falling precipitously in real terms), pulling down wages for all workers at the bottom. A gradual shift away from a higher-paid, highly unionized manufacturing economy, toward lower paid service-based industries further eroded wages and living standards. The upshot was declining family income, especially for low and middle wage earners, driving every available worker—and most parents—into the paid labor force.

These economic forces, combined with employment opportunities for women opened by the 1960s civil rights laws, changed the workforce dramatically, and the

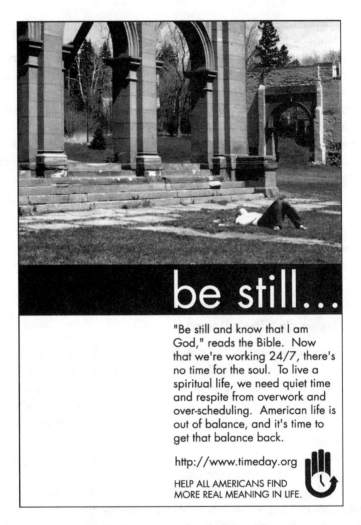

be still...

"Be still and know that I am God," reads the Bible. Now that we're working 24/7, there's no time for the soul. To live a spiritual life, we need quiet time and respite from overwork and over-scheduling. American life is out of balance, and it's time to get that balance back.

http://www.timeday.org

HELP ALL AMERICANS FIND MORE REAL MEANING IN LIFE.

new workforce, with nearly equal numbers of men and women, changed family life. The one thing that did not change was work conditions. As Eileen Appelbaum and her coauthors report in *Shared Work, Valued Care*, companies still operate on the model of an "unencumbered" worker: a husband employed full-time, full-year as breadwinner, without family responsibilities, and a wife as homemaker and caregiver at home. This model contemplates that all workers function as if each had a partner or caregiver at home, when in reality most parents are in paid employment.

The time crunch created by their dual "family" and "work" roles leaves most workers worrying that they do neither job well. It is a crisis that tears many families apart.

Evening/Weekend Hours and Opposite Shifts: Juggling Schedules to Make It Work

Respondents to the AFL-CIO's *Ask A Working Woman 2000 Survey*, a representative sample of working women, described the strains on their families. Two-thirds of women with children at home work full-time; more than one out of four regularly work nights or weekends; and nearly half of all women work different schedules from spouses or partners. A bus operator and single mother describes the concern: "One of the problems we have is we don't have a choice of the hours we're working. We're penalizing our kids."

Long work hours and opposite schedules wreak havoc on family life. Dr. Harriet Presser of the University of Maryland reports increased likelihood of separation and divorce for couples that work nights and rotating shifts. But workers are getting little help from their employers. Nearly one-third of working women say they do not even have paid sick leave *for themselves;* more than half have no paid leave to care for children or ill family members; and one-third have no flexibility or control over work hours. But workers believe they *should* get these benefits. In the AFL-CIO's September 2001 survey *Workers' Rights in America,* 90 percent of workers said it is essential or very important to have time off to care for babies or sick family members, and 90 percent said workers should be entitled to sick leave.

Union leaders know firsthand the toll that too many hours with too little control exacts from workers. In response, we are fighting to win core family-supporting benefits for all workers. And for nurses, cable splicers, machinists, waitresses and other employees, the efforts to gain control over work hours gone amok are paying off.

The Nursing Crisis: A Case Study in Unchecked Escalating Work Hours

Union nurses, as well as union members in other jobs, are deeply frustrated over work hours, and are having to resort to strikes, often long strikes, to bring those hours under control. Mandatory overtime, often because of short-staffing of nurses in hospitals, is the norm. A poll by the Federation of Nurses and Health Professionals (FNHP/AFT) in March 2001 found that 81 percent of respondents who worked in acute care facilities said their hospitals were understaffed or severely understaffed; over two-thirds (68.5 percent) had seen an increase in their overtime hours in the past two years; and nearly half (49 percent) had been *required* to work overtime for at least some of their overtime hours. Three quarters (72 percent) of those who refused overtime had been threatened with or suffered disciplinary consequences. Another poll reported by the SEIU Nurses Alliance found that nurses work an *average* of 6.5 overtime hours per week, or more than eight weeks of overtime per year.

Ironically, although health care facilities impose long hours in response to nursing shortages, overtime actually exacerbates those shortages. In a survey last year by Peter D. Hart Associates, 21 percent of nurses said they planned to leave the profession in the next five years because of job dissatisfaction, but three quarters said they would consider staying if conditions improved, primarily with regard to staffing and hours worked.

Too few nurses working too many hours pose risks to the safety and health of patients. According to a study in the October 2002 *Journal of the American Medical Association,* patients recovering from routine surgery at hospitals with fewer nurses per patient have a greater risk of dying. A patient's risk of death increased seven percent for each additional individual under one nurse's care. An examination released this year by the Joint Commission on Accreditation of Health Care Organizations (JCAHO) of 1,609 hospital reports of patient deaths and injuries since 1996 found the nursing shortage to be a contributing factor in roughly one quarter of the cases.

Nurses' unions are fighting hard to help their members rein in excessive hours. Members of the United American Nurses (UAN) have struck 50 times in the last three years over the issue. In one example, 1,200 staff nurses at the D.C. Washington Hospital Center waged a seven-week strike in late 2000, which was resolved with an agreement to limit mandatory overtime and allow nurses to refuse overtime due to fatigue, illness, and extenuating circumstances.

Nurses are also moving their fight to control work hours into Congress and state legislatures. At the federal level, the proposed "Safe Nursing and Patient Care Act" (H.R. 745, S. 373) would limit nurse overtime in hospitals and other health care facilities. Six states—Maine, Maryland, Minnesota, New Jersey, Oregon, and Washington—have enacted laws limiting overtime for nurses and other health care workers, and measures are under consideration in 17 additional states.

Reports from Other Industries

And it's not just nurses. Mandatory overtime is a problem for workers in many industries. The problem has been chronic in the telecommunications industry. In August 2000, a two-week strike of 37,000 Communications Workers of America (CWA) members working at Verizon facilities in the northeast led to a ground-breaking settlement limiting overtime. The agreement cut the number of mandatory weekly overtime hours for customer service employees from 15 to 7.5 and provided for a minimum notice of required overtime. In addition, caps on future overtime hours were negotiated to be phased-in over the life of the contract.

Unions have employed a variety of strategies across various industries to limit overtime, including increasing the premium for overtime, scheduling workers for overtime according to "overtime desired" lists, providing a system of "byes" allowing workers to refuse overtime a set number of times, and negotiating periods of time without overtime. Union contracts have also differentiated between types of overtime (voluntary, scheduled, and mandatory) and employed different methods to limit each.

The California Paid Leave Law: Another Way to Spell Relief for Overstressed Families

Since passage of the federal Family and Medical Leave Act (FMLA) in 1993, guaranteeing 12 weeks of unpaid leave for certain employees, millions of workers have taken unpaid leave when ill, or to care for babies or sick family members. But a major goal of the FMLA—to ease care giving burdens for workers—remains elusive for millions more who cannot afford time off without pay. "I was fired from my job when I had to care for a sick child," reports one woman, an assembly line worker. "Now I've been denied food stamps because I own a '95 van."

Recently, California took an important step in filling the gap between promise and reality under the FMLA. Acting in response to a campaign led by the California Labor Federation, California became the first state in the nation to pass a comprehensive paid family leave program. Beginning in July 2004, California workers will receive up to six weeks of partial wage replacement when they take leave to care for new children or ill family members.

Assembling a diverse coalition that included women's, seniors' and children's groups, and unions and family-friendly business owners, the California Labor Federation began its paid family leave campaign about two years ago. Legislation was introduced in the winter of 2002. The proposal encountered fierce opposition from much of the business community, even though the paid-leave program it creates is 100 percent employee funded. But despite business opposition, the bill passed earlier this year, and Governor Gray Davis signed it.

The old refrain "Eight hours for work, eight hours for rest, eight hours for what we will," expresses an ideal as urgent to working people now as it was 100 years ago. Without doubt, unions will be as important in today's struggle over work hours as they were in the struggle for the eight-hour day at the turn of the last century.

CHAPTER 25

It Would be Good for Business Too

SHARON LOBEL

Though business leaders have often opposed campaigns for shorter work hours, some of the most enlightened (see especially Benjamin Hunnicutt's examination of the Kellogg's six-hour day in Chapter 16) have found that shorter work time actually produces benefits in the form of more productive, happy, and loyal employees. While working on the PBS special, Running Out of Time, my colleague, Vivia Boe, interviewed Rudolph Ebneth, a manager at the giant BMW auto plant in Regensburg, Germany. "Our workers," said Ebneth, "have to work 400 hours less than their American counterparts. And they like having time for their families." A balanced life, he suggested, made them better workers. We invite American business leaders to join in the Take Back Your Time Day dialogue. We believe it's a win-win situation for workers and employers. —JdG t's a bird ... it's a plane ... No it's Workaholic! This superhuman being can work through anything—vacations, weekends, family events—all for the good of his or her company or organization. Indeed many employees need to be superhuman in order to endure the rigors of work in America. Consider what one manager at a large, global financial services company told Washington State University professors Mary Blair-Loy and Amy Wharton:

> *Especially in the past few years during downsizing ... I am doing the work of two or three people, with an intensive workload with no lull. Saturdays and Sundays are catch-up days. The past few years are characterized by lost vacations, working during vacation and holidays including Christmas Day, and late nights ... The phone never stops ringing. Once when I went to see my child play sports, I received five cell phone calls. When my spouse was undergoing major surgery, I was paged to call in to work.*

Workers such as these are often identified as organizational superheroes. One of my MBA students shared an e-mail that had been broadcast by a project manager to employees at a Fortune 25 manufacturing organization:

> *In a recent memo from our general manager, he talked about commitment, dedication, and flexibility. X showed us an example of this kind of behavior last week. He was scheduled for three days of vacation. The first day he showed up and I asked, "What are you doing here?" X said he needed to finish up some things for Y project. The next day he came to work again and said we really need to get this Z stuff done now. The third day it was an urgent need to get drawings out for review. Finally, on Friday, X took one vacation day. Thanks for all three of the above—commitment, dedication, and flexibility.*

In some sectors of American business, skeptics are beginning to question whether this is really the kind of role model we want to reward and emulate. In fact, researchers are finding that these superheroes are not all that they are cracked-up to be. For example, a cross-industry study by Work Family Directions demonstrated that managers who work more than 60 hours a week are *not* more committed to their organizations than those who work only 45 hours. But, the group working more than 60 hours differs in one very important respect: They report a 230% increase in burnout. They come home from work too tired to do what they want to do; and they are preoccupied with work at home and find it difficult to fulfill personal responsibilities.

Researchers have documented negative consequences of overwork for organizations, including increased error rates, involuntary turnover, overt and covert expressions of anger, reduced productivity, and poor employee health. Beyond these negative consequences, we are accumulating convincing evidence that reductions in overwork and overload have positive *benefits* for employers. Let's look at some of them.

Work Redesign

This is the most promising method to address work overload while benefiting employees and their organizations. In a typical example, managers ask employees to look at work practices through a *"work and personal life lens:"* What is it about the way people work that makes it difficult for them to fulfill dreams and responsibilities outside of work? Next, managers and employees identify important business goals. Finally, discussions address how to change work processes to enable a win-win for employees and their organizations.

Working with a group of engineers from Xerox Corporation, MIT researcher Lotte Bailyn and her colleagues asked the engineers to identify what aspects of their normal work prevented them from having enough free time outside of work. The engineers indicated that they needed more uninterrupted blocks of time during the day to get their work done. The group instituted a two-hour block of quiet time in the mornings. As a result, the unit had its first on time product launch and received numerous excellence awards. In addition, engineers found they were able to spend more time with their families in the evenings and on weekends, instead of having to play "work catch-up."

In another example of using a "work and personal life lens" to redesign work, Stew Friedman from Wharton Business School and Perry Christensen, a workplace consultant, described the process that occurred at a pharmaceutical company's 24-hour command center. Thirty employees monitor a hazardous manufacturing process, fire alarms, and other potential health and welfare issues for 8,000 employees. The number of "hot spots" monitored was set to increase from 10,000 to 20,000 over a period of two years. Financial constraints prevented hiring more people to match the increasing workload. The manager brought staff together and talked about the great responsibilities of the group, along with the increasing demands. Then, the manager asked the staff to design a solution that would meet the organization's needs, as well as employees' needs to reduce the impacts of added stress on their personal lives.

The staff developed a schedule that was predictable with more *concentrated time off* for each individual. After two years, the group had eliminated seven shifts, reduced error rates and overtime, reduced shutdown time, as well as the number of personal days taken by employees. Productivity increased and the center became a magnet for transfers and new hires. People wanted to work there!

At Eli Lilly, the philosophy of challenging work practices goes even further, as John Lechleiter, senior vice president of pharmaceutical products explains:

> *Employees need to see the boss challenge nonvalue work. For example, we do an annual planning process. I found that a group of people was working every weekend from January through March. I had never known that. I got them together and asked them to find some better, more simplified ways of*

getting the work done. I told them that the work wasn't worth it, so they sim-
plified the process and decided which areas needed less precision. It worked
out extremely well.

Rhona Rapoport of the Institute of Family and Environmental Research in London, Lotte Bailyn of MIT, and their colleagues describe how in one sales setting, employees who worked around the clock to complete proposals routinely received cheers from managers and coworkers in the morning. One manager, however, told his group he was disappointed in their behavior because "all-nighters" demonstrated a lack of planning. The team had to change its behavior to anticipate problems and plan to avoid all-nighters.

As a result of several work redesign experiments at Fleet Financial Group, using the "work and personal life lens" and team approach, researchers at the Radcliffe Public Policy Institute found that workers met productivity goals while reducing evening hours worked per week. Moreover, within three months, the percentage of people reporting difficulty getting a good night's sleep declined significantly. Since sleep-deprived workers make more errors and ultimately cost employers in quality and health care claims, measures such as these capture unexpected, but important, benefits.

I'm OK, You're OK

When employers institute policies that help employees voluntarily reduce stress and workload, employees get the message that the organization cares about its workers. Doug Lennick, the executive vice president of American Express, explains how a manager supported an employee's desire to spend one afternoon a week coaching his daughter's soccer team. "I can't tell you the commitment I have from [people] like that. They stay around. In order to grow a workforce you have to let them get something out of life." Research at Johnson & Johnson and FelPro shows that even employees who choose *not* to take advantage of available employer supports feel more committed to their organizations. They like working for an organization that treats people with respect.

The Fifth Dimension?

In the absence of an obvious productivity measure, face time—the amount of time during the day that an employee is visible to others—serves as a measure of commitment and performance. But, quantity of time does not equal quality of time; we know that people waste time at work. In fact, according to Sue Shellenbarger of the *Wall Street Journal*, people in many companies are working more "undertime." They leave the office for blocks of time or surf the internet while at work—all to compensate for heavier workloads and more stress. At the extreme, workers use clever acts of deception to look like workaholics. Try this one, for example. Empty the contents of your purse into your pockets. Leave the purse visibly on your desk. Then leave the office! How about buying one of those cups that keeps your coffee hot and let it steam away while you're out of sight?

Abandoning face time as a proxy for performance means that managers must take some time to define actual objectives, even in hard to measure jobs. They must focus on results and give employees more freedom in choosing how to meet those results. Says Gary Capelline, a former executive at Allied Signal:

> All I see is output. When that output occurs is quite immaterial to me. If some-
> one feels that they need to attend a school function for a child, or an event for a
> spouse, or something that they need to do for themselves, I'm quite relaxed about
> that. That doesn't mean I'm going to be relaxed with less profit at the end of the
> quarter. But I'm certainly relaxed giving as much leeway as I can for people
> being out of the office during the normal course of a working day.

In the end, having clear objectives motivates employees and provides an equitable measure of performance—outcomes that are certainly desirable for the organization.

Don't Vote Me Off the Island

There *are* alternatives to laying off employees and leaving the survivors with more work than they can handle. In fact, many employees may *voluntarily* accept reduced pay and work hours. Over 30 percent of respondents in a 1992 National Study of the Changing Workforce said they would give up pay or benefits or change employers for a better work-life balance. In surveys, both male and female professionals indicate a willingness to sacrifice increases in pay for more nonwork time.

Individuals who voluntarily work fewer hours lose the "luxury" of undertime. Researchers Mary Dean Lee of McGill University and Shelley MacDermid of Purdue reported that managers voluntarily working reduced hours accomplished more than most in a short amount of time. In addition, they were very flexible in responding to work demands and were viewed as highly committed and hard working. For the most part, they maintained or actually improved their individual performance while working fewer hours.

These data point to the flexibility of the American worker, especially in the face of an economic downturn. By avoiding mass layoffs, employers can reap positive impacts on morale and reduce costs of rehiring people during upturns.

Trim the Fat or Else—Choose Else!

A recent cross-industry survey found that 53 percent of employers are reducing staff. As medical and dental benefits cost employers about 28 percent of labor costs, and as health care costs rose 27 percent in the last year alone, employers have an obvious incentive to reduce these costs. Perhaps this is the single most signifi-cant reason that employers choose to lay off employees rather than spread the work out among more employees.

Still, there are other options for reducing employer health care costs. Healthy employees have fewer health care claims and we know that stress and overload have a negative impact on employee health. Increasing the employee's share of co-payments, deductibles, and so forth may be preferable to cutting a job. Flexible spending accounts can ameliorate the pain of additional expenses by helping employees pay for health care costs with pretax dollars.

Passing more costs to employees can reduce health care costs, but this measure will fail in terms of employee morale and commitment if the employer only passes on costs without offering positive changes. Employers have to prepare a package of measures that address employee and employer needs, fostering mutual respect. The work redesign efforts described earlier ought to form one pillar of the package.

Bullish on Growth

Although shareholders clamor for short-term results, the wise investor realizes that long-term growth fuels the national economy. Today's children will be future leaders and employees of American business. We need to invest in them for the long term. Researchers Jeanne Brett from Northwestern and Linda Stroh from Loyola found that managers who work the longest hours feel that "they do not really know their children" and that "their children are growing up without them." Some of these people have spouses or caretakers to fill in for them. But, nearly one-fifth of employed parents are single parents, many of whom struggle to find quality childcare. Investments that we make in time for our children, quality day-care, and education will yield the human resources we need to sustain successful organizations of the future.

New Role Models

The Workaholic superhuman we revere today is going to meet an unhappy fate. A new type of superhero is emerging in the American workplace. Consider these new role models:

Jim Goodnight, the CEO of SAS Institute in Cary, North Carolina, a highly suc-cessful software company, leaves the office most days at 4:30 P.M. He works a 35-hour week, and expects all other employees to do the same.

Mike Phillips, CEO of investment firm Frank Russell, says, "If somebody comes to me and says, 'I'm traveling too much,' I say, 'Well then don't travel so much.' And they say, 'But the business will suffer.' And I say, 'So the business will suffer. I'm not telling you to travel this much. And I'm the CEO. . . . You can delegate

more to your people and have them travel more, or just decide you're not going to do it. And I won't cut your bonus for doing that."

Larry Harrington, an Aetna Vice President of Customer Service, says, "We allow groups of employees to improve the way they work and challenge our practices. And we involve the lowest levels of the organization in our process redesigns. Those people have a better feel for what processes are stupid."

John Lechleiter of Eli Lilly declares, "I'm amazed at how many people at my level don't know what we are asking of our employees. We don't realize what we are asking people to do. I don't need six-digit precision. So, I find I have to foster good, clear communication about what we need and the level of precision needed."

Another model example comes from Professors Rapoport and Bailyn. In explaining why one woman failed her management review, her supervisor, a divisional manager said, "She probably thought it would be seen as a positive that she was willing to sacrifice her family for work. But she has gone through two divorces and who knows who is taking care of those kids . . . that's not the kind of person we admire."

In sum, many employees feel overworked and want to reduce their workload. By joining with them to find new ways to work, employers can avoid the negative consequences of overwork and reap the benefits of improved productivity and performance: improved recruitment and retention; lower training costs; better morale; higher job commitment; and less absenteeism and tardiness. What goes around comes around. With new role models arising to challenge the workaholic hero, we can choose what kind of legacy we want to leave for the future.

PART NINE

Rethinking Patterns of Culture

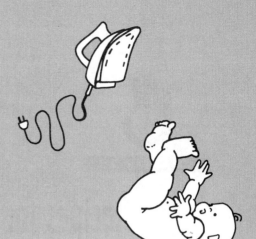

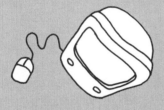

CHAPTER 26

Recipes for Relief

ANNA LAPPÉ

Author Frances Moore Lappé first gained international attention thirty years ago with her powerful book, Diet for a Small Planet. *In it, she suggested that a diet based far less on meat and far more on plants could solve the world's hunger problem and bring us all better health. Frances was part of the Simplicity Forum dialogue at Kalamazoo, Michigan, in March, 2002, that generated the idea of* Take Back Your Time Day, *and one of the first prominent Americans to officially endorse it. During the dialogue, we talked about the connection between overwork and time pressure on the one hand, and non-nutritious fast food on the other. As soon as the plan for this book took shape, I asked Frances to write a chapter about work and food. She would love to, she said, but she was too busy, with a hectic speaking schedule and her own needs to take back some time. She suggested that her daughter Anna, with whom she had just cowritten the book,* Hope's Edge, *write this chapter instead. "She's an excellent writer," Frances told me, betraying a mother's pride. But as you'll see, she wasn't exaggerating. —JdG*

Winding my way through Paris in a taxicab, I could smell croissants baking, espressos brewing, and that distinctive scent of McDonald's cheeseburgers frying.

I had been in Paris long enough to sense the connection the French still have to their food traditions. Around the corner from where I lived, the open-air market, one of dozens throughout the city, was packed every day. "Goutez! Goutez!" the vendors shouted, offering families, businessmen, and college students tastes of plums, pears, apples, and peaches. But that distinctive smell reminded me that those markets, the corner bistros, and cafés are slowly giving way to supermarket chains and glowing yellow arches.

Passing a pack of teenagers munching Big Macs, I asked my thirty-something Algerian cab driver how he explained this new found love for McDo's (as it's affectionately called in Paris). "Time," he said. "We have less and less of it." The honking traffic belted out the perfect soundtrack.

His words are even truer here at home. We work more hours and vacation less than any other industrialized country. If even the French feel pressured for time— this from the people who still believe in the hour-plus lunch break and collectively shut the country down for the month of August—no wonder we Americans feel doubly, triply, even quadruply so.

Since we're so often in a hurry, more and more of us are eating out—almost half of our food dollar now goes to food outside the home. When we do cook we're serving up more premade, processed food than ever before. Nutritionists warn that half of our children and teenagers eat less than one serving of fruit a day and nearly one-third eat less than one serving of vegetables (at least of the unfried variety).[1]

The impact on our health, waistlines, and bottom lines is alarming. The Centers for Disease Control report that 61 percent of us are overweight or obese, a figure nearly double what it was 25 years ago, and warn that the percentage of overweight children is the highest in history. Today, almost as many people in the United States die each year from obesity-related disease, as die from tobacco use.[2] As a nation, we now spend one out of ten of our health dollars on diabetes-related illnesses.[3]

In the face of this epidemic, there's been much hand-wringing and some action. The President has issued a call to exercise more without telling us where to find the time. Obese individuals, taking their cue from tobacco litigation, are suing fast food companies. School districts are sending out warning letters to parents of overweight children and reinstating physical education programs.

---

1. Data from Centers for Disease Control.
2. See the American Obesity Association for these and other statistics.
3. Surgeon Generals' Call to Action on obesity.

But these efforts don't get to the root of the crisis. Part of what prevents us from getting to the heart of the obesity epidemic is a hesitancy to talk about the *food* that's making us so obese. Many of the anti-obesity efforts have focused on turning couch potatoes into calorie-burners, like the government-sponsored www.verbnow.com campaign or Kidnetic.com, funded in part by Coca-Cola, Hershey, McDonald's, and PepsiCo, Inc.

Part of the problem is that we're also being taught what's good for us by the very folks offering up foods that are *not* good for us. I think of Coca-Cola's health education Web site where they deny any link between soft drinks and childhood obesity;[4] about McDonald's and Disney's exclusive ten-year agreement to promote each other's products;[5] or about the sugar industry's role in shaping national health guidelines.[6]

---

4. NCBA personal correspondence and marketing material.
5. *Fast Food Nation* has a good section on the connection between marketers for Disney and those for McDonald's, as well as the cross-promotion between companies.
6. *Food Politics* has a good analysis of the impact of corporate lobbying on food guidelines.

Another key part of what prevents us from getting to the roots of this epidemic is our reluctance to talk about *time*—how much of it we have or don't have, how we value it, and how we think about it.

Far Away Food

If we want to talk about what food we're eating, we need to talk about what food we're buying and where. It's no coincidence that the trend toward a processed fast food diet has coincided with concentration in food production and retailing. Today, nearly half of all the food sold in this country comes from just ten corporations.[7] Wal-Mart only started selling food in 1988, but by this year, had already become the country's largest food retailer, cashing in on $53 billion in sales.[8]

In many low-income communities, real grocery stores have become an endangered species. Where one is spotted, the options range from wilted lettuce to Ding Dongs. Take my hometown of Oakland, California. One of the city's poorest neighborhoods, West Oakland, has 24,000 residents and only one supermarket. In contrast, the community boasts 36 liquor and convenience stores that charge 30 to 75 percent more than supermarkets.[9]

It's true for most of us: We have to travel far to find decent food. With our crunched schedules, who has time? Then too, my overriding image of a typical American supermarket is of mayhem—kids pulling parents' pant legs crying out for what they just had to have. Marketers are smart; all the processed, sugary products are kids' eye level. No wonder, once shopping, we rush to stock up on food that keeps well, not necessarily that keeps us well.

Signs of Change

But, throughout the country, a quiet revolution is taking place. From farmers markets to food cooperatives to community-supported agriculture (CSA), people are reclaiming good, healthy food as a pleasure and as a right. They are realizing that even food shopping doesn't have to be a time sinkhole. It can be a way to enjoy time with our families, support local economies, keep family farmers on the land, and reconnect with food and those who grow it.

The USDA tells us that farmers' markets increased *79 percent* just from 1992 to 2002. Now, tens of thousands of people throughout the country can flock to their public squares, parks, and town centers to shop from farmers directly.[10]

---

7. Professor Tom Lyson at Cornell University is the national specialist on concentration in the food industry.
8. *Business Day* report on October 2, 2002.
9. Report provided by the People's Grocery project study by the University of California Cooperative Extension and Alameda County.
10. U.S. Department of Agriculture.

Today, more than three million Americans enjoy shopping in the nation's nearly 5,000 food cooperatives.[11] I think of my local Brooklyn co-op where I work a couple hours each month in exchange for access to affordable organic options and great products chosen carefully so as not to contain genetically modified organisms or chemicals that may be harmful to my health.

Nonexistent in the United States 15 years ago, community-supported agriculture—where people invest directly in a farm and get fresh produce throughout the harvest season—has grown to involve tens of thousands of families and more than 1,000 farms across the country. Last week at my neighborhood CSA, I was picking out my purple kale and Japanese eggplant along with local teenagers, young parents and their babies in strollers, and grandparents with their toddler grandkids.

Emerging across the country are also local initiatives stepping in to give urban communities access to healthy food. Back in West Oakland, the People's Grocery now offers organic food at affordable prices and, in the process, supports local African-American farmers. A few hundred miles south, Anna Marie "the Seed Lady of Watts" Carter, has been working in South Central Los Angeles for more than a decade, teaching gardening, seed sharing, and helping to ensure that folks in her community have quality food.

These efforts help to make shopping for food a way to connect with friends, family, community, and the people who grow our food, and help us to teach our kids that broccoli doesn't grow on Aisle 8.

No Time to Cook

In our time-pressed lives, the other big obstacle we sense to eating healthy food is finding the time to cook it. I like the advice of Julia Butterfly Hill—the infamous environmentalist who protested redwood logging by perching for 738 days in the branches of one of the ancient trees. Julia, whose schedule is about as grueling as a rock band's, suggests creating what she calls a "fast food kitchen." Hers includes keeping on hand basic spices and sauces, nut butter, grains and rice, and your favorite fruits and vegetables. Think about the basics that you need to make your favorite meals, and keep them handy.

I can vouch for the strategy. Since I've stocked my kitchen essentials, I've been able to whip up quick meals whenever I don't have the time to dive into something elaborate. In the time it used to take me to make Kraft Macaroni and Cheese, I can make a far healthier salad.

As a recovering kitchen-phobe, I can also attest to a strange phenomenon. In my former life as a college student and later as a graduate student, I never felt I had enough time and I never dreamed I'd spend it cooking! But once I started

---

11. American Academy of Family Physicians.

making meals, I noticed it actually felt like I was *gaining* time. Cooking became a way to pause during my day, do some good thinking, and spend time with friends. I'd finish cooking and be more relaxed and energetic than before. I came to see that it's not that I didn't have the time to cook; it's that I had never known the pleasures that cooking can offer us.

No Time to Eat

I recently heard a talk by Alice Waters—chef and midwife to the whole foods and local and seasonal eating movements—about the loss of family time around the table. Framed by brilliant red rhubarb stalks, Alice reminded us that throughout history meals were a time of community building and family knitting. The table is where our stories get passed down. But how many American families eat meals together anymore?

The crowd let out an audible gasp when she said that the typical family eats two meals together, at most, each week. No wonder recent studies have found that average parents spend 38.5 minutes a week in meaningful conversation with their kids.[12]

The time we take to eat, and what we have access to, in schools is even worse. When I think back to middle school lunchtime, I remember downing sodas and gobbling soggy French fries. In high school, we didn't even have a cafeteria. If we bought our food at school, it came out of vending machines. Vienna finger sausages and potato chips were the big hits.

But across the country, schools and concerned parents are starting to change what we generously call "school lunches." Just down the street from her Berkeley restaurant, Chez Panisse, Alice Waters helped bring to life an old idea: edible schoolyards. In less than ten years, Martin Luther King, Jr. Middle School has become the proving ground for school gardens, where kids grow their own food, harvest it, prepare it, and serve it together—on checked tablecloths and terracotta plates. The day I visited, the kids were preparing homemade tortillas and fresh salsa—a far cry from my soggy French fry lunches. But school gardens aren't just for crunchy Berkeley; they're appearing across the country.

Slow Food

Originating in Italy in 1986 and now creeping across our country, the Slow Food Movement is another "antidote" to the food-time crisis. Now numbering 60,000 on five continents, Slow Food folks believe in slowing down and appreciating food again. They appreciate valuing our health and connecting around a table and a good meal.

---

12. TV Turnoff Network Fact Sheets 2002.

But we don't need to join a movement to start eating together as families and friends around the table. It just takes the commitment. Think of it as an investment. Invest now and save later in quality relationships, strong bonds, and great health.

Time and Diet

Maybe one of the most debilitating ideas about food and time is about our diet itself. It seems every month another expert proclaims what's *really* good for us. This week we learn fat is great; last week it was the body's nemesis. Next week who knows? No wonder people throw up their hands! It feels overwhelming. Who has time to worry about it?

I remember watching Larry King ask fifties fitness guru Jack La Lanne this exact question on national television: "The experts say eat this, don't eat that. What's a person to do?" La Lanne's response? Simple, "If man made it," he said, "don't eat it!"

In other words, as long as our diet is based on whole, unprocessed foods, our bodies will have a healthy base. La Lanne reminds us that it doesn't take a PhD in nutrition, a complicated diet regimen, a special line of food products, or a huge investment in time to eat healthfully.

Unfortunately, not many of us hear La Lanne's mantra. Instead, we're inundated with advertising from a food and beverage industry that spends $30 billion to get us to consume their products.[13]

I'm thinking about what food we spend our time thinking about when I pick up *Harvesting Minds* by professor Roy Fox. In interviews with kids in rural Missouri, Fox asks about Channel One, the television program broadcast into half our nation's classrooms every day of the school year. Advertising peppers every twelve-minute news show. No wonder it's so hard to know what's good for us when even in our classrooms we're receiving advertising from Mountain Dew, Pizza Hut, Snickers, Snapple, Skittles, and McDonalds.

Fox meets eighth-graders who'd memorized Nike commercials, sing the jingle for Cinnaburst without missing a note, and recite commercials all the way to the vending machines during post–Channel One snack time. One girl tells Fox her dream: She flew to McDonald's and ate warm, crunchy French fries and a double cheeseburger. Then she flew home.

This middle school girl's dream is the best reminder for me of the urgency of rethinking time and food, of remembering the ideas we hold about how shopping, cooking, and eating affect our health, our family life, our communities—even what we dream.

I think back to the teenagers in Paris I'd seen munching their Big Macs. They may not yet be dreaming of McDo's, but unless we take action, it may just be a matter of time.

---

13. Roy Fox, *Harvesting Minds* (Westport, CT: Praeger Publishers, 2000).

CHAPTER 27

Time by Design

LINDA BREEN PIERCE

In chapter 13 of this book, Robert Bernstein shows how our dependence on automobiles has made us less effectively mobile—actually becoming a time sink and costing us nearly a fifth of our lives. Yet the issue goes far beyond cars and comes to include the entire way we've designed our cities. Although we can gain more free time by reducing work hours and cutting back on overscheduling, in the long run, we need to take a deeper look at how our cultural institutions and physical architecture add to our time stress. We may find that by reducing urban sprawl, we are not only cleaning up our air, saving energy, protecting the environment, and reducing global climate change, but also giving ourselves more time. Linda Breen Pierce gave up her successful law practice to find a simpler life with more time for herself and her husband, and for thinking about big ideas. —JdG

Time is an elusive asset that keeps slipping away, silently, unobtrusively, from our lives. We ask ourselves, "Where did the time go?" much like we wonder how a missing sock disappeared from the clothes dryer. In one sense, having an afternoon slip by in a flash feels good; at least we are not bored. Still, it's disappointing to arrive at the end of the day, week, or year and discover we have run out of time for what is most important to us.

Excessive work hours may be the greatest cause of time deprivation in America, but let me point out another, less obvious culprit. It pertains to the infrastructure of our society—the physical design and relationship between housing, work, transportation, recreation, civic activities, and the goods and services needed for daily living.

The Old and the New

In *The Geography of Nowhere*, author and self-described citizen-observer, James Kunstler, presents a disturbing portrayal of the landscape that has evolved in America since World War II: suburban sprawl created by people fleeing unattractive, densely occupied, noisy, soul-shattering industrialized cities. The suburban model idealizes large homes on expansive lots, set far back from the street, maximizing privacy and quiet; the larger the home and the lot, the better. Zoning restrictions against mixed uses have resulted in separate geographical areas for living, working, shopping, and recreating. With inadequate mass transit, the automobile is the primary link that connects these vital forms of living.

Walking or bicycling for transportation is generally unrealistic; the distances are too far and the journey is unsafe for all but the automobile, and even that is questionable. Consequently, we design public and private spaces to accommodate cars. We build wide streets to facilitate faster automobile speed. Highways and freeways connect residential and commercial areas. Garages have grown from one-car to massive three- and four-car spaces.

Suburban design encourages people to see their homes as the centers of the universe. They drive into attached garages using remote-controlled openers after long and exhausting commutes. Conversations with neighbors are short and infrequent. Instead, people isolate themselves within their homes.

There is a groundswell of dissatisfaction with the suburban way of life. People fill their homes with expensive furnishings and entertainment devices yet still feel isolated and lonely. They detest spending so much time in their cars, but accept it as part of life. When they do get home from work, they are unlikely to go out again; it's too much effort. Instead, they try to relax in their home-based media rooms and gyms, but at the cost of isolation from their communities.

New movements have formed to address the social, cultural, spiritual, and temporal shortcomings of suburban sprawl. One of the most visible movements is New Urbanism, a concept that advocates mixed-use, human-scale neighborhoods, towns, and cities that bear some or all of the following characteristics:

- Mixed residential, commercial, civic, and open space uses are encouraged, all within walking distance (5 to 10 minutes) of each other.

- Automobile traffic is accommodated, but does not dominate the landscape. Narrow streets and natural traffic-calming devices, such as fountains, curves, and medians, inhibit the speed of traffic. Garages are often placed behind the home (sometimes served by an alley).

- Walking and bicycling for both recreation and transportation are encouraged. Pathways for both are plentiful and safe.

- A diversified selection of housing—apartments, single-family homes, live/work units, and multi-family dwellings—serves a wide range of ages, lifestyles, and incomes.

- A town center or square provides a setting for civic functions and for businesses that offer goods and services for daily living.

- Abundant green spaces supply natural beauty and recreational opportunities.

- The aesthetics of the public realm are highly valued for their beneficial impact on psychological well being, civic pride, and commitment to the community.

- Certain design elements encourage community interaction and the feeling that the neighborhood and town are extensions of the home. For example, narrow, attractive, tree-lined streets with ample sidewalks entice people to go outside. Front porches and homes positioned at the front of the lot encourage people to engage in casual conversation with passersby. Smaller lots than the suburban model allow a greater number of people to live closer to each other.

- Ideally, work opportunities are integrated into the community to enable residents to walk, bicycle, or drive a short distance to work.

This movement is young, hardly a decade old. Few communities completely fulfill the New Urbanist ideal, but many have made substantial headway and hundreds of new projects are being developed. Some communities are built in undeveloped spaces; others involve redevelopment projects in existing towns and cities.

Livable towns are not limited to newly developed projects, but also include exist-ing neighborhoods and towns that meet most of the criteria for New Urbanism. The design of small American towns in the early part of the twentieth century shared many of these ideals and some have retained their character. Small or medium-sized university towns often incorporate some aspects of the New Urbanist model. Even some larger cities, like Portland, Oregon, include elements that create the feeling of a livable town.

America can look to Europe for many examples of livable towns. In July 2000 a League of Slow Cities (Citta Slow) was formed in Italy as an off-shoot of the Slow Food movement. The founders describe the movement as one in which towns and cities are brought to life by people "keen on time refound." These towns feature town squares, theaters, cafés, places of worship, shops, pedestrian access, and uncontaminated landscapes. This movement aims to improve the quality of life and conviviality of communities. For further information on the League of Slow Cities, see the Web site for the Slow Food Movement (www.slowfood.com).

What is Time, Anyway?

Where we live can affect how much time we have—or rather how much time we think we have. We can view time in a number of ways. There is raw time: 10 minutes is 10 minutes measured on the clock, an exact unit of measurement. But we don't always experience time in its raw form. For example, 10 minutes spent rushing to get dressed for work is *perceived* as less time than 10 minutes spent chatting with a friend after a leisurely meal, even though the clock insists it's exactly the same.

Sometimes there is no change in either raw or perceived time, but the quality of time shifts from "dead" time to "live" time. Dead time is time spent in an activ-ity that is not inherently pleasurable, fulfilling, or satisfying. Live time is the oppo-site; it has value in and of itself. For example, if you replace 30 minutes of driving in congested traffic with 30 minutes walking in a beautiful neighborhood, you experience a shift in the *quality* of time. Let's face it—we only have 24 hours a day; we cannot add time to our lives. The most we can do is change how we spend that 24 hours.

As noted above, the design of livable towns encourages community interac-tion. Stopping on a walk to the local grocer to chat with neighbors can have a calming effect and ironically, even though the trip takes longer, you often expe-rience a feeling of having more time, not less. It's as though your brain decides that if you have time to talk, there must be plenty of time. Some residents of liv-able towns describe the feeling of "time standing still."

WORK LESS, WATCH LESS

Don't be a couch potato.
Participate in Take Back Your Time Day
Turn off the tube and tune into our website

www.timeday.org

The Automobile Time Buster

One time difference between suburban sprawl and livable towns is the amount of time spent in the car. The average American drives twice as much as Europeans and Japanese and 75 percent of an American's trips relate to aspects of living other than work. Since livable towns integrate home living, socializing, shopping, civic functions, and recreation, walking short distances instead of driving is a viable alternative for many nonwork activities. For some people (especially home-based workers), work is a part of this integrated living model. All of this results in a significant reduction of raw transportation time.

While many people enjoy a Sunday drive in the country, most do not find driving for daily activities inherently rewarding. So besides reducing the raw time required for transportation, livable towns offer the opportunity to convert dead time (driving) to live time (walking in a beautiful community). Walking offers other benefits over driving—spontaneous socializing with friends and neighbors, excellent physical exercise, breathing fresh air, and a spiritual boost (especially if your walking environment is filled with a mixture of natural and man-made beauty). If you consider that a family can easily make 10 to 20 automobile trips a week, residing in a livable town can mean a substantial increase in quality time.

As the driver or passenger of a vehicle, you are subjected to both faster speeds and greater stimulation than if you are walking. Your brain needs to work harder as you focus on safety and process all that you see. In a car, you have a sense of rushing, for that is what is going on inside of you—a rush of sensory perceptions. Walking, on the other hand, necessarily slows your pace. Your senses are not bombarded with flashing images; instead, they absorb what you can comfortably assimilate. This contributes to the perception that time is moving more slowly and is expanding, not contracting.

Combine Activities to Free Up Time

There is more potential in livable towns for activities to serve more than one purpose and, thereby, save time. For example, in a traditional suburban neighborhood, you might drive to the gym for a workout, and then later drive to shop for dinner. In livable towns, you are likely to walk or ride a bicycle for your shopping, combining exercise with errands, netting additional time to spend with family or whatever else you want to do.

Save Time by Planning Less

The suburban lifestyle, with its emphasis on privacy and its dependence on the automobile, requires considerable planning and organization, a time-consuming activity in itself. You had better know what you are doing before you walk out the front door, because if you forget to pick up something, you will not want to jump back into the car if the destination is more than five minutes away. Due to the distances involved, you need to plan ahead, make lists, organize, and coordinate regularly with family and friends. Any unexpected change in plans involves even more lists and organizational tasks.

In livable towns, less planning is required because people, goods, services, recreation, and civic functions are close and accessible. If you can walk to the local grocer in five minutes, you can decide what you want for dinner an hour before you cook. You are more likely to get together with friends spontaneously, because you see them on the street or in the town center. Life is simpler. Lists no longer dominate your life. You don't need to excel at multitasking, but can focus on one thing at a time.

Share Resources and Save Time

American life has become increasingly complex and frenetic, in part due to the vast choices available to us. Whether we want to buy a stereo or plant a vegetable garden, researching the options can be overwhelming and time consuming. Community involvement in livable towns offers enormous potential to share resources—material goods, information and advice, or services—resulting in substantial time savings when researching and acquiring what we need or want. People who get together for a Friday afternoon beer are more likely to share infrequently-used tools than suburban neighbors who nod to each other on the way out of their driveways.

In livable towns, everything about the business of living changes. You don't have to solve all of life's challenges by yourself. Let's say you are having trouble with gophers in your garden. If you live in the suburbs, you might call or drive to a nursery to get advice, dig out a garden book, or surf the net. You may still do these things in a livable town, but you might just as easily find a solution in an informal chat with friends at the local coffee house.

When it comes to household projects, there is abundant opportunity to change dead time to live time in a livable town, again because people know each other. For example, the Johnsons may help the Smiths paint their home in the spring. During the following winter, the Smiths help the Johnsons refinish antique furniture that has been sitting in the attic for years. What could have been drudgery for both families evolves into working parties, a time for sharing and community.

Huge Time Savings for Parents

Perhaps the most dramatic time savings in livable towns occurs in families with children. Parents can give up their part-time jobs chauffeuring their kids to school, extracurricular activities, and friends' homes. Children can walk, bicycle, roller blade, or use their scooters to get where they want to go. This eliminates a dead activity (driving) for both parents and children, who then use their own motion power rather than ride in a car. Neighborhoods are designed to bring people out to the streets, increasing safety. Parenting becomes a village affair. If a kid acts up at the other end of town (usually a 10 to 15 minute walk), the parents will likely hear about it before that child gets home.

The Not So Big Town

Sarah Susanka, a Twin Cities architect and author of the bestselling book, *The Not So Big House*, contends that people are more comfortable living in homes with warm, inviting spaces designed to human-scale than in the large, expansive, formal, museum-like structures that reflect America's bigger-is-better mentality. Children know this for sure. Watch them play and you will see that they gravitate toward small, cozy spaces—the storage area under the stairwell, a small attic room, or an alcove.

Similarly, people are more comfortable in neighborhoods and towns designed to human-scale—places that are close and cozy and accessible. Livable towns not only restore quality time to our lives, but they also teach us something we once knew—a sense of place.

It's time to start building them.

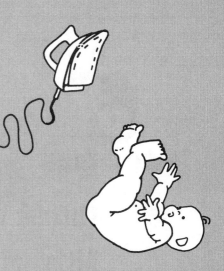

PART TEN

Changing Public Policy

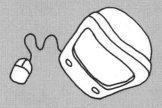

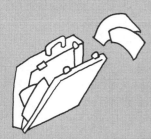

CHAPTER 28

Europe's Work-Time Alternatives

ANDERS HAYDEN

When I first read Anders Hayden's wonderful book, Sharing the Work, Sparing the Planet, it was an eye opener. Not only did he make a powerful case that one of the best things we could do for the environment was to work fewer hours, he also pointed out the vast difference between the U.S. (and Canada, since he is from Toronto) and Europe, where work time is concerned. One speech he cited, made by a European conservative, former Dutch Prime minister Ruud Lubbers, illustrated for me the chasm between European thinking and ours. According to Lubbers:

> It is true that the Dutch are not aiming to maximize gross national product per capita. Rather we are seeking to attain a high quality of life, a just, participatory and sustainable society. While the Dutch economy is very efficient per working hour, the number of working hours per citizen are rather limited. We like it that way. Needless to say, there is more room for all those important aspects of our lives that are not part of our jobs, for which we are not paid and for which there is never enough time.

Amen. —JdG

t's late October. You've been working hard all year and feel like you're ready for some time off. How about taking *the rest of the year*? If you've been working as much as the average American employee, you've already clocked as many hours as a full-time worker does over an *entire* year in many European countries.

Of course, Europeans don't just stop work nine to ten weeks before the New Year. Instead, European nations have introduced a wide range of shorter work-time policies. Their goals, which vary in importance in each country, include: improving the quality of life for working people, promoting work-family balance and gender equity, creating opportunities for skills-upgrading and lifelong learning, and reducing unemployment by better distributing the available jobs.

While Western Europe is not a worker's paradise, its various shorter work-time policies are valuable examples of ways in which public policies can foster "time affluence" alongside material affluence.

The Growing International Work-time Gap

One of the first products of the Industrial Revolution was a dramatic increase in work hours for most people, with 13- and 14-hour days, 70- or 80-hour weeks, or more, common in many countries in the nineteenth century. In response, working people embarked on a difficult struggle for work-time reduction, which, over time, has delivered achievements such as the eight-hour day, the two-day weekend, and paid vacations.

The United States was once an international work-time reduction leader. Henry Ford's auto plants introduced a 40-hour week in 1926, while German auto-workers had to wait until 1967 for a similar standard. In the 1930s, the U.S. and France were among the first countries to legislate a 40-hour week, and Congress seriously considered a 30-hour bill. By contrast, Saturday was a regular working day in the Netherlands until the 1960s, and Sweden did not reach a 40-hour standard until 1973.

After World War II, the American shorter work-time movement ground to a halt, while many European nations caught up with and surpassed American standards. From 1979 to 2000, France, Germany, the Netherlands, and Norway benefited from work-time reductions of nearly 10 percent or more (Table 1). Work hours have also fallen dramatically in South Korea and Japan, which now has a lower annual estimate than the United States.[1]

---

1. International work hours comparisons are imprecise due to differences in how hours are calculated in various countries. The Organization for Economic Co-operation and Development statistics provide a general idea of international comparisons, and a good sense of the trends within each country. Figures from the International Labor Organization show longer hour estimates for each country, but a similar difference between hours worked by Americans and by their counterparts in Europe.

TABLE 1: Average annual hours actually worked per person in employment

COUNTRY	1979	1990	2000	%CHANGE 1979–1990	%CHANGE 1990–2000	%CHANGE 1979–2000
Canada	1832	1788	1801	–2.4	+0.7	–1.7
France	1806	1657	1562*	–8.2	–5.7	–13.5
Germany (West)	1696	1548	1462	–8.7	–5.6	–13.8
Italy	1722	1674	1634*	–2.8	–2.4	–5.1
Japan	2126	2031	1840*	–4.5	–9.4	–13.5
Korea (South)	2734**	2514	2474	–8.0	–1.6	–9.5
Netherlands***	1591	1433	1343*	–9.9	–6.2	–15.6
Norway	1514	1432	1376	–5.4	–3.9	–9.1
Sweden	1516	1546	1624	+2.0	+5.0	+7.1
UK	1815	1767	1708	–2.6	–3.3	–5.9
U.S.A.	1845	1819	1877	–1.4	+3.2	+1.7

Source: OECD, 2001

*   1999 figures

**   1983 figure

*** Figures for the Netherlands are for dependent employment.
     Figures for all other countries are for total employment.

Bringing the Workweek Below 40 Hours

While many Americans long for the days when they worked *only* 40 hours per week, several European countries have recently reduced the standard workweek below 40 hours.

The boldest recent initiative is France's 35-hour week, which was announced in 1997 and became the legislated standard in 2000. The "shorter workweek" has taken many flexible forms, including extra days off (an average of 16 per year), shorter daily hours, and alternating four- and five-day weeks. In 2001, France's national planning agency found "indisputable" evidence that work-time reduction was creating vast numbers of new jobs, helping to bring unemployment down from 12.5 percent in 1997 to an eighteen-year low of 8.6 percent.[2]

A recent major study found that the majority of French workers (60 percent), said that shorter hours had improved their quality of *life*, versus only 15 percent with a negative experience. The effect on quality of *work*, however, has been more mixed. Roughly half said the 35-hour week had not changed their working conditions, with others equally divided over whether conditions had improved or deteriorated.[3]

Where complaints exist, increased workloads, as a result of insufficient new hiring, and the effects of increased work-time flexibility[4]—such as more evening and weekend work in return for shorter hours overall—are often the culprits. France's 35-hour week is still a work in progress.[5] But despite some concerns and controversies, it has delivered important employment and quality of life improvements overall.

Rather than a dramatic legislated leap forward, the Netherlands (36 or 38 hours), Denmark (37), Norway (37.5), and Belgium (39 in 1999, 38 in 2003) have relied on national agreements between employers and labor unions to gradually cut the workweek. By 1996, almost one-quarter of German employees enjoyed a 35-hour week through their collective agreement.

A shorter workweek is not only on the agenda in Europe's wealthier northern nations. In the 1990s, Portugal cut its workweek from 48 to 40 hours. Portuguese unions, like those in Greece, are now campaigning for 35 hours. Shorter hours are also gaining ground in Spain, where 1.4 million workers had a 35-hour week by the end of 2001.

Not all European countries have been making similar progress. For example, in the United Kingdom—Europe's "long-hours capital"—one in six employees works more than 48 hours a week. Still, on average, even British workers put in far fewer hours annually than do Americans.

Four to Six Weeks Vacations for All

Many Americans, who have no legally mandated right to paid vacations, suffer from "vacation deficit disorder." A typical U.S. worker earns only 13.8 vacation days per year, while 22.5 million private sector workers have no paid vacation at all.[6] President Bush, who took a full month off in 2001, is one notable exception.

---

2. Due to the global economic slowdown, French unemployment crept back up to about nine percent in 2002.

3. European Industrial Relations Observatory, October 2002. "Government issues assessment of 35-hour week legislation." European Industrial Relations Online http://www.eiro .eurofound.ie/2002/10/Feature/FR0210106F.html

4. The exchange of greater work-time flexibility for employers, which involves more variation in weekly hours in response to business needs and in return for shorter overall hours for employees, has been a controversial point in several European countries.

5. In October 2002, a newly-elected conservative government passed amendments to make the 35-hour week more "flexible" and allow more overtime. Critics of the changes fear that those firms that still have not moved to a 35-hour week will have no incentive to do so, leaving the workforce divided between 35-hour and 39-hour workers.

6. Average vacation days for an employee with five years of service in a medium or large firm, according to the Bureau of Labor Statistics. See also Helene Jorgense, "Give Me a Break: The extent of Paid Holidays and Vacations." *Center for Economic Policy and Research* (September 3, 2003). Economic Policy and Research Online http://www.cepr .net/give_me_a_break.htm

Across the Atlantic, the European Union (EU) Working Time Directives requires a minimum of four weeks paid leave each year for all employees, and several EU countries have five weeks (25 working days) of vacation by law. Dutch, German, and Italian workers have gained roughly 30 vacation days, on average, through collective bargaining (Figure 4).[7]

In 1998, a national strike shut down Denmark over the demand for a sixth week of vacation, later phased-in through five additional paid leave days. Some might think that Danish workers were asking for too much, but the strike is best seen as a struggle by working people to share in a booming economy, and *as an enlightened choice of time over money* as the way to take that share. In 2002, Sweden announced plans to catch up with its neighbor by phasing-in five more paid leave days, which employees can choose to take as vacation time, individual days off, or shorter daily work hours.

Paid Parental Leave

Spending time with newborn children is one of the most important reasons to scale back hours of paid work. The Family Medical and Leave Act gives American parents the right to a mere twelve weeks of *unpaid* leave after birth or adoption. In Western Europe, parental leave is generally much longer and *paid.*

Sweden's system is one of the most developed; parents can take 15 months of job-protected leave per child, at up to 80 percent of their previous pay. The leave can be taken flexibly, at any time, until the child reaches eight years of age. A "father's month" —30 days reserved for the father—encourages men to play a role in child care. In Norway, parents can take 42 weeks of leave at 100 percent of their previous wage, or 52 weeks at 80 percent. German parents have a very lengthy leave entitlement—up to three years, full-time or part time—but the rate of pay is relatively low: about $300 per month for two years or $450 per month for one year.[8]

The Right to Choose Shorter Hours with Equal Conditions

Some European countries, most notably the Netherlands, have recently shifted emphasis from collective work-time measures, such as a shorter standard work-week, to individualized options. In 2000, a new Working Hours Adjustment Act gave Dutch workers the right to reduce their hours of work, while part-timers can request longer hours. Germany introduced similar legislation later the same year.

---

7. Figure 4. Data from the European Industrial Relations Observatory, 2002. European Industrial Relations Online http://www.eiro.eurofound.ie/2002/02/Update/TN0202103U .html
8. Some critics say the German parental leave is actually too long, and in a climate of traditional "male breadwinner" values, encourages women to drop out of the workforce.

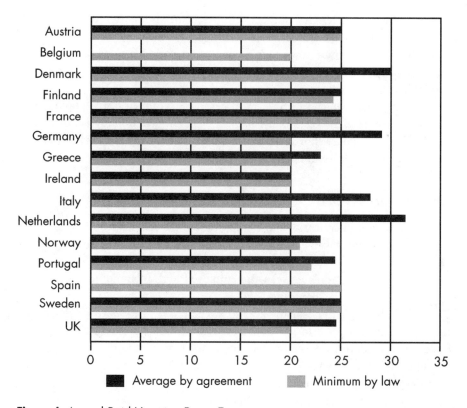

Figure 4. Annual Paid Vacation Days, Europe

If a Dutch or German worker wants a four-day week for four days' pay, for example, the employer can only refuse if he or she can show it is not possible without serious hardship for the firm. This promises to be a very significant reform, giving people more power to balance work with the rest of their lives.

The right to adjust one's work hours is part of the Netherlands' promotion of a "1.5 jobs model" for families—in which *both* men and women are empowered, and encouraged, to work 75 percent of their regular hours when they have young children. Some Dutch collective agreements also include "multiple choice" options— giving employees the choice between additional income, days off, or periods of leave. Among other uses, this could allow working parents to "buy time" while caring for children.

A 1996 Dutch law that outlaws discrimination between full-timers and part-timers in terms of hourly pay, benefits, and promotion opportunities makes the shorter-hours option more attractive. This principle of equal treatment for shorter-hour workers is now becoming law across Europe, in response to the 1997 EU Part-Time Work Directive.

Some other countries give workers with special needs the right to reduce their hours. Belgians over the age of 50 have the right to work an 80 percent or half-time schedule. The option of combining part-time work and a part-time pension for workers nearing retirement is also becoming more common in countries such as Germany.

Swedish parents can choose to work three-quarters of their normal hours until their children are eight years old. Norwegian parents with young children also have the right to choose shorter hours, and to combine part-time work with part-time, paid parental leave in flexible ways.

Career Breaks and "Job Rotation"

Several European countries allow employees to take breaks from their careers for training, family reasons, or other personal projects. In 1994, Denmark introduced an innovative system of paid educational, child-care and sabbatical leaves that allows "job rotation" between the employed and unemployed, and creates opportunities for skills upgrading.

Finland, the Netherlands, Norway, and Sweden have introduced similar measures, and Germany plans to do so. Each country's model differs slightly, but the basic idea is that an employee can take up to one year off and receive unemployment benefits or a paid allowance. The cost is balanced by the money saved when an unemployed person is hired as a replacement.

Belgium's "career break" program has evolved into a new "time credit" system. As of 2002, employees can take a one-year leave (full-time or half-time) from their job during their career and work a four-day week for up to five years, while receiving a paid allowance. In effect, this is like an extension of the public pension system, one that allows people to enjoy time off before retirement and to balance their careers with family responsibilities.

Fundamentally Different Cultures?

Some argue that inherent differences in national cultures, such as deeply-rooted differences in work ethic, are the reason why Europeans spend less time at work than Americans do. But this explanation is not entirely convincing. As mentioned, the U.S. was once an international work-time reduction leader. As late as the 1970s, Americans worked less and had a stronger desire for shorter hours than did Germans, for example.[9] If differences in work-time culture exist today, they are a recent development and not fundamental components of national character.

---

9. Bell, Linda, and Richard Freeman. "Why do Americans and Germans Work Different Hours?" *National Bureau of Economic Research Working Paper* No. w4808 (July 1994). Online http://papers.nber.org/papers/W4808

The work-hour advantage of some European countries *is*, however, related to "social democratic" institutions and policies, such as progressive taxation, public funding of health care and college education, and relatively low income inequality. Minimum wages in Europe are living wages, much higher than in the U.S., which help working people to have a decent life without excessively long hours.

A strong link also exists between work-time reduction and the percentage of workers covered by collective agreements,[10] which suggests that the relative weakness of American unions at present is a key factor in the growing international work-time gap.

However, widespread concern over the corrosive effects of long hours does give the U.S. Labor Movement—the folks who brought you the weekend and the eight-hour day—one important issue around which to rebuild.

NAME	**Take Back Your Time**
No.	One
WEEK	October 24, 2003

In	Monday	Did you know that
Out		the USA is the only
In		industrial country
Out		on earth with no
In	Tuesday	minimum paid
Out		vacation. While
In		Europeans get 5-6
Out		weeks of paid leave
In	Wednesday	a year, we average
Out		only two. And 26%
In		of working
Out		Americans got
In	Thursday	none at all last
Out		year. On average,
In		we gave back two
Out		holidays each
In	Friday	(worth a total of
Out		$20 billion) to our
In		employers, for fear
Out		of being labeled
In	Saturday	"slackers." Let's get
Out		in step with the
In		rest of the world.
Out		We need a break.
In	Sunday	
Out		
In		
Out		

Long Hours: The Price of Success?

Some people argue that long hours are necessary to succeed in the global economy. *The evidence suggests otherwise.* There is, however, a question of how one defines "success."

One point of comparison is unemployment. Some critics of work-time reduction note that the U.S. unemployment rate (5.6 percent in fall 2002) is lower than that in Europe's largest economies, Germany (9.8 percent) and France (9.0 percent). But these critics fail to recognize that unemployment in the Netherlands (2.9 percent) is only half that in the U.S., and is also lower in shorter-hours nations such as Denmark (4.3 percent), Norway (3.8 percent), and Sweden (5.1 percent)—not to mention the fact that if America's two million prisoners were

---

10. Organization for Economic Co-operation and Development. "OECD Employment Outlook." *OECD* (June 1998): 166–7.

added to the unemployment roles, its rate would be much higher, bringing us close to French and German levels.[11]

There's certainly no evidence here to suggest that only the American long-hours model can deliver low unemployment. In fact, work-time reduction has been an important job-creation tool in some countries, such as the Netherlands, although, on its own, it is no guarantee of low unemployment.

Now, what about productivity? Several shorter-hours innovators in Europe—Belgium, France, the Netherlands, and Norway—are actually more productive *per hour* of labor than is the United States.[12] Higher hourly productivity in these countries is almost certainly due, in part, to shorter work-time's beneficial effects on employee morale, less fatigue and burnout, lower absenteeism, higher quality of work, and better health.

Take Norway, for example. In 2001, its hourly productivity was 10 percent higher than the United States, but its annual Gross Domestic Product (GDP) per person was about 17 percent lower. The main difference was that Norwegians were working 29 percent fewer hours than Americans. (It's also worth noting that Norway's poverty rate is one-quarter, and its incarceration rate *one-tenth*, as high as the United States'.)

In the final analysis, the issue largely boils down to how nations choose to benefit from the capacity to produce more in each hour of labor. Is there more to the good life than maximizing output and consumption? Are work-family balance and a less stressful pace of life equally valuable? If so, then it's time to ask how the United States can regain its status as a world leader in creating not only material affluence, but time affluence, as well.

---

11. "Output, demand, and jobs," *The Economist* (October 31, 2002). http://www.economist.com.

12. Van Ark, Bart and Robert H. McGuckin. "International comparisons of labor productivity and per capita income." *Monthly Labor Review* (July 1999): 36–41. Online http://www.bls.gov/opub/mlr/1999/07/art3full.pdf. Van Ark's more recent calculations are reported in "Leisure often responsible for GDP gaps." *Toronto Globe and Mail* (July 8, 2002): B8.

CHAPTER 29

A Policy Agenda for Taking Back Time

JEROME SEGAL

Discussions of policy responses to long working hours and increasing time pressure often focus on two possibilities: a shorter work week (30, 32 or 35 hours) or longer vacations (or rather, some sort of minimum paid leave policy, as the U.S. now has none at all). But we needn't think so narrowly, as Jerome Segal points out in this chapter. As co-chair of the Simplicity Forum's public policy committee, Jerome was one of the founders of Take Back Your Time Day. He also writes eloquently about the issue in his book, Graceful Simplicity. *—JdG*

So, you want to take back your time? Well, broadly speaking, there are three different ways of doing that. You can . . .

1. Sell less of it: Work less at those things you get paid for.

2. Prevent other people (or circumstances) from extracting it: End those situations in which, against your will, you are forced to devote your time to things you would rather not do.

3. Use your time (at work or at home) in ways that make it truly and deeply your own.

One might say that these credos are responses to the three problems, *Overwork, Time Thievery,* and *Time Estrangement.* As a policy issue, the problem of *Overwork* represents well-established terrain. For much of the nineteenth century, and for the first third of the twentieth century, shortening the workweek was a central objective and accomplishment of the labor movement. But the problems of *Time Thievery* and *Time Estrangement,* as areas of public policy, have received far less attention.

So, let me consider them first. I won't try to be comprehensive, because one of the goals of Take Back Your Time Day is for *you* to get creative about solutions!

Time Estrangement

Time Estrangement, once you put aside humanity's external woes, such as war and disease, is a good contender for the central problem of human life. In other words, it could be described as *the absence of meaningful activity.* This is not simply a question of how much we work, but of whether or not, paid or unpaid, we find in life those activities which bring us most fully and deeply to life. It is the problem of whether or not we have found activities that allow for self-expression and self-realization, for growth and development. It is the problem of finding those activities that have such clear importance and significance in our lives that they impart a whole a sense of meaning and purpose.

Taken as such, *Time Estrangement* appears to be a basically individual problem. At that rate, what relationship does it have to public policy? What could be more removed from appropriate areas of state involvement than the questions of individual fulfillment?

But what happens if, after consulting widely among psychologists and psychiatrists, we reach the conclusion that, at least for the rich countries of the world, the absence of meaningful activity, is the central cause of mental illness and unhappiness. And let us say that we reach a further conclusion—that there is something of an epidemic of *Time Estrangement* in American life. Suppose we then ask, "Is there anything that government policy can do about this?" Perhaps there is. Let's consider some possibilities.

Work and Sabbaticals

Twenty-five years ago, Donald M. Fraser, a Congressman from Minnesota, introduced legislation to create "work sabbaticals" for everyone covered by Social Security. Here's how they would work. Social Security gives people the option when they reach age 62 to retire with partial benefits or continue working until 65 and retire with full benefits. Fraser reasoned that many people would treasure those three years of potential retirement not at age 62, but as a sabbatical during their working lives—as an opportunity to try something totally new, go back to school, or perhaps volunteer for some service that really made a difference in their lives.

Fraser proposed that every worker, after ten years of work, be eligible to take one of those three years off with partial benefits. After another ten years, he or she would become eligible for another sabbatical. Each person could do this up to three times during his or her work life. We could add a protection to this idea. After one year off, people would have the right to return to their old jobs. The result would be a kind of partially paid personal leave, allowing people to recharge, rethink, and redirect their work lives, and make them truly their own.

"Work sabbaticals" give people the opportunity to start in a new direction; however, except for the most entrepreneurial among us, they don't increase the supply of interesting, meaningful work. Here's a proposal that could.

We Americans talk a lot about family values, but our long working hours, the longest in the modern industrial world, mean families seldom see each other. If we want to strengthen American Families, there's no substitute for quality time together; time together keeps marriages and families together.

Only **25%** of American families eat together

Tax Credits for Contributions to Nonprofits

The nonprofit sector not only provides key services for the needy, but also provides meaningful jobs for a large number of Americans. In most cases, people who work for nonprofits could be making more money in the private sector. The fact that they chose "meaning" over "money" is a clear indication that the direct route to fulfillment (e.g. work that matters) is a powerful alternative to the standard path of high-income/high-consumption.

Nonprofits are largely supported by contributions which, in turn, are fostered by tax policies that make such contributions tax-deductible. Essentially, the government covers a portion of your contribution; therefore, we could expand the flow of resources to the nonprofit sector, and increase nonprofit job opportunities and service provision, by providing even greater tax incentives for contributions.

With the current tax deductions, people in higher tax brackets receive more government support for their contributions than do those in lower brackets, because they contribute more. By shifting to a tax credit (equal, say, to 50 percent of one's contributions), we could increase the extent of government support for people in lower tax brackets. Then, by making the credit refundable (i.e., if you don't owe any taxes, the government will reimburse you for 50 percent of your contributions up to a certain limit), we could empower poor and low income segments of our society to direct nonprofit growth to the areas they perceive as being most in need, at the same time increasing the supply of meaningful work.

Time Thievery

It's one thing to sell your time for things you would rather not be doing, but it's even worse to have to do it without being paid. *Time Thievery* comes in so many forms, we often don't recognize it. You could call it "hidden unpaid work."

1. The commute: For much of human history, work and home were either in one place or not far apart. Consider today's situation: a 30-minute commute comes to five hours a week, or 250 hours a year. That's the equivalent of more than six weeks of time theft (based on a 40-hour week). Solutions range from facilitating work at home, to flextime with a four-day week, to redesigning our cities, to new visions for transportation.

2. Phone solicitations: Here it's not just the amount of time, it's the intrusion. *By what right do they drag me to the phone for that @#%*&@ night after night!?* The solution is to require all solicitors to use a special electronic signal and for all phone services to give people the option to block them totally!

3. Tax preparation: It's not just doing the forms in April, it's living in the self-accounting mode all year long. Solution: Vastly expand the Standard Deduction so that most people don't lose anything by not itemizing or keeping records!

4. Trying to Get Health Insurance to Pay Up: What is more debilitating than spending hours chasing after Blue Cross, and the like? There are lots of solutions here. We could consider a system of nationalized health care, but there are alternative approaches, as well. For instance, we could dramatically reduce the role of so called "health insurance." Government could give everyone the option of very low-cost insurance that has two features. It would pay for *everything* in the rare year when catastrophe strikes and bills are really high, and it would pay nothing and have no intermediary role for run-of-the-mill expenses.

Most of the time, you simply pay the bill to the doctor you choose. By eliminating the middleman, this plan would reduce costs significantly, *and* by making doctors look patients in the eye, it would assist in eliminating some of the outrageous fees that are charged. People with low incomes would, of course, need additional protection, but such an option could also help many people (who work long hours solely to keep their health insurance) to achieve part-time alternatives.

5. Spending Every Night Wrestling with Your Kids over Their Homework: Why not make the school day an hour longer, and just eliminate most homework. Don't kids also deserve to be able to leave work at the workplace? Imagine the family with free time during weekday nights!

Overwork

Sometimes, overwork is voluntary, resulting from self-sacrifice or, simply, poor judgment. In its *involuntary* form, overwork comes in two varieties: economic necessity and being required by the people who control hiring and firing.

Required Overwork

In the United States, legislation established the eight-hour day and the 40-hour week. But these are *not* limits beyond which workers cannot be required to work; rather they are norms, above which employers must pay higher rates (e.g., time and a half). One solution for preventing overwork is to eliminate mandatory overtime, to enact worker's rights legislation that says that no worker can be penalized for refusing to work more than the standard hours. Another might be to increase the overtime premium to double pay instead of time and a half, thus discouraging the use of overtime.

Often, employers lay off workers, and then force others to work large amounts of overtime. They do so to avoid paying benefits to more workers. But, what if, instead of laying people off, they reduced working hours for all employees and provided work for more people?

It might actually be cheaper for the government to give tax credits to such companies, covering the additional benefits that such a strategy would require, rather than paying unemployment to laid-off workers. Because such tax credits would be targeted to companies actually engaging in work sharing, we would be assured that they increased employment.

This is a far less risky proposition than simply cutting all taxes with the hope that businesses would invest their newfound gains rather than simply enhance their CEOs' salaries or stockholders' profits.

Shorter Hours

Then there is the question of standard hours, themselves. For over a hundred years, increased leisure time, along with increased wages, was one of our measures of economic progress, and one of the ways in which we benefited from increased productivity. But, half a century ago, our society abandoned this objective. As a result, especially given the emergence of the dual-career family, we are an over-stressed, unbalanced society. Our most basic response, at this point, should be to make the expansion of leisure a fundamental social objective once again.

There are a wide variety of options here. We can pick up where we left off and aim for the 6-hour day and the 30-hour week. Alternatively, we could maintain the 8-hour day and aim for a 4-day week. But, my favorite approach is to gradually introduce more holidays.

Many workers now have 10 paid holidays a year. If we were to introduce 2 more per year, for each of the next 8 years, this would bring the total to 26, allowing for a 3-day weekend every other week.

Such an approach is gradual enough to be introduced without major disloca-tion, and is compatible with increasing wages during the same period while using only part of increased productivity for more leisure. Further, by allowing some workers to take off Fridays, and others to take off Mondays, and some the first and third weekends of the month, and others the second and the fourth weeks, we would still have almost a full workforce present on any given Friday or Monday. Thus, normal business functions could be maintained.

One further wrinkle is that we would maintain the 5-day school day, so parents could find themselves with 2 days a month in which the kids are at school and they are at home—alone!

Then there is the issue of paid vacation time. Most European nations have laws that entitle workers to paid vacations—6 weeks a year is quite common. It's time for statewide and national legislation that would begin with a guarantee of three or four weeks a year, and gradually expand that to at least 6 weeks (see also chap-ter 3).

But what about unpaid vacations, or more generally, *unpaid leave?* To what extent should workers have the right, for any reason whatsoever, to limit the amount of time they will put in on the job? Should they have a right to miss work on any given day? Or to decide at any point simply to stop work and go home, or go to the museum?

It sounds radical, almost impossible, and there is no problem in thinking up reasons why those responsible for producing goods or delivering services to the public couldn't function properly if everyone worked as much as he or she desired, whenever they wanted to.

Yet, it's worth keeping this standard of freedom in mind. Yes, there are good reasons why it isn't generally applicable, but we need a system that achieves a bal-ance between license and control. Thus, rights to take unpaid leave for family care, for pregnancy, for meeting with teachers, or for just sleeping late (occasionally) all have a place within a sane society.

Overwork from Necessity

Those suffering the most from overwork are often low wage earners, sometimes holding two or even three jobs. They try to cobble together a decent income, but their economic opportunities only allow them to meet their family's needs if they put in extraordinarily long hours.

Then, too, people are driven not just by their needs, but also by their aspirations, and even by their appetites. There is no public policy framework that can protect everyone from himself or herself, but we can do a lot better in providing a general framework for a decent life without overwork. The issues here involve the entire gamut of our approach to poverty and low incomes. Two elements stand out:

1. Minimum wages: This is a long established policy, but the actual level of the current minimum wage is so low that it fails to provide an income sufficient for core needs, even with two parents working full time. For instance, at 2,000 hours a year, a $5.50 minimum wage provides only $11,000 annual income. Here the "living wage" concept, enacted in many municipalities across the country, tries to set minimum wage levels (often only for certain classes of workers) on the basis of an assessment of the real costs of meeting core needs. Such "living wage" analyses have regularly concluded the need at least to double the minimum wage.

2. Earned income credit: Another feature of our existing policy framework provides low-income families with children a refundable tax credit. Over twenty million families currently benefit from the earned income tax credit, and it pays out varied amounts that rise to approximately $4,000 a year for families with two children. Within this existing framework it is possible to expand the program significantly, thus limiting the economic pressures towards excessive work hours.

Both of the above policy instruments focus on expanding the income of families. But, the other half of the equation, one often not thought about, is the cost side. *Why does it cost so much in America to meet rather simple needs?* Once stated in these terms, it becomes clear that the problem is not merely one facing those in poverty or with low incomes. There is intense economic pressure on most middle class families, as well.

For instance, consider what it costs to live in a safe neighborhood with access to good public schools. This is not a matter of having walk-in closets or three car garages. A neighborhood safe enough to send your kids out to play, a school free from violence, where children are enlivened by their education are not artificial desires or extravagant ambitions. They should be achievable objectives for all of us in this wealthiest of societies.

Yet, there is no doubt that the broad middle class often finds such neighborhoods and schools out of reach. In the area where I live, the Washington DC suburbs, the price of admission to such neighborhoods is a house that costs upwards of $300,000.

As a society, our primary response is individualistic. Each of us seeks higher levels of income so that we may move out and move up. Success is recognized by one's ability to live in those "better" areas. Yet, unless the supply of good neighborhoods is increased, the higher levels of income earned by working harder and longer result in a bidding war that pushes the cost of access still higher. Here, greater government investment in decent and affordable housing is essential.

Put in different terms, the problem of overwork cannot be separated from the cost of meeting core needs. If we are to address overwork as a social concern, and seek solutions—not for the few who win the competition, but for all of us—then we need radically new approaches and vast new levels of commitment to deal with fundamental social problems, such as schooling and violence.

Similar links between the cost of meeting core needs and the problem of insufficient leisure emerge in other sectors of consumption, as well. Consider, for instance, transportation. Today, the average American family devotes approximately 20 percent of its spending to transportation. This is more than it spends on food and clothing combined, and is approximately what is spent on shelter. Yet, transportation 100 years ago accounted for only one percent of household spending. It is easy to imagine that this is a matter of SUVs and other luxury indulgences. Yet, for most American families, that is not the situation.

What this makes clear, is that taking back your time, having time for life, is not a simple proposition. It engages the most fundamental aspects of our social organization and our cultural assumptions. Policy-wise, we can approach it incrementally, with this good idea and that, but at bottom, what taking back our time is about is a fundamental paradigm shift.

It is about keeping the question, "What is an economy for?" at the heart of our public discourse. It is about seeing that the answer to that question involves a vision of the good life balanced between meaningful work and leisure, friends, children and family, books and play, and religion and theatre. It is about being open-minded and creative as we look for new ways of making that life a possibility for all of us.

What's an Economy For?

DAVID KORTEN

Ultimately, if we look closely at American overwork and time pressure, and the stress they place on all of us and on our environment, we can't help but ask why our leaders seem so unwilling to change things. Even Robert Reich and Al Gore, whose recent books clearly address the problem, never seem to go where logic would carry them and call for U.S. work-time policies that approach those of Western Europe. Reich, in particular, worries that such policies could slow the remarkable growth engine at the center of the U.S. economy. Generally, the central argument against shorter work time is that it wouldn't be good for the economy. But, such an argument, as David Korten makes clear, puts the cart before the horse and fails to address the most important economic question of all—what's the economy for, anyway?

A former Harvard and Stanford Business School professor and overseas development officer, David Korten began asking that question years ago when he realized that he was encouraging developing countries to adopt our high-consumption lifestyle and it wasn't working out well at all. "We were seeing the environment trashed. We were seeing the destruction of the social fabric," he told me. In time, he came to believe that it was our way of thinking, not theirs, that was most in need of change. —JdG

Europe's Prized Leisure Life Becomes Economic Obstacle

—HEADLINE IN THE *WALL STREET JOURNAL*, AUGUST 8, 2002

A ccording to the *Wall Street Journal*, Europe is headed for trouble because Europeans put in fewer work hours than Americans do. It makes you wonder. The U.S. economy keeps growing and our productivity keeps increasing. So, each year we are richer than the year before. Yet, we are working longer hours to make ends meet and we can no longer afford things we once took for granted, such as leisure time, family life, education, health care, retirement, parks, clean water, and jobs that pay a family wage with benefits. What gives? What's an economy for?

Measuring Economic Performance

Most people, if asked to name the minimum essential characteristics of a healthy economy, would probably come up with a list something like the following:

- Every person has a secure, adequate, meaningful, and dignified means of living that meets basic needs for healthful food, clean water, clothing, shelter, transport, education, entertainment, and healthcare.

- Work arrangements allow adequate time for family and friends, participation in community and political life, healthful physical activity, learning, and spiritual growth.

- The environment is clean, healthy, and vibrant with a diversity of life.

- There is adequate long-term investment in education, physical infrastructure, and natural capital to secure the economic, social, and environmental health of future generations.

- There is equitable and democratic participation in ownership to secure the foundations of political democracy.

Again we note a curious fact. These are the basics we should expect of any economy, and they are within the material and technical means of almost every country in the world to achieve, even those we consider poor. Yet, the economies of many countries—especially the United States—are moving ever further from these standards.

The corporate media divert our attention away from this critical failure by focusing on the stock market and economic growth as the primary indicators of economic progress and well-being. This suits corporate interests, which are strongly

CHAPTER 30 / WHAT'S AN ECONOMY FOR?   221

linked to stock prices and growth in economic activity, but tells us nothing about the real health and well-being of people and nature.

Most stock index gains over the past twenty years have reflected an inflation of share prices far beyond underlying asset value. Most of the benefit has gone to the wealthiest one percent of households.

Indicators of economic growth, which report the market value of all monetized transactions, make no distinction between those that are beneficial or destructive to our well-being, or are simply defensive responses to the consequences of economic failure. For example, economists count the production and use of cancer causing toxins, the costs of treating the resulting cancers, and the clean up of toxic wastes all as economic gains. All contribute to corporate profits and may boost share prices, but come at great cost to our lives.

The same is true for increasing expenditures on security guards, alarm systems, law enforcement and prisons, gun sales to children, and military expenditures—all of which might be viewed as measures of social breakdown. When Enron was manipulating energy markets to gouge Californians, economists counted its treachery as a contribution to the economy.

The monopoly pricing of pharmaceuticals by drug companies similarly contributes to economic growth. The sale of timber from a clear cut counts as a gain, but nothing is deducted for the loss of services that the forest once provided, including contributions to soil and climate stabilization, flood control, species diversity, and recreation.

We, in America, know pretty much everything there is to know about making money, including hyping stock bubbles and cooking the corporate books, but we have turned economic purpose on its head—forgetting that *the purpose of an economy is to help us live fully and well.* We devote so much of our personal time—and life energy—to making money, we have forgotten how to live.

To take back our time is to take back our lives. To take back our lives we must replace what I call the global suicide economy (devoted to the service of money) with local living economies (devoted to the service of life).

Killing Ourselves for Money

The self-destructive dysfunction of the corporate global economy is centered in the global financial system, which holds both governments and corporations hostage to financial speculators for whom the long term rarely extends beyond next quarter's financial statement. If a government chooses to pursue policies that speculators consider unfriendly to their interests—for example, those protecting the environment, mandating a living wage for workers, or reducing working hours—the speculators dump its currency. The value of the currency falls. The economy takes a nose dive. And, the government loses the next election.

If a corporate CEO chooses to put the interests of workers, the environment, or even the long term viability of the company ahead of next quarter's share price, speculators will dump its stock. Its price falls. It becomes the target of a buyout or takeover. And the CEO loses his job.

The drive for growth in corporate earnings and market share to appease wealthy speculators creates a concentration of economic wealth and power. This translates into the political power of campaign contributions, lobbyists, and the threat of moving jobs away from any political jurisdiction that may resist corporate demands for subsidies, tax breaks, and immunity from regulatory oversight.

It also translates into a world divided between obscenely rich winners and desperately poor losers, and traps each of us in a life or death competition with our neighbors. Hopeful of being a winner and fearful of being a loser, we give our time—our life energy, really—to a system that is destroying the foundations of its own existence, as well as our families, our communities, the life support system of the planet, and the future of our children.

Fortunately, it doesn't have to be this way. The institutions of the suicide economy are human creations—the product of human choices. What humans have created, humans can change. It starts with taking back our time and redirecting it to economic choice that creates real value for ourselves, our families, our communities, our nation, our world, and the whole of life.

Consider the Possibilities

The quality of our living could be stunningly improved if we based economic decisions on life values rather than purely financial values. Consider what we might accomplish by changing the rules of the marketplace to actually honor a basic market principle called full cost pricing, one that eliminates the market distorting subsidies that encourage the destruction of life for financial gain.

Full cost pricing of energy, materials, and land use would expose the real inefficiencies of factory farming, conventional construction, and urban sprawl, and make life-serving alternatives comparatively cost-effective. Much of our food could be grown fresh on local family farms without toxic chemicals, and processed nearby. Organic wastes could be composted and recycled back into the soil.

Environmentally efficient buildings constructed of local materials and designed for their specific micro-environments, could radically reduce energy consumption. Much of our remaining energy needs could be supplied locally from wind and solar sources. Local wastes could be recycled to provide materials and energy for other local businesses.

There would be natural incentives to create compact communities that bring work, shopping, and recreation nearer to our residences—thus saving energy and

commuting time, reducing CO_2 emissions and dependence on imported oil, and freeing time for family and community activities. Land now devoted to roads and parking could be converted to bike lanes, trails, and parks.

By reducing waste, we, in America, would reduce our need to expropriate the material and energy resources of other countries, and eliminate the need to maintain a large military to secure such access. Poor countries could regain control of resources that are rightfully theirs, improve the lives of their own people, and, thus, reduce the threat of terrorism.

Instead of devastating the environment and dividing the world between the overworked and the under and unemployed, we could organize our economic lives to share paid work—providing every adult who wants a job with a secure and adequately compensated 20- to 30-hour workweek doing meaningful work that contributes to a vibrant community and a healthy environment.

Useful and Meaningful Work

Once we get clear that economic life should be about making a living for everyone rather than making a killing for lucky winners, we begin to see how much of the world's labor, energy, and material resources are being expropriated by the suicide economy for uses that are profitable for corporations, but harmful to life. This includes a major portion of the resources now devoted to automobiles, chemicals, packaging, petroleum, advertising and marketing, financial speculation, litigation, prisons, and the military.

This suggests a startling possibility. We might all be better off if the people now employed by these industries to do things harmful to our health and well-being were instead paid to do *nothing at all.*

The better answer, of course, is to offer the people employed in these industries meaningful family wage employment to perform beneficial work. At the same time, everyone's working hours could be reduced to share both leisure and paid employment equitably. It's all a question of how we choose, individually and collectively, to allocate our life energies.

We could, if we chose, redirect the life energy reclaimed from harmful work to beneficial work, such as providing elder and child care, managing community markets and senior citizen centers, educating our young people, counseling troubled youth and drug addicts, providing proper care for the mentally ill, maintaining parks and commons, registering voters, doing environmental restoration, running community recycling programs, retrofitting homes for energy conservation, and addressing countless other needs.

At the same time we could all have more time for recreation, quiet solitude, community service, political involvement, family life, and the disciplines and hobbies that keep us physically, mentally, psychologically, and spiritually healthy. Our paid work would be more fulfilling. Our lives, communities, and natural environment would be healthier.

A world no longer divided between the obscenely rich and desperately poor would know more peace and less violence, more love and less hate, more hope and less fear. The Earth could heal and provide a home for our children for generations to come. *And we would have more free time.*

Living Economics Emerging

The September 11, 2001 terrorist attack on America brought to the surface a great national hunger for meaning, community, and national purpose. Political leaders responded with war, a rollback of civil liberties, and calls to go shopping. There followed a wave of corporate scandals centered on massive accounting

70 YEARS IS LONG ENOUGH.

On April 6, 1933, the US Senate overwhelmingly passed a bill that would have made the official US workweek 30 hours, anything more would be overtime. In the 1930s, many companies, including the cereal giant, Kellogg's, adopted 30 hour work weeks, with great results for employment and community life. But today, despite a quadrupling of productivity, most of us can't get our work weeks down to 40 hours. We all need time for life.

WHAT GIVES?

participate in
TAKE BACK YOUR TIME DAY
www.timeday.org   OCTOBER 24, 2003

fraud that reached to the highest levels of the corporate and political establishment and shook our faith in the integrity of the system. The political power brokers responded with some minor rule changes and expressions of confidence in the system.

Meanwhile, community groups, local business owners, farmers, volunteers, members of religious orders and congregations, city officials, retirees, youth activists, and others are engaged in a far more constructive response—organizing to create local living economies comprised of locally-owned, independent enterprises that serve real needs, include all people, provide meaningful family wage jobs, reduce the human burden on the earth, and build communities connected to a place on the Earth.

They speak of real wealth as a sense of belonging, contribution, beauty, joy, relationship, and spiritual connection. And they are reaching out to like-minded people around the world, engaging in global cooperation to realize their dreams of a world of locally rooted living economies that meet the material needs of all people everywhere.

We have created a suicide economy based on absentee ownership, monopoly, and concentration of power, de-linked from obligations to people or place, that is killing us at an accelerating pace. It is the product of human choices motivated by a love of money. *Now we must make different choices motivated by a love of life to take back our time and reclaim our lives.*

So, the next time the *Wall Street Journal* tells us that taking back our time and our lives would be bad for the economy, take note that what is bad for the *suicide* economy might very well be good for the *living* economy—good for people and our planet. And that, after all, *is* what an economy is for.

Appendices

Organizing Take Back Your Time Day in Your Community

SEAN SHEEHAN

What will you do in your community to take part in Take Back Your Time Day? Of course, the options are many. The next two sections look at a couple of possibilities. These ideas are meant to be fun and creative, to get your imagination going. Sean Sheehan suggests one way of organizing a community meeting that can be both informative and enjoyable. You can adapt his plan or create your own from scratch. You'll note that this meeting takes place on Friday evening. It's for all those people who want to support Take Back Your Time Day, but just don't feel brave enough to skip work for even part of the day. What might work best is to hold campus teach-ins during the afternoon, and meetings in churches, union halls, and community centers or libraries during the evening. And don't be afraid to let the events continue the following day—it's a Saturday, and officially, it's Make A Difference Day. So you might want to make your difference by hosting a continuation of Take Back Your Time Day events—a community fair with tables, say. Of course, you could also hold your fair on Friday. The point is to make clear that the event is about taking back time. Be sure that it doesn't end without your getting names and contact information for everyone who attended so you can establish an on-going Take Back Your Time organization and continue to work on the issue. —JdG

Visualizing Take Back Your Time Day

Before you decide to organize a Take Back Your Time Day event at your college, with your religious congregation, in your union hall, or at your local library's meeting room, it would be helpful to get a picture of what one might look like. So, please close your eyes and picture this. Wait a second, unless the Time Day Handbook-On-Tape has already been released, you'll have to leave them open. Well, in any case, please take yourself to . . .

Place: Your place of work

Date: Friday evening, October 24, 2003 *(or, for subsequent years, the fourth Friday in October)*

Time: 6:42 p.m.

The sound of jingling keys echoes off the walls and you glance up to see a coworker pulling on her coat. You look at your watch in disbelief, and then grow concerned. Whatever could be the matter? A health problem? A family emergency?

"Rhonda, is everything OK," you call out.

"Yeah, why?" she turns, smiling. You breathe a sigh of relief.

"Well, it's barely dark. I mean, you haven't gone home before 9:00 p.m. all month, it doesn't look like you're bringing work home, and I know you have some big deadlines coming up."

"If it makes you feel better, I'm not going home," Rhonda smirks, and then adds, "and the fact that you know my work hours means you should come with me. C'mon, grab your coat—we're going to a Take Back Your Time Day discussion and I don't want to be late!"

Take Back Your Time Day? Something about it must have a struck a chord, because next thing you know you're walking alongside Rhonda toward the local library. You follow her into the library's community meeting room and glance at your watch—6:59 p.m. You made it!

Just inside the door, a tall fifty-something man, still wearing his jacket, stands talking to a seated younger couple. At the front of the room, the panelists have already taken their seats. You recognize a city counselor and surmise, based on attire, that two other panelists are a doctor and a minister. The remaining panelists are a mystery to you. Between you and the panel a few dozen people have filled up most of the rows of folding chairs. Who would have guessed this many people would come to the library to talk about time?

A cheerful woman named Florence Gardener, or so you gather from the nametag on her blouse, bounces up to you, offering greetings and handing you a blank nametag.

"As a way of getting to know each other, we're asking everyone to write their first name on these name tags. Then, we're writing a word that sums up one thing we'd really like to do if we had more time."

"For example," her colleague points out, "My name's Drew and my tag says 'Drew Family.'"

Your watch ticks a notch and, as if on cue, the MC calls the room to attention. You and Rhonda, now tagged 'Rhonda Cook,' slip into a row and take seats between Jackie Bicycle and Eric Meditate.

The MC enthusiastically announces that this is one of hundreds of such gatherings in cities and towns across the country. Each event is unique to its region's interests and resources, yet each holds the common theme that our overworked and overscheduled lifestyles are crowding out other values and activities we hold dear. She thanks the audience for taking time to attend and thanks the volunteers who pulled it all together. She also points out that while the event was orchestrated on a shoestring budget, three people donated 'gifts of time' to a silent auction to raise the meager funds needed to cover these costs. She encourages everyone to bid on the donated massage, driveway shoveling coupon, and guided backcountry hike at the booth by the exit.

The MC says that we'll be hearing from an array of experts and local leaders about the problem and prospects for solutions, but first she wants to know who has experienced a time crunch at some point in the past year. Every hand in the room shoots up.

"OK, we've all experienced a time crunch. That makes us all experts, so let's start by listening to what we all have to say."

She instructs everyone to break into groups of three, preferably not with a friend or acquaintance, and take a few minutes to elaborate on 'your chosen last name,' major obstacles in the way of having time for it, and what it would take to overcome those obstacles.

You take a few paces to your right and pull up a chair next to Dan Drums and Monica Study. Monica starts, explaining that her dream is to graduate from college, but she dropped out because she couldn't handle the study load combined with the full-time job she needed to pay for living expenses and the portion of tuition not covered by student loans. She's now taking a couple of community college classes, though even they've been tough to fit in between her jobs cashiering at a Big Box store outside of town and waitressing at a diner. She adds that she needs the jobs to help pay for her parents' medical expenses . . . and that she's worried about her looming student debt.

At that, Dan says his story now seems pretty petty, and that he's reluctant to even tell it, but you and Monica encourage him to go on. He shares how his greatest joy as a kid came from playing drums in the school band and that he has longed to recapture that feeling for many years now. Last year, he saved up and bought a very expensive drum set, but his marketing job typically works him 8 to 8 and has him on the road virtually every weekend. In other words, he's never home during the hours that his condo complex would allow him to play his drums.

You share your story with Dan and Monica.

The next hour consists of brief yet powerful presentations from the panel. The Doctor talks about "hurry sickness" and other health risks resulting from overwork, such as fast food and lack of sleep. The minister reflects upon the importance of the Sabbath and how we've lost both that day of rest and the time we need to set aside for spiritual matters. A professor from the university talks about the social impact of our work-and-spend culture, and a representative from the Sierra Club talks about the environmental impacts.

Just when you think you can't take anymore bad news, the final two panelists talk about solutions. A former big shot at the phone company talks about his decision to downshift from the rat race and rekindle his relationship with his wife and kids. He talks about the flextime and telecommuting possibilities with his current job and emphasizes that he's never regretted the time-money trade-off. Then, a soft-spoken immigrant single mom and union steward talks about how she is organizing against mandatory overtime on her job, because she wants to be home when her 12-year-old son gets out of school. She doesn't pull punches about the hardships and challenges she faces as a result, yet she has no doubt that she's making the right choice.

The MC wraps up the event with an exciting description of next spring's Take Back Your Time policy conventions and next fall's 'Billion Hour March.' She encourages everyone to sign up to help plan or promote this next generation of events and also to fill out a pledge card describing what they're personally committing to do for Take Back Your Time Day and beyond. The pledge cards ask participants to make two commitments to themselves, one personal and one external.

These commitments can be as simple as reflecting on the evening's event and discussing it with a friend or loved one. Or they can be as dramatic as looking for a new job and writing a letter to the editor, businesses, or policymakers about time issues. It's up to the participants to decide for themselves, although the MC does point out that pens, paper, and relevant addresses have been provided on a back table for people who wish to take a letter-writing route.

The room slowly begins to empty amidst the buzz of excited voices. Many congregate around the letter-writing table and "gift of time" silent auction booth. You turn to Rhonda and ask what she plans to do.

Organizer Qualification Test—Do You Have What It Takes?

While the preceding description took place in a library meeting room, it just as easily could have occurred at a college, place of worship, union hall, or even someone's living room. It could have also followed a number of different formats and featured different types of speakers.

There are also two crucial differences between the sample description and reality. First, invigorating events don't materialize from thin air—they require planning.

Secondly, you didn't learn about Take Back Your Time Day 18 minutes before the event; you're learning about it today! Because you're learning about it today, *you* have the opportunity to help organize an event in *your* community.

Do you have what it takes? Here's a short quiz to help you find out.

1. Are you concerned about America's time crunch and the impact it's having on families, communities, workers, our health, and the environment?

2. Do you have an hour or more a week you could put into organizing a community event?

3. Do you have two or three friends who could do the same?

If you answered "yes" to all of the above questions, congratulations! You're qualified to coordinate a Take Back Your Time Day event.

If you answered "no" to any of the above questions, it sounds like you might personally benefit from a Take Back Your Time Day event in your community even more. If you can't take a lead role yourself, please pass out copies of this Handbook to leaders of labor, church, family, or environmental organizations and tell them you'd love to see a Time Day in your community.

Ten Tips for a Successful Day

10. Tap local experts and celebrities to attend and offer remarks.
This will help to develop coalitions, attract publicity, and build credibility.

9. Invite local organizations to tie their issues to time.
If you invite the coordinator of a local community service network to talk, for example, be clear that the purpose is not to talk about community service in general. They are invited to talk about how community service projects could be improved if people had more time.

8. Leave room for interaction.
We've all worked. We've all experienced a time crunch. That makes us all experts. Let's listen to what we all have to say.

7. Props for props.
Nametags with time desires are one idea. Time Day pledge cards, letter-writing tables, and "gift of time" silent auctions are others. What props and interactive exercises can you think of?

6. Don't set the bar too high.
If you work yourself to death on this event, or even just show up looking a bit ragged, people might suspect hypocrisy . . . and they'd be right.

5. Don't set the bar too low.

The key here is to remember that you don't need to do it all yourself. People are really excited about this topic. Your job is simply to connect their skills and passion to the aspect of the event that suits them best . . . then let them run with it.

4. Feeling overwhelmed? Do what you can.

If you don't have time to reach out to local organizations and venues, don't sweat it. Even hosting a small discussion with a handful of friends and friends of friends can be a great way to plant the seed for future endeavors.

3. Feel free to disregard any of the first seven tips.

It's your community, you know it better than I do. If your better judgement tells you otherwise, listen to it.

2. Address as many issues and audiences as possible, including those outside of your 'usual circle.'

Take Back Your Time Day offers a rare opportunity for environmentalists to see eye-to-eye with family values advocates, doctors with labor advocates, and maybe even politicians with those on the other side of the aisle. Make the most of it.

1. Don't take it too seriously.

If people wanted to be stuffy, they could spend another day at work. Be sure to have fun.

Timeline for a Successful Take Back Your Time Day

Obviously, the earlier you begin planning, the better—both for the event's effectiveness and for your own sanity. For the purposes of this sample timeline, we thought Independence Day was a fine time to begin thinking about our freedom and what we choose to do with it. If you can start organizing in the spring, by all means, go for it. Don't worry if, on the other hand, you can't start until September; you still have time to pull off a solid event.

July

Goals for the month:

1. Assemble organizing committee of two to four people.

2. Select time and venue for Time Day event

How?

- Talk to friends and other folks in your community—we'll help connect you!

- Solicit faith committees, unions, forward-thinking businesses, and environmental groups to cosponsor the event, and offer a representative to the organizing committee.

- Poke into Take Back Your Time Day Web information at www.timeday.org

- Appeal to people from your zip code on the New Dream Action Network white pages on www.turnthetide.org

Agenda list for first meeting:

- Assign roles (logistics, publicity, volunteer coordinator, organization liaison).

- Brainstorm what your Time Day event could look like, what issues should be covered, which organizations and local celebrities should be invited.

- Brainstorm possible locations, dates, and times. Leave with a plan to pursue top venue options.

August

Goals for the month:

1. Outline event format and invite speakers.

2. Solidify preparatory and promotional to do list.

How?

Logistics: Finalize details on venue's dos and don'ts and obtain public transit directions, driving directions, and parking instructions. Check in with other members of organizing committee.

Publicity: Talk to local bookstores and libraries about hosting a Time Day Handbook book release event in September and using it to promote your October 24 event. Be sure to post details of all events at www.timeday.org.

Volunteer coordinator: Place a listing in community newspapers, e-mail lists, and bulletins of local civic, faith-based, and other groups, announcing the

Time Day event and calling for volunteers to help with baked goods, 'gifts of time' for a silent auction, and event support. Such organizations often publish or meet monthly and may require some lead time to announce the fair.

Organizational liaison: Prioritize the organizations and local celebrities from July's brainstorm and invite them to participate by (1) cosponsoring Time Day and giving employees the opportunity to take the day off, either with or without pay; (2) providing a staff member or volunteer to represent their group on the day of the fair; and (3) helping to publicize the event.

September

Goals for the month:

1. Build momentum for the event.

2. Attract media attention.

How?

Everyone: Attend the September book event and talk up your October 24 event.

Logistics: Check in with other members of the coordinating team and help out where needed.

Publicity coordinator: Fax or mail PSA, calendar announcement, and/or press release to all local radio, television, and print media. Create a local speakers contact list for the media.

Volunteer coordinator: Solicit more volunteers, including live music, if appropriate. Field calls and emails from prospective volunteers and direct them to assist logistics, publicity, and organization coordinators, as appropriate.

Organization liaison: Follow up with the initial wave of invitations and continue to expand list of invitees to cosponsor the event (i.e., help to publicize and provide volunteers). Be sure to reach Rotary Clubs, Women's Clubs, Girl Scout troops, etc. Put interested groups in touch with your publicity and volunteer coordinators.

October

Goals for the month:

1. Make a big splash with your Time Day event and have fun doing it!

2. Walk the talk—make time for what you want to do!

How?

Everyone: Execute the to-do list you came up with in August.

Logistics: Double-check venue details. Check in with other members of the coordinating team and help out where needed.

Publicity coordinator: Follow up with press contacts (see Eric Brown's chapter about "getting media" for more detailed tips).

Volunteer coordinator: Follow up with volunteers and make sure everyone is clear and comfortable with their assignments.

Organization liaison: Follow up with organizations and make sure they are clear and comfortable with their commitments.

November

Goals for the month:

1. Launch a Handbook discussion group to meet weekly throughout November and/or January.

2. Set up a committee to plan local preparation for next spring's Take Back Your Time policy conventions and another for next fall's "Billion Hour March."

How?

Logistics: Organize a meeting of this year's Time Day organizing committee and people interested in being on next year's committee to do a post-mortem on this year's event and set next year's plans in motion.

Publicity coordinator: Send photos and a report of your event to the national Time Day committee to post on the Web site.

Volunteer coordinator: Thank all volunteers for their contributions and catalog their contact information and interests for future organizing purposes.

Organization liaison: Thank all organizations for their contributions and invite them to participate in the Handbook discussion group and future organizing efforts.

Everyone: Pat yourselves on the back and make time for what you want to do.

Teach-ins and Study Circles

CECILE ANDREWS

In this essay, Cecile Andrews offers suggestions that can make your teach-ins or meetings more lively and inclusive. You'll see that some of her ideas are different from Sean Sheehan's. She likes smaller panels, for instance. But there are no "right" ideas in these essays that need to be followed by everyone. Discuss the possibilities with other members of your local time day committee. Think about who your audience is and what your setting is. Some audiences will want formal presentations, others more personal dialogues, yet some combination of the two should be part of your event. Many people really want facts to chew on, but they also need time to discuss them with others. Consider all the ideas here and then plan your event. If you decide on a larger panel like the one Sean suggests, make sure the panelists all have something different to say, and ask them to tell stories and be personal as much as they can to help hold the audience's interest. Good luck! —JdG

The Philosophy

To paraphrase Einstein, if you want a different result, you have to change the way you do things. In our efforts to educate people, we can't keep teaching in the same old competitive, didactic way. We have to try something different.

For instance, the primary teaching technique—found at almost all levels of education—is that of overwhelming students with information. We seem to believe that facts alone will change people. Yes, some people *are* changed by information, but most students just spit the facts back and go on about their business.

Further, our conventional education focuses primarily on the individual learner, but we need to change society. How can we both transform people's lives and change the wider society? Fortunately, we don't have to start from scratch. We have a long, albeit hidden, history of education for social justice. How many people know that a few months before her *history changing* action, civil rights champion Rosa Parks had been to a school called Highlander—a school for social change that continues to exist today?

Founder Myles Horton created a school rooted in the idea that wisdom lies in the people. Highlander has been credited with being at the heart of the civil rights movement, perhaps our greatest American social change campaign. People came together at Highlander and found the answers to their problems themselves. Most of all, they left Highlander inspired and emboldened, ready to dive into their communities and take action!

This is the core of educating for change—the belief that the answers lie within the people, and that when people come together in a participatory, democratic setting, they find the answers themselves. It is a turning away from reliance on experts and authorities; it is helping people learn to think for themselves and act for the common good.

We don't really have a name for this kind of education. *Folk* education thrives in Denmark, but people in the U.S. assume it means basket weaving or line dancing. Some are familiar with Brazilian educator Paulo Freire's *popular* education, but, again, the word *popular* doesn't convey the right message. So what can we call it? The best I've been able to come up with is *community education:* education by the people, for the people, and of the people. It's education that can happen in the community, that can create community, and that can benefit the community. Community education evokes excitement, concern, involvement, and participation; it inspires action and reflection and more action.

Community education is built on respect for the individual *within* the community. Its foundation rests in the absolute belief in the dignity of the individual, but it goes further, assuming that people learn and change best in community, that people are most fulfilled when they contribute to the common good.

If we are really going *to take back our time,* we need to embrace this alternative approach to education. Conventional education is part of the status quo that promotes a feverish striving and straining to get ahead. We need education that inspires people to question, to reflect, to discern what is in their own true best interest and in the best interests of the greater good. We need education that leads people to action—action to change their own lives, as well as change society.

The Strategies

This is the basic philosophy of community education: *wisdom lies in the people*. So how do we do it? Here are the essential ingredients:

Analysis of the Personal Story: In Paulo Freire's words, we must move beyond *reading the word* to *reading the world*. People's ideas and values must emerge from an analysis of the lessons of their own lives. When people suffer from chronic sleep deprivation, for instance, they shouldn't just take the doctor's medication, they should ask themselves what caused their problem. They must try to discern what their experience is telling them—that you'll get sick when you work longer and longer hours.

To find answers to these questions, people must have a chance to tell their own stories. Telling your story is like writing—you learn in the telling. The act of listening calls forth a deeper wisdom.

Small groups: One of the most effective tools of community education is the small group. It's hard to tell your personal story to a big group. (For one, there's never enough time for everyone to talk.) The larger the group, the more we become guarded; the smaller the group, the more we become intimate. Further, it's easier to form community in a smaller group. When you're sitting nose to nose with others, you become fond of them. So no matter what the size of the whole group, break up periodically into groups of three to four. Always take turns going around the circle giving people three minutes to tell their story with no interruptions. (In the beginning, people use egg timers until the three minutes becomes automatic.)

Action and Reflection: To really change, people must try out their ideas and then reflect on the outcome. People need to see life as an experiment; certainly, we learn the most from our mistakes and failures. In community education people commit to an action and return to reflect with the group.

Critical Thinking: In community education, nothing is accepted as a given. Every conventional idea is probed and tested. Most important, we must seek out *alternative* sources of information from our standard media—stories that help us spot deception and manipulation. Luckily, as more and more Web sites bring us dissident information, this is getting easier. The problem is that there's so much! But when you have a *group* of people reading and searching and sharing, the group becomes sort of an *information cooperative* with everyone contributing what they've read and discovered, and no one needing to read everything. Together people search for what's really going on, moving beyond the deceptions, seeing through the *manufactured consent*.

Absolute Safety: If people are to learn to speak up, they need to know that aggressive attacks, sarcasm, sneering, and competitive debates are not allowed. Of course, you can disagree with others, but you can do it without trying to demolish their ideas. The leader of the group establishes rules and models of behavior that value the voice of every person and refuses to allow anyone to silence another. When people don't feel that they're being heard, they quit speaking up. If we are to gain the courage to speak up in the larger society, we need a safe place to practice!

The Activities

Teach-ins: The marks of a rousing and inspiring teach-in are the *personal story, presentation of suppressed information,* and *commitment to action.*

Effective teach-ins should have speakers who have not only *studied* an idea, but have *lived* it. For Take Back Your Time Day teach-ins, you need people who have suffered from overwork but who have also made changes—limiting their work hours, changing jobs, cutting back to part time, quitting, or developing their own small business. We need to hear people say, "Yes, having more time is wonderful!" Next, you need some experts who can summarize what's going on in places like Europe and in this country. Finally, you need to rouse response in the participants.

Here is a suggested agenda:

1. Begin with the personal presentations. Have a panel of no more than three. Try to have the people represent different groups. Don't just have lawyers or corporate executives, have some "working people," as well, if you can. Try for gender, racial, and age diversity. Give each person strict time limitations: perhaps 5 to10 minutes, depending on the setting. (Talk with them earlier, and make sure you don't have someone deadly dull!) Save questions and comments until later.

2. Next, the participants in the audience should gather in small groups (of three) to respond with their own stories. Do this immediately, while everyone is still inspired by the speakers. With only three people in a group, everyone gets to talk and be heard. You'll see the energy of the audience go up immediately.

3. Next, move from the personal to the political realm and bring in the expert. People need to hear about the alternative approaches in Europe. This speaker can take clarification questions from the audience.

4. At this point, move to open discussion in the large group, exploring ways to work toward policy change.

Have someone facilitate a large group discussion about the issues such as:

What will be the arguments against shorter work time and how would you answer them?

What would be the best tactic—to begin with a shorter workweek, longer vacations, or more holidays?

It's helpful to have a few people in front who can give some "expert" testimony on the questions. You might want to have someone from government, labor, or professional organizations talking about strategies. The people in the audience should be restricted to no more than three minutes or else someone will go on and on, becoming irritating and taking up valuable time. (You need a strong timekeeper.)

5. Finally, a teach-in should end with people making a commitment to some sort of action: to talk to someone, to read something, to get a study circle going, to form a committee in their professional organization, etc. People should turn back to their small groups to discuss possibilities, and then close the meeting by returning to the large group with people (volunteers) standing up and announcing their plans. By talking first in a small group, everyone makes a commitment, and by closing with the large group, the meeting ends on a high note with lots of energy! Obviously it's best to have a room with movable chairs, but people can still talk in small groups of three in fixed seats.

Study Circles

Although workshops and teach-ins are important to rally people, more effective change comes from getting people involved in longer term study and conversation. The study circle is a form of adult education and social change that is used extensively in Sweden. (Indeed, Sweden has been called a *study circle democracy*.)

The study circle takes the same basic format as the teach-in, but lasts over a period of weeks and occurs in a small group of four to eight people.

Here is a format:

First Meeting

1. Begin the first meeting with personal stories: people go around the circle talking about their own experiences with time. Beginning with the personal involves people at a deeper level.

2. At the first meeting, present people with some questions for them to explore in the following weeks. Have them clarify the questions and suggest some of their own.

Some possible questions include:

How does lack of time hurt people, the community, and the planet?

Why do we put up with our time famine? Is there something in our national character that has lead to this?

What do you think people will do with extra time? Is there a danger they will just use the time to shop more? What can we do to keep that from happening?

What arguments against shorter work time do you anticipate? How would you respond?

These questions can be addressed one per week over a period of five weeks—long enough to build a sense of community, but not so long that people feel they can't commit the time. (After five weeks, study circles often go on indefinitely.)

3. Present the idea of "research." During the week, people discuss the questions with friends and coworkers. The focus is on listening, not on arguing. (You'll not only be gathering information, but listening to others—a form of social change in itself!) Each week people return to report on their "research." They also report on newspaper and magazine articles they've seen.

Subsequent Sessions

1. Begin by discussing personal struggles with taking back your time. Have people go around the circle with each having three minutes to report.

2. Next, report on your talks with people in the community.

3. Report on reading.

4. Bring together all of the information and discuss that week's questions.

Summary

People who experience this kind of education find themselves enlivened and enlightened. They not only have new ideas, but a new energy and commitment to bring about change in their own lives and in the wider society. Teach-ins and study circles can be exciting experiences of personal and social transformation. We need these for the long haul because what we are doing is starting *a national conversation* about "taking back our time." People are just beginning to think about this issue. Our goal is to keep the conversation going and rally support for policy changes.

We can keep our spirits up by remembering Margaret Mead's words: "Never doubt the ability of a small group of thoughtful, committed citizens to change the world; indeed, it is the only thing that ever has."

How to Pitch (Not Place) a Story

ERIC BROWN

By all accounts, Eric Brown, who once starred as "the dim-witted son" (People Magazine's description of his role) in the TV sit-com, Mama's Family, was an excellent actor. It takes a lot of smarts to appear dim-witted on TV, but he'd have been hard pressed to match his current skills as Communications Director for the Center for a New American Dream. In the past few years, Eric has placed (oops! that should be "successfully pitched") hundreds of stories about the Center and its remarkable work in thousands of newspapers. I see one in my local paper every couple of months. In the course of that work, he's learned a lot about how to do it right. —JdG

You're in luck. If you have decided to organize Take Back Your Time Day in your community, you have a ready-made story that a variety of news media are likely to be interested in. If you play your cards right, you have a terrific chance of getting some press.

There are whole books about grassroots media relations, so this chapter is by no means a definitive text on the subject. Nevertheless, I hope that it can be a useful tool for people with very little experience in reaching the media, and may even provide an entertaining diversion for seasoned, crusty, battle-scarred communications professionals.

On Bended Knee

I love reporters. This isn't "spin," I swear. Reporters are smart, curious, interesting people who could make a lot more money doing almost anything else, but the vast majority of them do what they do because they love their jobs. Remember this: They're not your enemy. They tend to be very nice, much like yourself (I'm assuming you're nice). If you cut them, they usually bleed. If you tickle them, most will laugh.

Next to the message itself (and you've got a great one), the relationship you establish with reporters is the single most important factor that will determine whether you will get coverage for this event. And since much of your time will be spent talking to reporters, it behooves you to get to know and like them. I mean, what's not to like about someone who calls you up, respectfully asks your opinion, and then prints it in a newspaper for your mother to read and brag to her friends about? Oh, and I almost forgot: reporters are also incredibly overworked, and this, as it turns out, is very lucky for you (more on this later).

Exploding the Myths

In my travels, I occasionally hear the cynical musings of people (some of whom are communications people) quite frankly laboring under a pile of misconceptions about the news media. Here are a few key misconceptions and why they're wrong:

Myth #1: Reporters are Lazy

Mallarky. Reporters are anything but lazy. In fact, they're extremely hard working and are invariably time starved. If you think most reporters are going to just reprint your press release, you are sadly mistaken. I suppose it happens from time to time because reporters are under the gun, but this is no strategy for success. Reporters are very busy, so the more help you can provide coming up with pithy quotes, people with interesting experiences for them to interview, and reliable statistics, the easier it will be for them to do a good story.

More important to you, though, is that overworked, overstressed reporters will arch their eyebrows (the sound of an arching eyebrow over the phone is a beautiful thing) and lean in hopefully when you call them and say that you're working on a campaign to help Americans have more free time (for more on this, see Myth #3).

Myth #2: You Can "Place" a Story

Never happens. Nobody calls a reporter and "places" a story. I don't know where people get this nutty idea. You pitch, you cajole, you wheedle, whine and beg, but you don't "place." The fact is that getting media, even for a great idea with a great message like Take Back Your Time Day, takes work. Don't go gallivanting around town bragging to your friends about how you're going to "place" a story in the *New York Times,* or the *Ypsilanti Times,* for that matter. Still, getting a great story in the paper can also be as straightforward as calling the right reporter and letting them know about this very cool movement. Just don't say you "placed" the story. It makes my teeth itch.

Myth #3: Reporters Don't Have a Point of View

Ha! Reporters try to be objective, and if a story is controversial they'll try to get both sides, but every reporter has a point of view. Most environmental reporters, for example, have some kind of interest in the environment. Most TV reporters like television. Restaurant writers? They tend to like good food. It doesn't take long to figure out which reporters are likely to write about Take Back Your Time Day. Start reading the paper, watching the news, listening to local radio. Do your homework. Find out who covers issues related to work and family life and get a sense of the reporter's point of view. These are people you want to get to know, and they're the ones most likely to cover your Take Back Your Time Day efforts. And don't forget columnists. They're actually *encouraged* to have a point of view, and churning out a column day after day isn't easy. They need help. Get to know your local columnists and give a call to the ones most likely to be sympathetic to your work on Take Back Your Time Day.

It's the Message, Stupid

If you don't have a compelling message, you will fail—and that's a promise. I spent one very eventful year as a Capitol Hill press secretary, and the highlight of that exciting time was the thirty minutes Paul Begala spent addressing a group of press secretaries on the topic of message. (Paul Begala and his partner James Carville were Bill Clinton's Mutt and Jeff media team in the 1992 elections, and now cohost CNN's *Crossfire.*) I took copious notes that day (in fact, I keep the original yellow tablet from that day in 1997 in my office), and I've taken Mr. Begala's lesson on message to heart. Over the years I've adapted the lesson here and there, and borrowing largely from the master himself, this is what I now try to teach others. With apologies to Paul, here goes.

A message is:

1. *A story.* "John de Graaf is working his butt off so you don't have to" is a story about John's crusade to help Americans have more free time to improve their quality of life, protect the environment, and build a better society. "Eric Brown left his pressure cooker job as a congressional press secretary to work for the Center for a New American Dream because he

loves the group's mission, and by the way, they work a 32-hour week" is a story about a guy who took a risk that paid off. These are stories about real people doing things differently that are compelling and that immediately draw you in.

2. *Brief.* This always freaks people out, but a good message is easy to digest. Watch the evening news tonight and see how long the sound-bite of the President (or more likely the bystander describing the 50-car pile-up) is. If it's more than eight seconds, give me a call and I'll send you a dollar. Resist the temptation to blather on. We all want to cram everything plus the kitchen sink into our press releases and all our materials, but it will be much, much better if you can come up with a nice, clean, brief message. It's hard to do, but it's worth it.

3. *Unique.* "Dog bites man" seldom makes the newspaper, but "man bites dog" gets the front page above the fold. Here's a rundown of stories in today's issue of the *Washington Post* that's sitting on my desk: "A Monument to Eco-Mindedness—Takoma Park Silo to Fuel Corn-Burning Stoves," about the efforts of some enterprising citizens to take an unusual step to combat global warming; "Women Rise in Corporations," about a report that details how women are finally beginning to crack the glass ceiling; and "Egon Kafka, The Man Who Couldn't Stop Taking Buses," about a distant relative of Franz Kafka who has a collection of 112 buses. Why did these stories get written? Because they're interesting. They draw you in and make you want to know more. They're *unique,* or in some way (as in the case of the women-in-corporations story) show the beginning of some kind of cultural shift or new trend. *Take Back Your Time* is unique. At a time when people are working more than ever, the movement toward working *less* is unique. What else might be unique about your event? Easy question—the people who are bucking the trend, whose story you will tell to reporters eager to find something unique to write about. (This is fun, isn't it?)

4. *Relevant.* If your message isn't relevant to the reporter's readers or to the producer's viewers, you're toast. Fortunately, Take Back Your Time Day is even relevant to your family pet (see Chapter 7), so you're in luck. Just make sure that you don't gloss over the relevance of your campaign. The really compelling thing, for example, is not that John de Graaf is working his butt off, but that it may help each and every one of us have more free time to do the things that really matter. That's personally relevant to me, and it makes me want to learn more.

5. *Emotional and Evocative.* Which is a catchier message, "John de Graaf has embarked upon a campaign to promote free time" or "John de Graaf is working his butt off so you don't have to"? How about, "Eric Brown decided to cut back on work and found a job that lets him do that" versus "Eric Brown left his pressure cooker job as a congressional press secretary to work for the Center for a New American Dream because he loves the group's mission, and by the way, they work a 32-hour week"? The message with emotion, passion, and some colorful imagery is way better than a dry recitation of the facts. Paint a picture with words. Can't you see John working his butt off? I know I can. Don't you picture the emotional pressure cooker of working on the Hill and the tremendous relief of suddenly working a 32-hour week? Me, too.

6. *Repetitive.* This chapter has two themes. First, you need to establish and cultivate relationships with reporters, and I have hammered that home in one way or another in no less than eight separate places so far. Second, message is everything, and counting conservatively, there are at least ten places where I've stressed the need for understanding and communicating a strong message. This is a damn repetitive chapter, but I like to think that when you're done reading it, you'll have a sense of what I think your approach to getting press should be. I may not convince everyone who reads it, but there will be little doubt about my position. Your message to reporters should be equally clear, and the way you do that is by repeating yourself. You don't have to use the same words all the time, but in one way or another you need to say "we need more free time" a million different times in as many interesting ways as you can.

7. *Forward Thinking.* All good messages and good campaigns are about the future. Whether it's about protecting the environment, creating healthy and happy communities, building the framework for a just society, or just about any important idea I can think of, the implicit and often explicit message is that we're doing what we can to make the future a better place for our kids and grandkids. "John de Graaf is working his butt off so you don't have to" is about the future. It's about how much time our children will get to spend with their parents; it's about our ability to engage civically; it's about our capacity to protect the environment—it's about what the future could look like. It's a hopeful, positive, powerful message. That's why you're reading this book, and that's why I'm writing this chapter.

Now Go Get Media

When I was twelve years old, I lived in a residential neighborhood in Queens, New York, and one day on the way home from the neighborhood park, I came across a chicken. It was alive and looked healthy, and I've always been a real softie for animals, so I took it home, fed it some Quaker Oats, and put it in the garage until I could figure out what to do with it. Then I picked up the phone (I swear, I swear, I swear, this is the absolute honest truth), and I called the *New York Daily News*. Even then, I knew that "Boy Finds Chicken in Queens" was newsworthy. And sure enough, the paper sent out a photographer, my friends and I were in the paper the next day, and my PR career was born.

If you are holding a Take Back Your Time Day event, you are sitting on the equivalent of "Boy Finds Chicken in Queens," and your next step is to pick up the phone. Having read and absorbed whatever wisdom I've been able to impart, you've learned to love reporters, you're getting a sense of how they think and what they need, and you've begun to understand how to frame your message. Now make a list of reporters you'd like to talk to and pick up the phone.

Write a press release (don't tell anyone, but I use pretty much the same format every time—here's a sample: www.newdream.org/campaign/kids/polls.html) so you can send the reporters something they can look at, and give them a call. Call in advance of the event so they can feature the people in *your* community who are working hard on Take Back Your Time Day so we don't have to (your release isn't about John de Graaf, it's about someone in your community—local newspapers always want a local hook if possible), let them know about the teach-in, the speakers, and the other stuff, but make sure they understand the real *story*—the brief, unique, relevant, emotional and evocative, forward-thinking *story*, that makes the event worth participating in.

That's all there is to it, really. It's a lot of work, but you have a really terrific chance of getting your message out if you try hard enough. Be persistent but respectful. Don't get discouraged if people say no. A lot of them will. But my feeling is that more of them will be interested in telling the Take Back Your Time Day story because it's a great story that readers, viewers, and listeners will be very interested to learn about.

If you have any questions, drop me an e-mail at eric@newdream.org and I'll be happy to help. Have fun. Now get out there and work your butt off so I don't have to.

References

CHAPTER 1

Bluestone, Barry, and Stephen Rose. "Overworked and Underemployed: Unraveling an Economic Enigma." *The American Prospect* 31 (1997): 58–69.

Bond, James T., et al. *The 1997 National Study of the changing Workforce.* New York: Families and Work Institute, 1998.

Hochschild, A. *The Second Shift.* New York: Penguin, 1989.

Jacobs, J. A., and K. Gerson. "Who Are the Overworked Americans?" *Review of Social Economy* LVI(4)(1998): 443–459.

Juster, F. T., and F. P. Stafford. *Time, Goods and Well-Being.* Ann Arbor, MI: Survey Research Center, Institute for Social Research, University of Michigan, 1985.

———. "The Allocation of Time: Empirical Findings, Behavioral Models, and Problems of Measurement." *Journal of Economic Literature* 29(2) (1991): 471–522.

Leet, L., and J. B. Schor. *The Great American Time Squeeze.* Washington, DC: Economic Policy Institute, February 1992.

———. "Assessing the Time Squeeze Hypothesis: Estimates of Market and Nonmarket Hours in the United States, 1969–1989." *Industrial Relations* 33(1) (1994): 25–43.

Mishel, Lawrence, et al. *The State of Working America 1998–99*. Ithaca: Cornell University Press, 1999.

Rifkin, Jeremy. *The End of Work: The Decline of the Global Labor Force and the Dawn of the Post-Market Era*. New York: Tarcher/Putnam, 1995.

Robinson, J.P., and G. Godbey. *Time for Life: The Surprising Ways Americans Use Their Time*. State College, PA: Penn State Press, Second Edition, 1999.

Schor, J.B. *The Overspent American: Upscaling, Downshifting and the New Consumer*. New York: Basic Books, 1998.

———. *The Overworked American: The Unexpected Decline of Leisure*. New York: Basic Books, 1992.

CHAPTER 2

Bluestone, Barry, and Stephen Rose. "Overworked and Underemployed: Unraveling an Economic Enigma." The American Prospect 31 (1997): 58–69.

Bond, James T., et al. *The 1997 National Study of the Changing Workforce*. New York: Families and Work Institute, 1998.

Dodson, Lisa, Tiffany Manuel, and Ellen Bravo. *Keeping Jobs and Raising Families in Low-Income America: It Just Doesn't Work*. Cambridge: Radcliffe Institute for Advanced Study/Harvard University, 2002.

Labor Notes. Labor Notes Online. http://www.labornotes

Mishel, Lawrence, Jared Bernstein, and Heather Boushey. *The State of Working America: 2002–2003*. Ithaca: Economic Policy Institute/Cornell University, 2003.

CHAPTER 4

Aakerstedt, T. *Work Injuries and Time of Day: National Data*. Stockholm: Symposium on Work Hours, Sleepiness and Accidents, 1994.

Altman, M. and L. Golden. "Over-Supply of Labor: Behavioral Economic Roots of Labor Supply, Overwork and Overemployment." *Global Business & Economics Review-Anthology:* forthcoming 2002.

Babbar S., and D.J. Aspelin, "The Overtime Rebellion: Symptom of a Bigger Problem?" *The Academy of Management Executive* (February 1998): 68–76.

Bailyn, L.R. and T. Kochan. *Integrating Work and Family Life: A Holistic Approach*. Sloan Foundation Work-Family Policy Network: September, 2001.

Baker, K., J. Olson, and D. Morisseau. "Work Practices, Fatigue, and Nuclear Power Plant Safety Performance." *Human Factors* 36 (1994): 244–57.

Bell, L., "The Incentive to Work Hard: Differences in Black and White Workers' Hours and Preferences." In *Working Time: International Trends, Theory and Policy Perspectives*. London: Routledge, 2000.

Berg, P., T. Appelbaum, and A. Kallenberg. *Shared Work, Valued Care: New Norms for Organizing Market Work and Unpaid Care Work*. Washington, DC: Economic Policy Institute, 2002.

Bigler, R. *Workers' Rights Unions Give Workers the Power to Fight Forced Overtime*. Labor Research Association, September 12, 2002.

Boodman, S. G. "Your Doctor is a Rookie. He's Been on Duty More Than 30 Hours." *The Washington Post* (March 27, 2001): 12–18.

Circadian Learning Center. *The Business of 24/7 Operations*. Lexington, MA: 2002.

Cutler, D., and B. Madrian. "Labor Market Responses to Rising Health Insurance Costs: Evidence on Hours Worked." *RAND Journal of Economics* 29(3) (1998): 509–30.

Ehrenberg, R. and P. Schumann. "Compensating Wage Differentials for Mandatory Overtime." *Economic Inquiry* 22(4) (1984): 460–478.

Families and Work Institute (FWI). *Feeling Overworked: When Work Becomes Too Much*. New York: 2001.

Fenwick, R. and M. Tausig. "Scheduling Stress: Family and Health Outcomes of Shift Work and Schedule Control." *The American Behavioral Scientist* 44(7) (2001): 1179–1198.

Galinsky, E. and J. T. Bond, eds. *The National Study of the Changing Work Force, 1997*. New York: Families and Work Institute, 1998.

Gander, P. H., A. Merry, and J. Weller. "Ours of Work and Fatigue-Related Error: A Survey of New Zealand Anesthetists." *Anaesthesia and Intensive Care* 28(2) (2000): 178–83.

Golden, Lonnie. Flexible Work Schedules: "What Are Workers Trading Off to Get Them?" *Monthly Labor Review* 124(3) (2001): 50–67.

———— and H. Jorgensen. "Time After Time: Mandatory Overtime in the U.S. Economy." *EPI Policy Brief*. Washington, DC: Economic Policy Institute, 2001.

Hanecke, K., T. Silke, T. Friedhelm, H. Nachreiner, and Grzech-Sukalo. "Accident Risk as a Function of Hour at Wrok and Time of Day as Determined from Accident Data and Exposure Models for the German Working Population." *Scandinavian Journal of Work Environment Health* 24(3) (1998): 43–48.

Hansen, F., *FLSA Compensation and Benefits Review* 28(4) (1996): 8–14.

Hayashi, T., Y. Kobayashi, K. Yamaoka, and E. Yano. "Effects of Overtime Work on 24-Hour Ambulatory Blood Pressure." Journal of Occupational and Environmental Medicine. 38(10) (1996): 1007–11.

CHAPTER 6

This chapter includes several exceprts from Betsy Taylor's recently published book:

Taylor, Betsy. *What Kids Really Want that Money Can't Buy.* New York: Warner Books, 2003.

CHAPTER 12

Kawachi, I., and B.P. Kennedy. *The Health of Nations: Why Inequality is Harmful to Your Health.* New York: New Press, 2002.

CHAPTER 14

Hutchins, Claire, Joe Kita, *Five Minutes to Orgasm Every Time you Make Love: Female Orgasm Made Simple.*

CHAPTER 21

House, Henry, Henry Kimsey-House, Phil Sandahl, Laura Whitworth, *Co-Active Coaching.*

CHAPTER 24

AFL-CIO. "Workers' Rights in America: What Workers Think About Their Jobs and Employers," September 2001.

AFL-CIO. "Ask a Working Woman Survey 2000." Poll conducted by Lake Snell Perry & Associates, 2000.

Aiken, Linda H., Sean P. Clarke, Douglas M. Sloane, Julie Sochalski, and Jeffrey H. Silber. "Hospital Nurse Staffing and Patient Mortality, Nurse Burnout, and Job Dissatisfaction," *Journal of the American Medial Association* 288 (16) (2002).

Appelbaum, Eileen, Thomas Bailey, Peter Berg, and Arne Kalleberg. "Shared Work, Valued Care: New Norms for Organizing Market Work and Unpaid Care Work." *Economic Policy Institute* (January 2002).

Bravo, Ellen, Mark Greenberg, and Cindy Marano. "Investing in Family Well-Being, a Family-Friendly Workplace and a More Stable Workforce: A 'Win-Win' Approach to Welfare and Low-Wage Policy," Summer 2002.

California Labor Federation. "Paid Family Leave," September 23, 2002.

Communications Workers of America (CWA) News. "Strikers Win Groundbreaking Agreement: Job Security, Card Check, Less Overtime Among Victories at Verizon," September 2000.

Federation of Nurses and Health Professionals (FNHP/AFT). A Mandatory Overtime Survey: March–April 2001.

Joint Commission on Accreditation of Healthcare Organizations. "Health Care at the Crossroads: Strategies for Addressing the Evolving Nursing Crisis," August 2002.

Labor Project for Working Families. A Work/Family Database: Best Union Contracts Online. http://laborproject.berkeley.edu/contracts.html

Peter Hart Research. Poll for the Federation of Nurses and Health Professionals, April 2001.

Presser, Harriet. "Nonstandard Work Schedules and Marital Instability." *Journal of Marriage and Family* 62 (February 2000): 93–110.

Service Employees International Union. State Legislation to Limit Mandatory Overtime Online http://www.seiu.org/health/nurses/mandatory_overtime/mot_factsheet.cfm

United American Nurses. Mandatory Overtime Online http://www.nursingworld.org/uan/uamand.htm

CHAPTER 26

Additional Resources

Local Harvest (a list of local green markets, food coops and CSAs). Online http://www.localharvest.org

Community Support Agriculture. Online http://www.csacenter.org

Slow Food Movement. Online http:///www.slowfood.com

Recommended Reading

Diet for a Small Planet by Frances Moore Lappé

Hope's Edge: The Next Diet for a Small Planet by Anna Lappé and Frances Moore Lappé

Fast Food Nation by Eric Schlosser

Food Politics by Marion Nestle

The Food Revolution by John Robbins

Index

About the Authors

Cecile Andrews is a former college administrator, founder of the Simplicity Study Circles Movement, codirector of Seeds of Simplicity, and author of *Circle of Simplicity*.

Robert Bernstein has degrees in Physics from MIT and the University of California and is the Conservation Chair and Transportation Chair of the Sierra Club's Santa Barbara (CA) Group.

Stephen Bezruchka, MD, MPH, is a senior lecturer in the Department of Health Services in the School of Public Health and Community Medicine at the University of Washington.

Barbara Brandt, of Cambridge, Massachusetts, is the National Staffperson for the Shorter Hour Working Group and the author of *Whole Life Economics*.

Eric Brown is a former actor, Congressional press secretary, and currently the Communications Director for the Center for a New American Dream.

Kirk Warren Brown is a member of the psychology faculty in the Department of Clinical and Social Sciences at the University of Rochester.

Barbara Z. Carlson is a cofounder of Putting Family First and coauthor, with William Doherty, of *Putting Family First*.

William Doherty is a professor in the Department of Family Social Science and director of the Marriage and Family Therapy Program at the University of Minnesota. He is a cofounder of Putting Family First, a grassroots organization of parents.

Carol Eickert is a social policy analyst with the Public Policy Department of the AFL-CIO.

Lori Ericson is a writer in Cedar Rapids, Iowa.

Camilla Fox is National Campaign Director for the Animal Protection Institute in Sacramento, California.

Larry Gaffin is a career counselor and founder of the Center for Life Decisions in Seattle.

Beverly Goldberg is the Vice President of the Century Foundation in New York City and the author of *Age Works: What Corporate America Must Do To Survive the Graying of the Workforce.*

Lonnie Golden is Associate Professor of Economics at Penn State University, Abington College, and author/editor of many books and articles about work-time.

Anders Hayden, of Toronto is former research and policy coordinator for the 32 Hours Coalition, a Canadian Shorter Work Hours Group, and is the author of *Sharing the Work, Sparing the Planet.*

Benjamin Kline Hunnicutt is Professor of Leisure Studies at the University of Iowa, and the author of *Work Without End* and *Kellogg's Six Hour Day.*

Tim Kasser is Associate Professor of Psychology at Knox College in Galesburg, Illinois and author of *The High Price of Materialism.*

David Korten is the author of *When Corporations Rule the World* and *The Postcorporate World,* chair of the board of the Positive Futures Network, a former professor at the Harvard Business School, and development officer for the Ford Foundation and the U.S. Agency for International Development.

Anna Lappé, of Brooklyn, NY, is a writer, activist, and public speaker on food and nutrition issues, coauthor of *Hope's Edge: The Next Diet for a Small Planet,* and cofounder of the Small Planet Fund (www.smallplanetfund.org).

Sharon Lobel is a professor of management in the Albers School of Business and Economics at Seattle University and holds a PhD from Harvard University.

Paul Loeb is the author of *Soul of a Citizen: Living with Conviction in a Cynical Time* (www.soulofacitizen.org) and three other books on citizen involvement.

Irene Myers is a career coach in Seattle, Washington.

Karen Nussbaum is the Assistant to the President of the AFL-CIO, the founder of 925—the National Association of Working Women—and former director of the Women's Bureau in the U.S. Department of Labor.

Carol Ostrom is a staff writer at the *Seattle Times*.

Christine Owens is the Director of Public Policy at the AFL-CIO and an attorney.

Linda Breen Pierce is a writer and former attorney, the author of *Choosing Simplicity* and *Simplicity Lessons*, and founder of the Simplicity Resource Guide (www.gallagherpress.com/pierce).

Charles Reasons is a professor in the Department of Law and Justice at Central Washington University and the author of *Race, Class and Gender in the United States*.

Vicki Robin is the coauthor of the best-selling *Your Money or Your Life*, president of the Seattle-based New Road Map Foundation, founder of the Conversation Cafes Movement, and chair of the Simplicity Forum.

Joe Robinson, of Santa Monica, California, is a former magazine editor, author of *Work to Live* and founder of the Work to Live Campaign (www.worktolive.info).

Jonathan Rowe, is Director of the Tomales Bay Institute in Pt. Reyes Station, California, a former assistant to Senator Byron Dorgan, and coauthor of *Time Dollars*.

Jerome Segal is a research scholar in the School of Public Affairs at the University of Maryland, author of *Graceful Simplicity*, and cochair of the Public Policy Committee of the Simplicity Forum.

Bob Sessions is Professor of Social Sciences at Kirkwood Community College in Cedar Rapids, Iowa and author of *Working in America*.

Juliet Schor is Professor of Sociology at Boston College and the author of *The Overworked American* and *The Overspent American*.

Barbara Schramm is a holistic health educator and counselor in Portland, Oregon.

Suzanne Schweikert, MD, is an Obstetrician-Gynecologist with the Center for Behavioral Epidemiology and Community Health at San Diego State University and is currently completing her Masters in Public Health.

Sean Sheehan is the Outreach Director for the Center for a New American Dream in Takoma Park, Maryland (www.newdream.org).

Betsy Taylor is the former director of the Center for a New American Dream and the Merck Family Fund, and the author of *What Kids Really Want That Money Can't Buy.*

David Wann, of Golden, Colorado is a writer, video producer, environmental scientist and former EPA official, and coauthor of *Affluenza: The All-Consuming Epidemic.*

Rabbi Arthur Waskow directs the Shalom Center in Philadelphia (www .shalomctr.org) and was the founder of the Free Time/Free People Campaign (www.FreeOurTime.org).

Art Credits

Take Back Your Time Day posters were designed by graphic design students at the University of Minnesota Duluth. Larger versions of the posters are available for download via the Web site at www.timeday.org.

Chapter 19
page 142, Maggie Schwalm

Chapter 20
page 151, Heather Mueller
page 152, Leah Senn

Chapter 21
page 159, Karoline Faber

Chapter 22
page 162, Gary D. Flavin

Chapter 23
page 171, Abby Liljequist: design,
Jenny Kampinen: illustration

Chapter 24
page 174, Katie Just

Chapter 25
page 184, Foua Khang

Chapter 26
page 188, Scott A.Bader

Chapter 27
page 197, Shannon N. Faber

Chapter 28
page 209, Luke Scanlon

Chapter 29
page 213, Kate C. Haraldson

Chapter 30
page 223, Daniel E. Bergh

Chapter 30
page 225, Stephanie L. Magedanz

Part Openers
Valerie Winemiller,
Seventeenth Street Studios

Berrett-Koehler Publishers

Berrett-Koehler is an independent publisher of books and other publications at the leading edge of new thinking and innovative practice on work, business, management, leadership, stewardship, career development, human resources, entrepreneurship, and global sustainability.

Since the company's founding in 1992, we have been committed to creating a world that works for all by publishing books that help us to integrate our values with our work and work lives, and to create more humane and effective organizations.

We have chosen to focus on the areas of work, business, and organizations, because these are central elements in many people's lives today. Furthermore, the work world is going through tumultuous changes, from the decline of job security to the rise of new structures for organizing people and work. We believe that change is needed at all levels—individual, organizational, community, and global—and our publications address each of these levels.

To find out about our new books,
special offers,
free excerpts,
and much more,
subscribe to our free monthly eNewsletter at

www.bkconnection.com

Please see next pages for other books
from Berrett-Koehler Publishers

Affluenza
The All-Consuming Epidemic

John Graaf, David Wann, and Thomas Naylor

Based on two highly acclaimed PBS documentaries, *Affluenza* uses the metaphor of a disease to tackle a very serious subject: the damage done by the obsessive quest for material gain that has been the core principle of the American Dream. The authors explore the origins of affluenza, detail the symptoms of the disease, and describe number of treatments options that offer hope for recovery.

Hardcover, 275 pages • ISBN 1-57675-151-1
Item #51511-415 $24.95

Paperback, 288 pages • ISBN 1-57675-199-6
Item #51996-415 $16.95

Whistle While You Work
Heeding Your Life's Calling

Richard J. Leider and David A. Shapiro

We all have have a calling in life. It needs only to be uncovered, not discovered. *Whistle While You Work* makes the uncovering process inspiring and fun. Featuring a unique "Calling Card" exercise—a powerful way to put the whistle in your work—it is a liberating and practical guide that will help you find work that is truly satisfying, deeply fulfilling, and consistent with your deepest values.

Paperback original, 200 pages • ISBN 1-57675-103-1
Item #51031-415 $15.95

Bringing Your Soul to Work
An Everyday Practice

Cheryl Peppers and Alan Briskin

This new book addresses the gap between our inner lives and the work we do in the world. Case studies, personal stories, inspirational quotes, reflective questions, and concrete applications navigate readers through the real and troubling questions inherent in the workplace.

Paperback, 260 pages • ISBN 1-57675-111-2
Item #51112-415 $16.95

Berrett-Koehler Publishers
PO Box 565, Williston, VT 05495-9900
Call toll-free! **800-929-2929** 7 am-9 pm Eastern Standard Time

Or fax your order to 802-864-7627
For fastest service order online: **www.bkconnection.com**

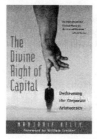

The Divine Right of Capital
Dethroning the Corporate Aristocracy

Marjorie Kelly

In *The Divine Right of Capital,* Kelly argues that focusing on the interests of stockholders to the exclusion of everyone else's interests is a form of discrimination based on property or wealth. She shows how this bias is held by our institutional structures, much as they once held biases against blacks and women. *The Divine Right of Capital* shows how to design more equitable alternatives—new property rights, new forms of corporate governance, new ways of looking at corporate performance—that build on both free-market and democratic principles.

Hardcover, 300 pages • ISBN 1-57675-125-2
Item #51252-415 $24.95

Paperback, 288 pages • ISBN 1-57675-237-2
Item #-52372-415 $17.95

By David Korten

When Corporations Rule the World
Second Edition

Korten offers an alarming exposé of the devastating consequences of economic globalization and a passionate message of hope in this extensively researched analysis. He documents the human and environmental consequences of economic globalization and explains why human survival depends on a community-based, people-centered alternative.

Paperback, 400 pages • ISBN 1-887208-04-6
Item #08046-415 $15.95

The Post-Corporate World
Life After Capitalism

The Post-Corporate World presents readers with both a profound challenge and an empowering sense of hope. It is an extensively researched, powerfully argued, eye-opening critique of how today's corporate capitalism is destroying the things of real value in the world—like cancer destroys life—including practical alternatives that will help restore health to markets, democracy, and every day life.

Paperback, 300 pages • ISBN 1-887208-03-8
Item #08038-415 $19.95

Berrett-Koehler Publishers
PO Box 565, Williston, VT 05495-9900
Call toll-free! **800-929-2929** 7 am-9 pm Eastern Standard Time

Or fax your order to 802-864-7627
For fastest service order online: **www.bkconnection.com**